THE
GRASSES
OF
MISSOURI

Revised Edition

Clair L. Kucera

UNIVERSITY OF MISSOURI PRESS

COLUMBIA AND LONDON

Library of Congress Cataloging-in-Publication Data

Kucera, Clair L.
    The grasses of Missouri / Clair L. Kucera. — Rev. ed.
    p.   cm.
    Includes bibliographical references (p.   ) and index.
    ISBN 0-8262-1164-X
    1. Grasses—Missouri—Classification.   2. Grasses—Missouri—
Identification.   I. Title.
QK495.G74K8   1998
584'.9'09778—dc21   97-52226
                                                              CIP

Designer: Susan Ferber
Typesetter: Crane Typesetting
Printer and binder: BookCrafters
Typefaces: Adobe Garamond and Adobe Garamond Semibold

The University of Missouri Press gratefully acknowledges the assistance of the Missouri
Prairie Foundation in publishing this book.

Illustrations from the Hitchcock-Chase Collection of Grass Drawings, courtesy the Hunt
Institute for Botanical Documentation, Carnegie Mellon University, Pittsburgh, PA,
indefinite loan from Smithsonian Institution.

Illustrations on pp. 263 and 274 reprinted from *The Grasses of Texas,* by Frank W. Gould, by
permission of the Texas A&M University Press, copyright 1975.

To my grandchildren,
Christina and Matthew.

CONTENTS

PREFACE

This revision of *The Grasses of Missouri* was undertaken to update advances in classification and to recognize published changes in nomenclature since the first edition. A third purpose was to include additions to the flora, as well as to exclude or otherwise qualify those taxa of doubtful status.

Significant changes in grass classification have taken place in the past several decades. Such changes reflect a consolidation of viewpoints, aided by increased emphasis placed on phyletic criteria. Much of the early impetus was initiated by European botanists including Avdulov (1931), Prat (1932), and Pilger (1954), among others. In North America, important contributions to grass systematics were made by Stebbins (1956), Reeder (1957), and Brown (1958). Key criteria described and evaluated in these works included characteristics of leaf anatomy, epidermal cells, lodicules, and embryo; identification of non-Kranz and Kranz syndromes based predictably on a combination of anatomical and photosynthetic attributes; and cytological data such as chromosome size and number. From these studies, more comprehensive interpretations of grass phylogeny were made possible, replacing variably artificial treatments with their emphasis on morphology, especially that of the spikelet and inflorescence. One such work addressing the new criteria for North American genera served as a focus for further evaluation and refinement (Stebbins & Crampton, 1961).

In the first edition, the author followed the then standard treatment, *Manual of the Grasses of the United States* (Hitchcock as revised by Chase, 1951). The system included two subfamilies, the Festucoideae and the Panicoideae. The current work essentially follows the outline of Clayton & Renvoize (1986). A few of the changes effected in this revision are readily noted. Six subfamilies are represented in the Missouri flora. The additions are derived solely from the breakup of the traditional Festucoideae, resulting in smaller but more cohesive alliances. The Panicoideae group remains intact at this level, attesting to a more natural assemblage. With the new alignments, some tribes have been expanded in number of constituent genera, others reduced or abandoned, and the residual genera transferred to other tribes or used as the basis of new ones. Eighteen tribes are listed here, compared to twelve in the earlier edition. Generic revisions are accompanied by brief commentary or explanation supported by citation in most cases. Such changes include mergers as well as delineation and transfer of the affected species or section to another genus. Eighty-seven genera are included in this treatment, five of which represent taxonomic transfer.

Name changes engendered by current taxonomic revision as well as previous oversight or illegitimate application of rules of botanical nomenclature are frequently necessary, albeit contributing to an already burdensome synonymy. In order to provide orientation and equivalence for the reader, names most widely employed from well-known manuals and monographs are included at the ends of species descriptions.

This text is a compilation of the native and naturalized species presently known to occur in the state. Roadside waifs and ephemerals of sporadic occurrence and uncertain tenure are also acknowledged, but qualified as such. Working keys and accompanying descriptions, with line drawings for most species, are included to assist the observer in identifying unfamiliar taxa. It is hoped that these aids will promote greater interest in the uncultivated grasses of Missouri and the Poaceae in general.

This book was brought to completion though the help and interest of many persons. I wish to express my deep appreciation to George Yatskievych of the Missouri Botanical Garden for his timely advice on systematic matters, and to Curator Robin Kennedy for herbarium assistance at the University of Missouri–Columbia. Paul McKenzie, Bill Summers, Douglas Ladd, Stanford Hudson, and Wallace Weber provided distributional data, including several state records, and their generosity is gratefully acknowledged. I thank Brad Jacobs, Ann Wakeman, and Nancy Brakhage for their collection information for several species. Brenda Graves-Blevins and Josephine Johnson at Ellis Library at the University of Missouri–Columbia were most helpful in locating and accessing various sources in the literature. Special appreciation is expressed to Marcia Nelson for valuable assistance in collating the final bibliography. Preparation of the preliminary draft by Rosemary Crane, Barbara Culbertson, and Carol Bobbitt is most appreciated. Acknowledgment is made concerning the reproduction and use of line drawings from the *Manual of the Grasses of the United States*. Most of the illustrations were obtained from this source. I wish to thank Bill Dierker and Rhett Johnson for providing several additional drawings selected for the book, and Walter Schroeder, Department of Geography, for assistance in map preparation. Appreciation is expressed to Karen Farley and Traci Wagner at Secretarial and Office Support Services, University of Missouri, for preparing the final disk copy for publication. My sincere thanks are extended to Director Beverly Jarrett, Managing Editor Jane Lago, Production Manager Dwight Browne, and Editor Julie Schroeder, of the University of Missouri Press, for their guidance and generous support through the period. Last, I would like to express my appreciation to members of the Missouri Prairie Foundation for assistance in the publication of this work.

C. L. K.
Division of Biological Sciences
University of Missouri–Columbia
1998

THE GRASSES OF MISSOURI

INTRODUCTION

The Poaceae constitute a large and distinctive family with an estimated 620 genera and 8,000 to 9,000 species. The grasses are the most cosmopolitan of flowering plants, occurring in the widest range of ecological conditions for plant growth. In some regions, especially in midcontinents where there are typically subhumid to semiarid climates, native grasses are the principal life form, in extensive areas of prairie, savanna, and steppe, or their relict examples. Many grass species have special economic importance for man, including maize, wheat, and rice. Other cultivated grasses include the well-known sorghums, sugar cane, a host of bamboos, and numerous forage, turf, and landscape species. Because of its adaptiveness, diversification, and geographic distribution, the grass family is the subject of detailed systematic study and the source of broad academic interest.

The grass plant has characteristic features readily distinguishable from other flowering plants, although the Cyperaceae (sedges) and the Juncaceae (rushes) appear somewhat grasslike. Several vegetative characters of the grass plant are useful supplementary aids in recognition and separation from members of other families. Leaf arrangement is *2-ranked*, alternating from opposite sides of the *culm*, or stem, in contrast to the three-ranked condition of sedges. The grass culm is jointed, generally hollow or sometimes pithy, and more or less round in cross-section. In rushes, the stem is round in cross-section and hollow but lacks the conspicuous joints or nodes of the grass plant. The leaf of grasses consists of a *blade* and a *sheath*, the latter encircling the culm. The sheath of most grasses is "open" in which the margins are not fused but merely overlap, contrasting with the "closed" sheath of sedges and most rushes (Figure 1a,b). Several grasses have closed sheaths, including *Bromus, Glyceria,*

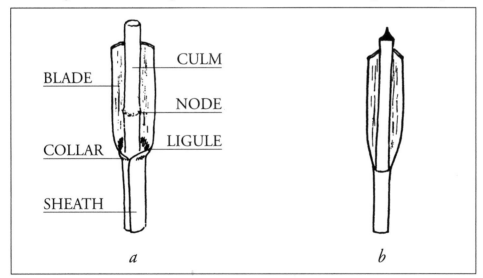

FIG. 1. a. Grass culm with "open" sheath showing overlapping margins; b. sedge stem with "closed" sheath.

and *Melica.* The outer junction of the leaf blade and the sheath is called the *collar.* On the inner side is the *ligule.* It varies in size, shape, and texture and is an important and reliable character in grass classification (Figure 2a). In *Sorghastrum*, the ligule is an expanded rigid projection, whereas in *Dactylis* it is similarly large but hyaline. The ligule consists of a tuft of hairs in many genera, especially of the tribe Eragrostideae. Some genera, particularly of tribe Triticeae, are characterized by the presence of *auricles*, two small curved appendages, one on each side of the collar (Figure 2b).

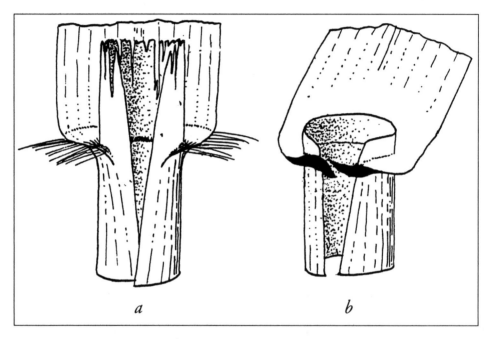

FIG. 2. a. Ligule, membranous example with lacerated margin; b. auricles (shaded) at each side of collar.

The *spikelet* is the basic unit of the inflorescence. It consists of one to several *florets*, each of which encloses the true flower, the whole subtended by two bracts called *glumes*. In some species one or both glumes are absent. A generalized spikelet with several florets is depicted in Figure 3a. The florets are attached at the joints of the *rachilla*, the central axis of the spikelet, in an alternating 2-ranked arrangement. An extracted floret is shown in Figure 3b, consisting of two bracts, the *lemma* and *palea*, and the flower. The lemma is usually the larger and is on the side away from the rachilla. The spikelets of certain grasses or groups bear *awns*, which are mostly solitary projections of the midvein of either glumes or lemmas, or both. Awns vary in length, thickness, and form (straight, geniculate, twisted, etc.) and are a useful aid in identification. The perfect or bisexual *flower* consists of stamens and pistil (Figure 3c). In some genera the flowers are unisexual with plants being either monoecious, as in *Tripsacum*, or dioecious, as in *Buchloe*. The most common number of stamens is three, but sometimes there are as many as six *(Zizania)*. The filament of the grass stamen is typically delicate and flexible. The pistil consists of a feathery, usually 2-parted stigma and a 1-seeded ovary, the latter developing as the *grain* or *caryopsis*. At the base of the ovary, two minute scales, or *lodicules*, are sometimes present in

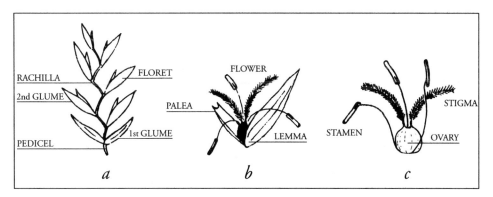

FIG. 3. a. Spikelet consisting of six florets on the expanded rachilla, subtended by the two glumes; b. floret consisting of lemma and palea, and flower; c. flower with three stamens and pistil showing 2-parted stigma and ovary.

some species. These are vestigial parts of an ancestral perianth. Most grasses are wind-pollinated, with insect-pollination reported for a few species in closed rainforest communities.

Basic inflorescence types in grasses include the *spike, raceme,* and *panicle.* There are variations in which panicles or racemes sometimes appear spikelike. The inflorescence of timothy, *Pheum,* is a panicle; however, because of the much-reduced dense branching, it is similar in general appearance to the true spike, which has sessile spikelets on a simple axis, as in *Triticum.* The most common inflorescence in grasses is the panicle, which is characterized by compound branching. In addition to the terminal inflorescence, axillary flowering is sometimes developed. One section of *Panicum (Dicanthelium)* commonly has terminal as well as reduced axillary panicles, the first typically appearing as a vernal phase, the latter developing later in the season. *Cleistogamy* occurs in some grasses, in which the spikelets are generally concealed in axillary or basal sheaths. The florets remain closed, so that the flowers are self-pollinated, as in *Danthonia.*

Many of our native grasses have statewide distribution. Others are restricted to a particular section such as the glaciated prairie region, the Ozarks, or the southeastern lowlands, while a few species are distinctly local and frequently limited to a single collection site. A considerable number of species are adventives. Some are highly invasive and have spread widely from the point of ingress. Introductions intended for domestic use occasionally escape cultivation to become established, especially in areas of disturbance. In the interest of conserving space in this treatment, since one of its purposes is to serve as a field manual, distributional maps are not included. Rather, general, regional, or specific county designations for each species are emphasized. The following map of the counties is provided with letter-number axes, accompanied by a table of coordinates for locating each county.

INDEX MAP

MAP 1

COUNTIES

THE VEGETATION OF MISSOURI

Geologic history, parent materials, seasonal climates, and diverse landscapes are significant factors contributing to the rich and varied flora of Missouri. In addition to physical factors, historical variables such as fire and grazing are modifying influences affecting local vegetative structure and composition.

Glacial drift of pre-Illinoian age covered approximately one-third of the state (Map 2). Loess deposits of the postglacial period accumulated on the drift area to varying depth. The interstream topography of this region is flat to variably rolling, in some places marked by considerable dissection. Bordering the Missouri River in particular, loess deposits of great depth occur, producing a distinctive hill-and-bluff topography. Soil profiles tend to be deep, porous, and well drained. Diminishing

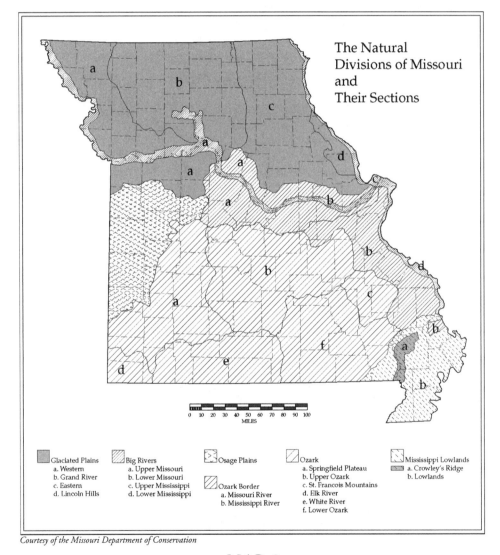

The Natural
Divisions of Missouri
and
Their Sections

Glaciated Plains	Big Rivers	Osage Plains	Ozark	Mississippi Lowlands
a. Western	a. Upper Missouri		a. Springfield Plateau	a. Crowley's Ridge
b. Grand River	b. Lower Missouri		b. Upper Ozark	b. Lowlands
c. Eastern	c. Upper Mississippi	Ozark Border	c. St. Francois Mountains	
d. Lincoln Hills	d. Lower Mississippi	a. Missouri River	d. Elk River	
		b. Mississippi River	e. White River	
			f. Lower Ozark	

0 10 20 30 40 50 60 70 80 90 100
MILES

Courtesy of the Missouri Department of Conservation

MAP 2

accumulations of wind-carried loess produced a mantle over extensive areas of till, becoming finer in texture with increasing distance from the source, west to east. On the more level terrain, as in the eastern one-third of the drift region, subsoils derived from fine loess are characterized by high clay content and low permeability. Here, soils may become seasonally waterlogged, particularly in the non-growing season, effecting anaerobic conditions in the lower profile.

South of the glacial boundary there was a much longer history of soil genesis and uninterrupted plant occupancy. Parts of the eastern Ozarks, centered in Iron, Madison, and St. Francois Counties, are among the oldest land areas in North America. In this highland region, weathering of residual substrates dates back to periods of uplift in the Paleozoic and Precambrian eras. Nonresidual or transported materials are of lesser extent and include local loess deposits and stream alluvia.

Bordering the Mississippi Lowlands of southeastern Missouri, with the lowest average elevation in the state, Crowley's Ridge is a disjunct landform ranging across Stoddard County to northern Dunklin County. Small spring-fed drainages traverse the lower slopes, and in conjunction with coarse-textured soils provide numerous moist and well-drained plant habitats. To the west in the White River watershed of Missouri and Arkansas, a terraced landscape of thin, droughty soils occurs over extensive areas dissected by deep valleys. This upland derives from extensive dolomite outcropping of Ordovician age, capped here and there by attenuated knobs and ridges of cherty limestone from the Mississippian period. In this region of numerous caves and springs, clear-running streams are commonplace. North and west of the White River system, the landscape becomes less rugged, and stream cutting less advanced. This region, called the Springfield Plateau, constitutes the western Ozarks border, transitional with the more open "prairielike" terrain and soils of the Osage Plains. This natural division in turn lies in contact with the southern limits of glacial advance in western Missouri (Thom & Wilson, 1980).

Mean annual rainfall varies from 80 to 90 centimeters in northwestern sections along a gradient to over 125 to 130 centimeters in the southeastern lowlands. This regional difference in precipitation is due to typically drier winters toward the north and west and reflects greater continental influences. Amounts received in spring and summer are more similar throughout the state, averaging from about 60 to 70 centimeters. In the northwest, a relatively greater percentage of the annual precipitation occurs in the growing season, suggesting a climate more favorable for grassland than deciduous forest.

The general pattern of Missouri vegetation (Map 3) is a depiction of its presettlement status constructed from several sources. Tallgrass prairie occurred extensively in the drift region and south of the glacial boundary in the Osage Plains and westernmost parts of the Springfield Plateau. Only isolated remnants of prairie exist today in the drift area. Some examples of flat "claypan" prairie still persist in the eastern division, including Callaway, Adair, Audrain, Macon, and Randolph Counties. South of the drift border in the western section of the state, the remaining prairie is more extensive and widespread. Here the soils are frequently shallow, stony, or with rock outcroppings. In the White River region distinctive glade communities are found. A complement of prairie grasses and herbs occurs on typically thin soils in association with woody species of small stature, including eastern red cedar, yellow wood, and smoke tree.

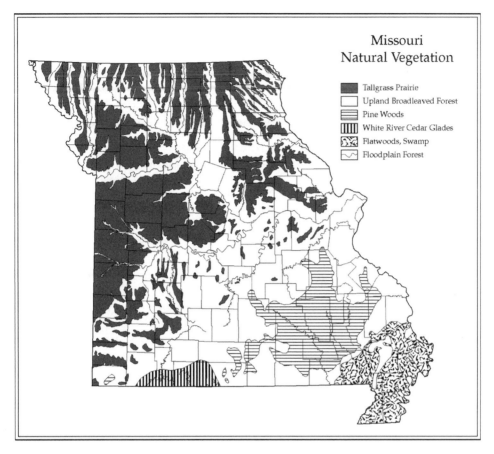

MAP 3

The principal grass species of the Prairie Association in Missouri include the bluestems, *Andropogon gerardi* and *Schizachyrium scoparium;* Indian grass, *Sorghastrum nutans;* wild rye, *Elymus canadensis;* June grass, *Koeleria pyramidata;* dropseed, *Sporobolus heterolepis;* switchgrass, *Panicum virgatum;* sloughgrass, *Spartina pectinata;* and sideoats grama, *Bouteloua curtipendula.* The last is prevalent in limestone prairies and glades and on loessial bluffs. Other species are less widely distributed. Bluejoint, *Calamagrostis canadensis,* occurs mainly in damp swales of the drift region. Another species having mainly a northern distribution, occupying swales and bottomlands, is the common reed, *Phragmites australis.* Porcupine grass, *Stipa spartea,* a species of the dry upland, is found in the western and northern parts of the state. Some grasses that are more common in the nation's semiarid western plains occur as natives in northwestern Missouri. These are restricted to loessal hills bordering the Missouri River, mainly in Atchison and Holt Counties, and include alkali sacaton, *Sporobolus airoides;* the grama grasses, *Bouteloua gracilis* and *B. hirsuta;* and buffalo grass, *Buchloe dactyloides.* Other plains species found in these habitats include soapweed, *Yucca glauca,* and loco weed, *Oxytropis lambertii* (Map 3).

The Oak-Hickory Association is the principal upland forest type in Missouri. It occurs throughout the state and is most extensive and best developed in the Ozarks region. Several oak species are widespread and common, including white oak, *Quercus alba;* northern red oak, *Q. rubra;* and black oak, *Q. velutina.* The bur oak, *Q. macrocarpa,* is also common, occurring generally on lower ground or along streams. Post oak, *Q. stellata,* and chinquapin, *Q. muhlenbergii,* are found in xeric habitats, the latter generally on calcareous soils. A principal hickory of upland sites is shagbark, *Carya ovata.* Bitternut hickory, *C. cordiformis,* is also generally distributed but occupies more moist sites. Common species of sloughs and prairie drainages are pin oak, *Q. palustris,* and shingle oak, *Q. imbricaria.* These oaks are less important in stands toward the south, particularly in the Ozarks region. Common Ozark species include scarlet oak, *Q. coccinea;* southern red oak, *Q. falcata;* and blackjack oak, *Q.marilandica,* the last more wide-ranging. Blackjack oak, post oak, and also black hickory, *C. texana,* are characteristic of dry woodland on cherty limestone soils. Prime examples are found in the White River region, occurring in an abrupt contact zone with the more open glade communities. Southwestward extensions of this hardwood complex occur in Oklahoma and Texas.

Sugar maple, *Acer saccharum,* and basswood, *Tilia americana,* are frequent dominants in a secondary association usually restricted to more mesic sites compared to those of the widespread oak communities. Associated species are northern red oak, white oak, bitternut, and red elm, *Ulmus rubra.* Species with local ranges in Missouri include American beech, *Fagus grandifolia,* and American holly, *Ilex opaca.* Both are limited to several southeastern counties and are best known from moist, sandy habitats of Crowley's Ridge (Map 3).

The main distribution of shortleaf pine, *Pinus echinata,* in Missouri is confined to the Ozarks region, in the eastern and southern counties. It is the only native pine in the state. Stands of mixed oak and pine occur on xeric ridges and slopes having typically thin, acid soils. Extensive pineries were once an abundant resource in the timber industry. One remnant stand of large specimens can be observed in Shannon County, north of Eminence. The map indicates the principal range of pine in Missouri; however, scattered trees and isolated stands occur also in adjacent areas outside the depicted boundary.

The Mississippi Lowlands provide distinctive plant habitats not found elsewhere in the state. Flatwoods and swamp vegetation were typical before drainage, but important areas still remain. Forest species include bald cypress, *Taxodium distichum;* tupelo, *Nyssa aquatica;* sweet gum, *Liquidambar styraciflua;* overcup oak, *Quercus lyrata;* cherry bark oak, *Q. falcata* var. *pagodaefolia;* and swamp cottonwood, *Populus heterophylla.*

Floodplain forests of varying extent and species representation are found in bottomlands and along banks of permanent waterways ranging from small streams to the major river systems. Important species in this community type include eastern cottonwood, *Populus deltoides;* black willow, *Salix nigra;* sandbar willow, *S. interior;* sycamore, *Platanus occidentalis;* river birch, *Betula nigra;* silver maple, *Acer saccharinum;* hackberry, *Celtis occidentalis;* green ash, *Fraxinus pennsylvanica;* and American elm, *Ulmus americana.*

Numerous grasses are ubiquitous components of the ground cover in Missouri forests and woodlands, in a broad spectrum of varying moisture and light conditions. In drier and more open sites, common genera include *Danthonia, Aristida, Panicum, Paspalum, Sporobolous, Schizachyrium,* and *Andropogon.* In protected, more moist phases of the forest continuum, *Bromus, Poa, Diarrhena, Cinna, Elymus, Paspalum, Panicum, Muhlenbergia,* and *Leersia* are frequently represented. Some genera have aquatic representatives, notably *Glyceria, Alopecurus, Poa, Paspalum, Zizania,* and *Phragmites.* In old-field and roadside habitats, broomsedge, *Andropogon virginicus,* is a distinctive successional type, mainly in the several Ozark divisions, often in association with purple top, *Tridens flavus,* dropseed, *Sporobolus asper,* and *Aristida oligantha.* The grasses by their adaptiveness and widespread presence through a wide range of habitats constitute a cohesive network in the vegetation continuum. A more comprehensive discussion of the species composition of native communities in the state is provided by Nelson (1987).

Synoptic List of Missouri
Subfamilies, Tribes, and Genera

I. SUBFAMILY BAMBUSOIDEAE

Tribe 1. BAMBUSEAE
    1. *Arundinaria* Michx.

Tribe 2. ORYZEAE
    2. *Oryza* L.
    3. *Leersia* Sw.
    4. *Zizania* L.
    5. *Zizaniopsis* Doell & Aschers.

Tribe 3. DIARRHENEAE
    6. *Diarrhena* P. Beauv.

Tribe 4. BRACHYELYTREAE
    7. *Brachyelytrum* P. Beauv.

II. SUBFAMILY POOIDEAE

Tribe 5. STIPEAE
    8. *Hesperostipa* (Elias) Barkworth
    9. *Piptatherum* P. Beauv.

Tribe 6. POEAE
    10. *Festuca* L.
    11. *Lolium* L.
    12. *Vulpia* K.C. Gmel.
    13. *Cynosurus* L.
    14. *Puccinellia* Parl.
    15. *Poa* L.
    16. *Dactylis* L.
    17. *Sclerochloa* P. Beauv.

Tribe 7. MELICEAE
    18. *Glyceria* R. Br.
    19. *Melica* L.

Tribe 8. AVENEAE
    20. *Arrhenatherum* P. Beauv.
    21. *Avena* L.
    22. *Trisetum* Pers.
    23. *Koeleria* Pers.
    24. *Sphenopholis* Scribn.
    25. *Holcus* L.
    26. *Aira* L.
    27. *Anthoxanthum* L.
    28. *Phalaris* L.

29. *Agrostis* L.
30. *Calamagrostis* Adans.
31. *Apera* Adans.
32. *Cinna* L.
33. *Alopecurus* L.
34. *Beckmannia* Host
35. *Phleum* L.

Tribe 9. BROMEAE
36. *Bromus* L.

Tribe 10. TRITICEAE
37. *Elymus* L.
38. *Hordeum* L.
39. *Agropyron* Gaertn.
40. *Secale* L.
41. *Triticum* L.

III. SUBFAMILY CENTOTHECOIDEAE

Tribe 11. CENTOTHECEAE
42. *Chasmanthium* Link

IV. SUBFAMILY ARUNDINOIDEAE

Tribe 12. ARUNDINEAE
43. *Arundo* L.
44. *Phragmites* Adans.

Tribe 13. DANTHONIEAE
45. *Danthonia* DC.

Tribe 14. ARISTIDEAE
46. *Aristida* L.

V. SUBFAMILY CHLORIDOIDEAE

Tribe 15. ERAGROSTIDEAE
47. *Distichlis* Raf.
48. *Tridens* Roemer. & J.A. Schultes
49. *Triplasis* P. Beauv.
50. *Leptochloa* P. Beauv.
51. *Eragrostis* von Wolf
52. *Eleusine* Gaertn.
53. *Sporobolus* R. Br.
54. *Crypsis* Aiton
55. *Calamovilfa* (A. Gray) Hack. ex Scribn. & Southworth
56. *Muhlenbergia* Schreb.

Tribe 16. CYNODONTEAE
57. *Chloris* Sw.
58. *Schedonnardus* Steud.
59. *Gymnopogon* P. Beauv.
60. *Cynodon* L.C. Rich.
61. *Spartina* Schreb.
62. *Bouteloua* Lag.
63. *Buchloe* Engelm.

VI. SUBFAMILY PANICOIDEAE

Tribe 17. PANICEAE
64. *Panicum* L.
65. *Sacciolepis* Nash
66. *Echinochloa* P. Beauv.
67. *Brachiaria* (Trin.) Griseb.
68. *Eriochloa* Kunth
69. *Paspalum* L.
70. *Setaria* P. Beauv.
71. *Paspalidium* Stapf
72. *Stenotaphrum* Trin.
73. *Digitaria* Haller
74. *Pennisetum* L.C. Rich. ex Pers.
75. *Cenchrus* L.

Tribe 18. ANDROPOGONEAE
76. *Saccharum* L.
77. *Miscanthus* Anderss.
78. *Microstegium* Nees
79. *Sorghum* Moench
80. *Sorghastrum* Nash
81. *Bothriochloa* Kuntze
82. *Andropogon* L.
83. *Schizachyrium* Nees
84. *Arthraxon* P. Beauv.
85. *Coelorachis* Brongn.
86. *Tripsacum* L.
87. *Zea* L.

KEY TO TRIBES

a. Culms woody, persistent, to 5 m tall or more; some leaf blades with short petiole-like constriction at base; flowering infrequent or sporadic ....1. *Bambuseae,* p. 25
a. Culms herbaceous, renewable each year; leaf blades not petiolate; flowering on a regular basis
  b. Spikelets several-flowered
    c. Culms to 3–5 m tall or more at flowering maturity, reedlike, with leaf blades distributed uniformly from base to terminal plumelike panicles.........12. *Arundineae,* p. 133
    c. Culms of varying height, usually not more than 1–2.5 m tall at maturity
      d. Culms with closed sheaths, the margins fused or connate (in our genera)
        e. Lemmas mostly awned from notched apex, sometimes awnless; lemma margins firm ....9. *Bromeae,* p. 100
        e. Lemmas awnless, with thin, scarious margins ....7. *Meliceae,* p. 65
      d. Culms with open sheaths, the margins overlapping but not connate
        f. Glumes relatively long, mostly exceeding the lowermost floret, and sometimes all florets of the spikelet
          g. Awns arising from bidentate apex of lemma; low grasses with dense basal clusters of narrow curling leaves..............................13. *Danthonieae,* p. 136
          g. Awns arising from below simple apex on back of lemma, or awnless...........
          ....8. *Aveneae,* p. 69
        f. Glumes relatively shorter, sometimes bristlelike or absent, if sometimes longer, spikelet 1-flowered
          h. Inflorescence a terminal spike; spikelets sessile, alternating on opposite sides of the jointed rachis..10. *Triticeae,* p. 111
          h. Inflorescence not as above, consisting of slender compact to open panicles
            i. Spikelets with lower 1 to several florets sterile, only upper ones fertile
            ....11. *Centotheceae,* p. 130
            i. Spikelets with all florets mostly similar and fertile
              j. Spikelets sparsely distributed on close-ascending branches of narrow, wandlike panicles; caryopsis beaked, conspicuously plump at maturity, not enclosed by lemma and palea.....3. *Diarrheneae,* p. 34
              j. Spikelets in compact to open panicles, not noticeably sparse; caryopsis not as above
                k. Lemmas mostly 5-nerved; ligule membranous .....6. *Poeae,* p. 41
                k. Lemmas mostly 3-nerved; ligule consisting mostly of cilia or hairs ....15. *Eragrostideae.* p. 144
  b. Spikelets 1-flowered, sometimes with 1 to several sterile florets (bracts)
        l. Glumes absent or obsolete; grasses of aquatic habitats and damp ground..2. *Oryzeae,* p. 27
        l. Glumes present (first glume sometimes minute or obsolete)
          m. Lemmas with tri-parted awn..............14. *Aristideae,* p. 138
          m. Lemmas with single awn or awnless
            n. First glume minute or obsolete; rachilla joint a conspicuous extension behind palea......4. *Brachyelytreae,* p. 36
            n. First glume not reduced; rachilla joint not extended.
              o. Spikelets separating above the glumes at maturity, the latter persistent on the pedicel
                p. Florets firm, apically awned, mostly terete, fusiform to narrow-cylindric............5. *Stipeae,* p. 38

p. Florets variably awned or awnless, not terete or fusiform, more or less laterally compressed

  q. Glumes relatively large, equal to or exceeding the single floret; lemmas 3–5-nerved or more, awn, if present, mostly dorsal ....8. *Aveneae,* p. 69

  q. Glumes highly variable, sometimes equal to floret; lemmas 1–3-nerved, awn, if present, apical

    r. Inflorescence mostly paniculate, with compact to open branching; ligule mostly a fringe of hairs...15. *Eragrostideae,* p. 144

    r. Inflorescence variable, including dense spikelike racemes, digitate or approximate, or sometimes consisting of short spikes or open panicles with spikelike branching; spikelets often arrayed on one side of the rachis; ligule a minute membrane with ciliate fringe ....16. *Cynodonteae,* p. 119

o. Spikelets separating below the glumes, falling entire

    s. Spikelets in pairs, the lower one sessile and fertile, the upper mostly reduced and sterile, or staminate (see *Miscanthus* and *Saccharum*); inflorescence including simple racemes, spikes, or panicles, the spikelets sometimes unisexual as in *Tripsacum* and *Zea*...18. *Andropogoneae,* p. 264

    s. Spikelets not in pairs, uniformly fertile; inflorescence consisting of spikes, panicles, or spikelike racemes, the spikelets bisexual, with sterile lemma usually similar to and opposite second glume; spikelets sometimes subtended by bristles or enclosed in bristly involucres or spiny burs..........................17. *Paniceae,* p. 203

KEYS TO GENERA

e. Spikelets distinctly awned

Tribe 7. MELICEAE
Key to Genera

Tribe 8. AVENEAE
Key to Genera

a. Spikelets with mostly 1 perfect floret, sometimes with 2 sterile lemmas (bractlike) beneath and appressed to fertile floret

  b. Spikelets with sterile lemmas below the fertile floret

  b. Spikelets lacking sterile lemmas

    d. Spikelets ovate to lanceolate, glumes not obovate

      e. Inflorescence cylindrical, compact, a spikelike panicle

      e. Inflorescence paniculate with open to short-compact branching, not spikelike

        g. Spikelets separating above the persistent glumes

          h. Florets lacking tuft of hairs at base

            i. Lemma with slender awn; plants annual

a. Spikelets usually with 2 or more perfect florets

      k. Spikelets separating below the glumes, falling entire

        l. Spikelets narrow-ovate to lanceolate

      k. Spikelets separating above the persistent glumes

n. Glumes small, usually less than 1 cm long

 o. All lemmas awnless ....23. *Koeleria,* p. 72

 o. Upper and/or lower lemmas awned

  p. Lemma of upper floret with delicate awn, the lower sometimes awnless; annual ....26. *Aira,* p. 78

  p. Lemmas of 1 or more florets awned; perennials

   q. Spikelets 3–4-flowered, the awns from below the split apex of lemma........22. *Trisetum,* p. 69

   q. Spikelets 2-flowered, the lower floret staminate, its lemma with bent awn from near base ....20. *Arrhenatherum,* p. 69

Tribe 9. BROMEAE

One genus of native and introduced species in Missouri ....36. *Bromus,* p. 100

Tribe 10. TRITICEAE
Key to Genera

a. Spikelets single at each joint of rachis

 b. Lemmas bilaterally symmetrical with centered keel ....39. *Agropyron,* p. 125

 b. Lemmas somewhat asymmetrical with keel displaced toward one side

  c. Glumes broadly ovate, 1-nerved ....41. *Triticum,* p. 126

  c. Glumes narrow-lanceolate, 3-nerved ....40. *Secale,* p. 126

a. Spikelets 2 to several at each rachis joint, sometimes only 1 spikelet perfect, the others reduced, sterile, but similarly awned

  d. Perfect spikelets 1-flowered, 1 at each rachis joint with 2 lateral spikelets, these reduced, awned ....38. *Hordeum,* p. 121

  d. Perfect spikelets 2- to several-flowered, more than 1 at each rachis joint ....37. *Elymus,* p. 111

Tribe 11. CENTOTHECEAE

One native genus in Missouri..42. *Chasmanthium,* p. 130

Tribe 12. ARUNDINEAE
Key to Genera

a. Lemmas with silky hairs; rachilla glabrous; tall exotic species ....43. *Arundo,* p. 133

a. Lemmas glabrous; rachilla with long dense hairs; tall native species ....44. *Phragmites,* p. 133

Tribe 13. DANTHONIEAE

One native genus in Missouri...45. *Danthonia,* p. 136

Tribe 14. ARISTIDEAE

One native genus in Missouri..46. *Aristida,* p. 138

Tribe 15. ERAGROSTIDEAE
Key to Genera

a. Spikelets 1-flowered

 b. Inflorescence a short, compact cylinder, spikelike ....54. *Crypsis,* p. 175

 b. Inflorescence variable, with open to relatively compact branching, but not cylindrical

  c. Lemmas awned from apex ....56. *Muhlenbergia,* p. 178

  c. Lemmas awnless

   d. Lemmas with conspicuous tuft of hairs at base, one half or more the length of body ....55. *Calamovilfa,* p. 178

   d. Lemmas lacking tuft of hairs, sometimes with merely short-pilose hairs

e. Lemmas 1-nerved, lacking tuft of hairs.............................53. *Sporobolus,* p. 167
e. Lemmas 3-nerved, sometimes with pilose hairs............56. *Muhlenbergia,* p. 178
a. Spikelets 2- to several-flowered
    f. Spikelets unisexual; plants dioecious, low perennials spreading by rhizomes....
    ....47. *Distichlis,* p. 144
    f. Spikelets with perfect florets (except *Eragrostis reptans,* a dioecious annual)
        g. Sheaths inflated, partially enclosing inflorescence........49. *Triplasis,* p. 148
        g. Sheaths not noticeably inflated
            h. Inflorescence a panicle with compound branching, but sometimes spikelike
                i. Lemmas with solely villous nerves, sometimes extended with a 3-parted apex...48. *Tridens,* p. 144
                i. Lemmas not as above, apex simple, acute ....51. *Eragrostis,* p. 153
            h. Inflorescence consisting of few to numerous simple branches or spike-like racemes
                j. Racemes few, subdigitate, more or less confined to summit of flower stalk ....52. *Eleusine,* p. 166
                j. Racemes numerous, spread along the main axis, not digitate ....
                ....50. *Leptochloa,* p. 149

Tribe 16. CYNODONTEAE
Key to Genera

a. Plants dioecious; staminate spikelets in short 1-sided spikes to 1.5 cm long.........................
....63. *Buchloe,* p. 200
a. Plants with perfect spikelets; spikes more than 1.5 cm long
    b. Spikes several, digitate or subdigitate
        c. Spikelets 2-flowered, awned, the upper floret sterile.......................57. *Chloris,* p. 190
        c. Spikelets 1-flowered, awnless ....60. *Cynodon,* p. 192
    b. Spikes several to many along a central axis, not digitate
        d. Spikes with numerous imbricated spikelets, short-pendulous, flaglike, or spreading-ascending
            e. Spikelets with 1 to several sterile, awned florets above the fertile floret; plants to about 0.5 m tall...62. *Bouteloua,* p. 196
            e. Spikelets lacking sterile florets; plants 1.5–2.5 m tall ....61. *Spartina,* p. 196
        d. Spikes slender, as sparsely flowered simple branches of terminal panicles, the branching remote to relatively close
            f. Spikelets awned; leaf blades relatively stiff, short; branching close ....
            ....59. *Gymnopogon,* p. 192
            f. Spikelets awnless; leaf blades thin, becoming involute; branching remote ....
            ....58. *Schedonnardus,* p. 192

Tribe 17. PANICEAE
Key to Genera

a. Spikelets 1 to several, enclosed in a spiny bur or bristly involucre, at maturity the assemblage falling together
    b. Spikelets in a bristly involucre, the bristles generally hairlike, free to their base ....
    ....74. *Pennisetum,* p. 259
    b. Spikelets enclosed in a spiny bur, or, if a bristly involucre, the bristles weakly connate at base ....75. *Cenchrus,* p. 262
a. Spikelets not in spiny burs or involucres
    c. First glume absent or minute
        d. Spikelets ovate-orbicular, plano-convex, the flat side away from the rachis; inflorescence consisting of spikelike racemes.....................................69. *Paspalum,* p. 239

  d. Spikelets mostly elliptic, biconvex

    e. Fertile lemma apiculate, with abrupt tip..............................68. *Eriochloa,* p. 236

    e. Fertile lemma not apiculate ....73. *Digitaria,* p. 255

 c. First glume present, conspicuous

    f. Spikelets subtended by several free, persistent bristles ....70. *Setaria,* p. 248

    f. Spikelets not subtended by bristles

      g. Panicles mostly dense, usually compact; fertile lemma distinctly plano-convex ....66. *Echinochloa,* p. 228

      g. Panicles variable; fertile lemma biconvex

        h. Inflorescence consisting of spikelike racemes; spikelets mostly sessile or short-pedicellate

          i. Spikelets appressed to a broad, thick rachis, falling with rachis joints.. ....72. *Stenotaphrum,* p. 255

          i. Spikelets not appressed or imbedded in rachis, the latter not jointed

            j. Spikelike racemes with short bristlelike tip of the rachis extending past uppermost spikelet..............................71. *Paspalidium,* p. 253

            j. Spikelike racemes lacking bristlelike tip.........67. *Brachiaria,* p. 234

        h. Inflorescence mostly open panicles, if narrow, spikelike, then second glume inflated or saccate

          k. Second glume saccate, broader than the sterile lemma............... ....65. *Sacciolepis,* p. 228

          k. Second glume not saccate, similar to the sterile lemma.............. ....64. *Panicum,* p. 203

Tribe 18. ANDROPOGONEAE
Key to Genera

a. Some spikelets with perfect (bisexual) florets

 b. Both spikelets of pair pedicellate, perfect.....................................77. *Miscanthus,* p. 267

 b. Lower spikelet of pair sessile, the upper one pedicellate

  c. Both spikelets of pair with perfect florets

    d. Inflorescence a dense terminal panicle; tall perennials...........76. *Saccharum,* p. 264

    d. Inflorescence consisting of short racemes, subdigitate; low running annual............. ....78. *Microstegium,* p. 267

  c. Spikelets dissimilar, the sessile one with perfect floret, the pedicellate one usually reduced, sterile, sometimes staminate, or absent

    e. Spikelets recessed in a smooth, narrow, cylindrical rachis ....85. *Coelorachis,* p. 279

    e. Spikelets in spreading racemes or panicles

      f. Spikelets in feathery racemes, the latter single on each peduncle, axillary, from bractlike sheaths along the culm..............................83. *Schizachyrium,* p. 277

      f. Spikelets in several subdigitate racemes or in branching panicles

        g. Inflorescence a terminal, dense, pyramid-shaped panicle

          h. Pedicellate spikelet somewhat turgid; forage and grain plants or aggressive weeds ....79. *Sorghum,* p. 269

          h. Pedicellate spikelet absent, the pedicel bearded; native prairie species..... ....80. *Sorghastrum,* p. 270

        g. Inflorescence consisting of few racemes, subdigitate or approximate, sometimes spatheate, or, if paniculate, pedicellate spikelet present, not turgid

          i. Inflorescence paniculate, with numerous branches............................ ....81. *Bothriochloa,* p. 273

          i. Inflorescence consisting of few racemes, subdigitate, sometimes partially enclosed in spathelike sheaths

j. Leaf blades short, ovate with cordate base; annual, rare adventive ...
....84. *Arthraxon,* p. 279

j. Leaf blades narrow, elongate; native perennials of prairies, glades, and old fields ....82. *Andropogon,* p. 273

a. All spikelets unisexual; plants monoecious

k. Spikelets in spikelike racemes, the staminate immediately above the pistillate ones on the same rachis; at maturity the hard, seed-bearing portion of the rachis fragmenting readily ....
....86. *Tripsacum,* p. 281

k. Staminate spikelets in terminal racemose panicles or tassels, the pistillate spikelets on a variably modified rachis from lower sheaths, the whole assembly on abbreviated peduncle and enclosed in 1 to several appressed spathes or husks........................
....87. *Zea,* p. 181

Description of Genera and Species

TRIBE 1. BAMBUSEAE

1. ARUNDINARIA Michx.

Woody perennials, spreading by slender rhizomes; canes variably branching, with some leaves much reduced; larger leaf blades with constricted, petiole-like base; sheaths crowded, overlapping; panicles terminal, sometimes axillary; spikelets several-flowered, compressed-keeled, separating above the glumes; glumes pointed-acuminate; lemmas tapering, awnless. $x = 12$; non-Kranz.

Arundinaria is the only native genus of woody bamboos in North America. Other genera are horticultural introductions, mostly from eastern Asia.

1. Arundinaria gigantea (Walt.) Muhl. ssp. **gigantea** GIANT CANE. Fig. 4.

Plants forming extensive clumps or colonies; culms hard, coarse, 1.5–6.5 m tall; sheaths hispid, with auriculate bristles 5 mm long or more; leaf blades lanceolate, 1–3 cm wide, petiolate; rudimentary leaf blades not petiolate; spikelets large, to 6–7 cm long, mostly short-pubescent.

Southeastern United States, from Florida to Texas, north to southern Missouri, Ohio valley, and mid-Atlantic region.

Missouri. River bottoms and spring branches, southern Ozarks to Mississippi River, generally south of a line from McDonald to Perry Counties, sometimes forming dense colonies; reported also for Dallas County (DeBellis 1906 IPM/UMO), where probably adventive. Flowering infrequent or rare, in summer.

A. gigantea ssp. *tecta* (Walt.) McClure, with a restricted southern and eastern range, is a smaller taxon than ssp. *gigantea,* separated also by differences in rhizome anatomy including air channels (*A. tecta* (Walt.) Muhl.) (McClure, 1973). Although no specimens of ssp. *tecta* have been collected in Missouri, the most probable sites are aquatic habitats in the Mississippi Lowlands section of the state.

FIG. 4. **Arundinaria gigantea** ssp. **gigantea.** Flowering shoot, × ½; two views of floret, × 2.

TRIBE 2. ORYZEAE

2. ORYZA L.

Annuals and perennials; panicles terminal, large, with nodding or spreading branches; spikelets 1-flowered, laterally compressed, separating below the glumelike bracts (sterile lemmas); true glumes reduced to a broadened flange at summit of pedicel; fertile lemma and palea nearly equal. $x = 12$; non-Kranz.

1. Oryza sativa L. CULTIVATED RICE. Fig. 5.

Annual; culms coarse, erect, to 2 m tall; leaf blades elongate, about 1 cm wide or more; panicles large, 15–30 cm long, the branches somewhat drooping; spikelets 6.5–8 mm long; fertile lemmas flattened, oblong, appressed-pubescent, with abrupt tip to sometimes short-awned; sterile lemmas much smaller, 1.5–3 mm long, awnless.

Eastern Asia and other warm regions; cultivated in the southern United States, sometimes occurring as a waif.

Missouri. Grown as a crop in the Mississippi Lowlands and, to some extent, northward along the Mississippi River, where reported as an escape, but not persistent. Flowering in summer and fall.

3. LEERSIA Sw.

Perennials; panicles consisting of short, spikelike racemes toward ends of spreading or ascending branches; spikelets 1-flowered, laterally compressed, falling entire; true glumes and sterile lemmas lacking; fertile lemma broad, keeled, usually ciliate; palea narrower, nearly as long as lemma. $x = 12$; non-Kranz.

Key to Missouri Species

a. Spikelets broad-ovate, 4–5 mm long, almost as wide.....................................1. *L. lenticularis*
a. Spikelets narrower, less than 2 mm wide
    b. Plants stiff, with harsh leaf blades and sheaths; panicles with numerous branches, some
      of these whorled ....2. *L. oryzoides*
    b. Plants slender, delicate; panicles sparsely flowered, with few distant branches ....
      ....3. *L. virginica*

1. Leersia lenticularis Michx. CATCHFLY GRASS. Fig. 6.

Plants erect, 4–10 cm tall; foliage mostly glabrous, the leaf blades 1–2 cm wide; ligule about 1 mm long, truncate; panicles open, flexuous, with crowded imbricated spikelets toward the ends of the slender branches; spikelets (the fertile floret) conspicuously flat, elliptic to oval, 4–5 mm long, fringed with stiff cilia, awnless.

Mid-Atlantic and Gulf regions, west to Minnesota and Texas.

Missouri. Bottomland forests, swampy meadows, riverbanks, and marshes; scattered but most common in the eastern counties. Flowering in summer.

2. Leersia oryzoides (L.) Sw. RICE CUTGRASS. Fig. 7.

Plants erect to somewhat spreading or decumbent, to 1 m tall or more; foliage harsh, strongly scabrous to touch; leaf blades about 1 cm wide, panicles spreading, drooping; spikelets compressed, strongly flattened, about 2 mm long, the keel fringed with cilia. A late-season form, with panicles entirely or partially enclosed in the sheath, is sometimes treated as f. *inclusa* (Weisbord) Dörfl.

FIG. 5. **Oryza sativa.** Plant, × ½; spikelet, × 5.

FIG. 6. **Leersia lenticularis,** × 1.

Widespread in the United States and southern Canada; reported also from Europe.

Missouri. Pond borders, sloughs, marshes, and flatwoods, generally distributed. Flowering in late summer and fall.

3. Leersia virginica Willd. WHITEGRASS. Fig. 8.

Plants slender, erect or sometimes decumbent near the base, rooting at the lower nodes, to 1 m tall; leaf blades to 1 cm wide or more, only slightly scabrous; panicles diffuse, with few spreading branches; spikelets somewhat overlapping, 3–4 mm long, about 1 mm wide, with sparse cilia on keel.

Eastern and central United States, west to South Dakota to Texas.

Missouri. Low woods, creek banks, and spring branches, generally distributed. Flowering in summer.

4. ZIZANIA L.

Annuals and perennials; panicles large, terminal, with spreading or ascending branches; spikelets unisexual, 1-flowered, falling entire; glumes reduced or lacking; staminate spikelets acuminate, pendulous, from the lower branches, the lemma awnless; pistillate spikelets linear, firm, stiffly ascending from the upper branches of same panicle, the lemma long-awned. $x = 15$; non-Kranz.

1. Zizania palustris L. var. **interior** (Fassett) Dore NORTHERN WILD RICE. Fig. 9.

Annuals; culms somewhat coarse, erect, becoming decumbent near base, frequently 2 m tall or more; leaf blades to 3 cm wide, ligule conspicuous, 1 cm or more in length; staminate spikelets pendulous; about 10 mm long, awnless; stamens 6, the anthers 4–5 mm long; fertile lemma of pistillate spikelets linear, firm, 1.5–2 cm long with abrupt apex ending in a long, straight awn. *Z. aquatica* L. var. *interior* Fassett.

North central United States and southern Canada. Typical *palustris,* cited for Illinois but not for Missouri, occurs farther east and south than var. *interior.* Wild rice is an important food plant for waterfowl. In the northern United States and adjacent Canada the grain is harvested and marketed for human consumption.

FIG. 7. **Leersia oryzoides.** Plant, × ½; spikelet, × 5.

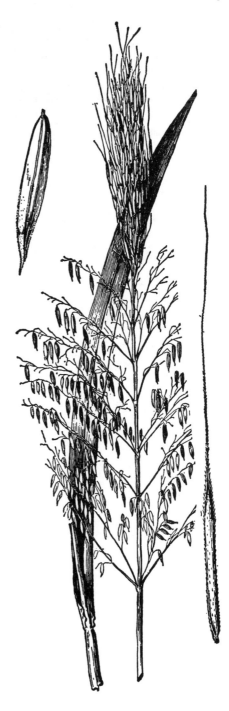

FIG. 8. **Leersia virginica**, × 1.

FIG. 9. **Zizania palustris** var. **interior.**
Panicle, × ½; pistillate spikelet and
staminate spikelet, × 5.

Missouri. Sloughs, marshes, and stream banks; widely scattered, reported for Clay, Jackson, Newton, Greene, Butler, Dunklin, New Madrid, St. Charles, and Clark Counties. Flowering in summer.

5. ZIZANIOPSIS Doell. & Aschers.

Perennials; panicles large, terminal, with whorled branches; spikelets unisexual, 1-flowered, falling entire; glumes lacking; staminate spikelets occurring below the pistillate ones on the *same* branches of the panicle; lemmas of staminate spikelets awnless or merely awn-tipped, those of the pistillate spikelets short-awned. $x = 12$; non-Kranz.

1. Zizaniopsis miliacea (Michx.) Doell & Aschers. Southern Wild Rice. Fig. 10.

Plants spreading by rhizomes; culms erect, 2–3 m tall or more; leaf blades elongate, scabrous, about 2 cm wide; ligule conspicuous, about 2 cm long; panicles large, to 50 cm long, with whorled, nodding branches; staminate spikelets conspicuously nerved, about 7–8 mm long, the lemma and palea about equal, apiculate; stamens 6, the anthers large, about 5 mm long; pistillate spikelets also conspicuously nerved, about the same length as the staminate spikelets; lemma with awn 2–3 mm long; palea only slightly longer than lemma; grain plump, about 3 mm long, with stiff, persistent style.

Southern and mid-Atlantic region, west to Oklahoma and Texas.

Missouri. Aquatic habitats including creek banks, sinkhole depressions, and swampy ground; infrequent and limited to the eastern Ozarks and Mississippi Lowlands, including Shannon, Oregon, Butler, Stoddard, Dunklin, Pemiscot, and New Madrid Counties. Flowering in late spring.

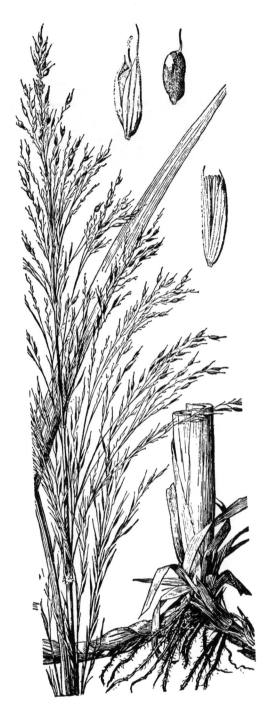

FIG. 10. **Zizaniopsis miliacea.** Plant, × ½; staminate
spikelet, pistillate spikelet, and ripe caryopsis, × 5.

TRIBE 3. DIARRHENEAE

6. DIARRHENA P. Beauv.

Perennials; panicles narrow, with few, ascending branches; spikelets few-flowered, remote, scattered along the slender axis, separating above the persistent glumes, glumes unequal; lemmas 3-nerved, with a stiff, pointed apex, palea shorter than the lemma; grain plump, with noticeable beak. x = 10, 19; non-Kranz.

1. Diarrhena americana P. Beauv. BEAK GRAIN. Fig. 11.

Plants sometimes forming extensive colonies, spreading by rhizomes; culms leafy, reclining to erect, 50–100 cm tall; leaf blades dark, shiny green with a conspicuous midvein, elongate, 1–2 cm wide, tapering toward the base; panicles wandlike, slender, with several short, closely ascending branches; spikelets few, 3–5-flowered, shattering readily; florets plump; glumes unequal, the 1st 1-nerved, the 2nd 3-nerved; lemmas prominently 3-nerved, oblong to obovate, 4–10 mm long, acuminate or abruptly pointed.

Plants with lemmas 7–10 mm long and the apex acuminate are referred to var. *americana;* those with mostly shorter lemmas, 4–7 mm long, obovate, the apex with abrupt beak, are separated as var. *obovata* Gleason.

Eastern and central United States, west to South Dakota and Texas.

Missouri. Wooded limestone slopes and ravines; generally distributed as var. *obovata,* absent extreme southeast; var. *americana* reported for Christian, Ozark, Stone, and Taney Counties. Flowering in June–September.

Fig. 11. **Diarrhena americana** var. **obovata.** Plant, × ½; spikelet and floret, × 5.

TRIBE 4. BRACHYELYTREAE

7. BRACHYELYTRUM P. Beauv.

Perennial, consisting of a single species; panicles slender, sparsely flowered; spikelets 1-flowered, separating readily above the persistent glumes; glumes unequal, reduced; lemma distinctly nerved, awned; palea tightly enclosed by lemma; rachilla with conspicuous extension behind the palea. $x = 11$; non-Kranz.

1. Brachyelytrum erectum (Schreb. ex Spreng.) P. Beauv. var. **erectum** Fig. 12.

Plants solitary or few in loose clumps, from short, knotty rhizomes; culms leafy, erect, to 1 m tall, sheaths somewhat pubescent; leaf blades thin, lax, to 1 cm wide or more; panicles narrow, with short, ascending branches; spikelets about 10 mm long; glumes reduced, acuminate, the 1st sometimes obsolete; lemmas narrow, pubescent on the conspicuous nerves, and with distinct callus at base; awn of lemma straight, slender, 1–3 cm long.

Eastern and central United States, west to Kansas and Oklahoma; also eastern Asia, representing wide-ranging disjunction for a native species.

Missouri. Moist, wooded slopes and ravines, mostly on calcareous soils, generally distributed. Flowering in June–July.

FIG. 12. **Brachyelytrum erectum** var. **erectum.** Plant × ½; branchlet with glume of two spikelets, and floret, × 5.

TRIBE 5. STIPEAE

8. HESPEROSTIPA (Elias) Barkworth NEEDLEGRASS

Perennials; panicles narrow, strict to somewhat open with spreading branches; spikelets 1-flowered, readily separating above the glumes, glumes unequal, papery, exceeding the lemma; floret terete, elongate, with sharp, hairy callus, the lemma terminating in a twisted, persistent awn. x = 9, 10, 11, 12; non-Kranz. *Stipa* L. in part.

1. Hesperostipa spartea (Trin.) Barkworth PORCUPINE GRASS. Fig. 13.

Plants forming loose clumps; culms erect, 50–100 cm tall; leaf blades narrow, becoming involute when dried; ligule membranous, conspicuous, about 5 mm long; panicles narrow, flexuous, sparsely branched; spikelets large, to 4 cm long excluding awn; glumes thin, long-acuminate, somewhat unequal, both exceeding floret, the latter narrow, cylindrical, about 2 cm long, with tufted, sharp-pointed base; awn of lemma geniculate, noticeably twisted, 12–15 cm long. *Stipa spartea* Trin.

Widespread through the northern United States and adjacent Canada from Pennsylvania to Montana, south through the Ohio valley to Oklahoma and New Mexico.

Missouri. Upland prairies, roadsides, and open areas; widely scattered, north and west of a line from Newton to Moniteau to Shelby and Schuyler Counties. Flowering in May–June.

The small genus *Nasella* (Trin.) Desv., centered in South America, is another member of the Stipeae. *N. trichotoma* (Nees) Hack. ex. Arech., commonly known as serrated tussock grass, was reported for Missouri as a contaminant in fescue seed imported from Argentina in 1989. While no specimens of this invasive species have been observed to date under field conditions, its establishment remains a possibility, especially in or near St. Louis and Jefferson Counties, where contaminated seed was initially brought into the state. Serrated tussock grass is described as a bunch grass with elongate, stringlike leaf blades becoming involute upon drying. The drooping panicles are deciduous at maturity, much branched, with a purplish hue. *Nasella* differs from *Hesperostipa*, with which it is closely allied, by its somewhat asymmetrical lemma with an off-center awn.

9. PIPTATHERUM P. Beauv. RICEGRASS

Perennials; panicles narrow, spikelike to more open with spreading branches; spikelets 1-flowered, separating above the glumes; glumes nearly equal, enlarged, mostly exceeding the floret; lemma indurate, variably pubescent, awned, enclosing the palea. x = 11, 12; non-Kranz. *Oryzopsis* Michx.

1. Piptatherum racemosum (Smith) Barkworth Fig. 14.

Plants forming tufts, rhizomatous; culms slender, erect, to 1 m tall; leaf blades becoming longer on upper culm, soft-pubescent on lower surface, 1–1.3 cm wide; panicles with few ascending branches, sparsely flowered; spikelets about 8 mm long; glumes conspicuously nerved, awn-tipped; lemma acute-elliptic, with inrolled margins, becoming dark at maturity; awn of lemma straight, 10–20 mm long, jointed, and breaking from body, leaving a stipe about 1 mm long at apex. *Oryzopsis racemosa* (Smith) Hitchc.

Fig. 13. **Hesperostipa spartea.** Plant, × ½; glumes and floret, × 2.

Fig. 14. **Piptatherum racemosum.** Panicle, × ½; floret, × 5.

Eastern United States from New England to South Dakota, south to Kentucky. *Missouri.* Woodlands, limestone slopes, and bottomlands; sporadic and infrequent, Clark and Shannon Counties, and more recently Callaway County, scattered colonies at confluence of Smith and Cedar Creeks (Wakman s.n. and McKenzie 1742 MO, UMO). Flowering in summer.

TRIBE 6. POEAE

10. FESTUCA L. FESCUE

Perennials, forming clumps and loose tufts, or sod-forming; auriculate leaf blades sometimes present (Subgenus Schedonorus); panicles mostly terminal, narrow, compact, to diffusely spreading; spikelets several-flowered, separating above the persistent glumes; glumes narrow, acute, mostly unequal; lemmas 5-nerved, acuminate or pointed, or sometimes awned from the apex. $x = 7$; non-Kranz.

Festuca is a large, wide-ranging genus of approximately 350 species characteristic of temperate regions and montane zones, some with considerable forage and range value.

Key to Missouri Species

a. Leaf blades usually flat, to 5 mm wide or more
  b. Plants forming dense clumps; auricles usually present; introduced forage species
    c. Florets 7–10 mm long ....1. *F. arundinacea*
    c. Florets generally smaller, 5–7 mm long ....2. *F. pratensis*
  b. Plants forming sparse clumps or solitary; auricles absent; native woodland and prairie species
    d. Panicles open, with diffuse branching; spikelets mostly sparse....3. *F. subverticillata*
    d. Panicles contracted, usually dense; spikelets crowded ....4. *F. paradoxa*
a. Leaf blades mostly inrolled, stringlike, 1–2 mm wide, the upper leaves sometimes wider with flat blades
    e. Basal sheaths reddish brown, becoming fibrous or stringy; plants forming a turf
    ....5. *F. rubra*
    e. Basal sheaths not reddish or fibrous; plants forming dense clumps
      f. Leaf blades involute, stringlike, about 1 mm wide ....6. *F. ovina*
      f. Leaf blades stiff, tough, mostly wider ....7. *F. longifolia*

1. Festuca arundinacea Schreb. TALL FESCUE. Fig. 15.

Plants forming loose to dense tufts; culms erect, to 1 m tall or more; foliage glabrous; leaf blades 5 mm wide or more; auricles ciliate, sometimes only one present; panicles somewhat spreading, to 25–30 cm long, with branches densely floriferous; spikelets 5–7-flowered; glumes unequal, with scarious margins; lemmas glabrous, 7–10 mm long, awnless or rarely with minute awn. *F. elatior* L. var. *arundinacea* Schreb.; *Lolium arundinaceum* (Schreb.) S.J. Darbyshire.

Widespread in the United States, introduced from Europe as a forage species.

Missouri. Fields, meadows, pastures, and waste areas, common and widespread. Flowering in May–June.

2. Festuca pratensis Huds. MEADOW FESCUE

Plants resembling no. 1 but differing in the shorter culms, less robust habit, and more contracted panicle branches; creeping rootstocks sometimes present; spikelets 6–9-flowered; lemmas about 5–6 mm long, awnless or with short awn from tip. *F. elatior* L. var. *pratensis* (Hudson) A. Gray; *Lolium pratense* (Hudson) S.J. Darbyshire.

Formerly treated under *F. elatior* as variants, *F. pratensis* and *F. arundinacea* constitute diploid and hexaploid complexes respectively, producing sterile hybrids (Terrell, 1967). More recently, these species (Subgenus Schedonorus) have been transferred to genus *Lolium* L. on the basis of general correspondence in a number of morphological as well as significant nonmorphological criteria, summarizing the

FIG. 15. **Festuca arundinacea.** Plant, × ½; spikelet and floret, × 5.

works of several authors (Darbyshire, 1993). The importance of this merger is recognized as a contribution toward a more monophyletic classification; however, the traditional separation of *Festuca* and *Lolium* based on distinctive inflorescence types (panicle vs. spike) is provisionally retained here. Widespread in cooler regions of the United States; introduced from Eurasia as a forage species.

Missouri. Fields, pastures, and roadsides, generally widespread. Flowering in late spring and early summer.

3. Festuca subverticillata (Pers.) E. Alexeev NODDING FESCUE. Fig. 16.

Plants solitary to loosely tufted; culms to 1 m tall; foliage glabrous or with slight pubescence on lower sheaths; leaf blades thin, lax 3–10 mm wide; panicles open, diffuse with few spikelets toward the ends of branches; spikelets elliptic; few-flowered about 4–7 mm long; glumes unequal, the first awl-shaped, 2.5–3 mm long, the second wider and longer; lemmas glabrous or nearly so, 3–4 mm long, awnless. *F. obtusa* Biehler.

Eastern United States to the Midwest.

Missouri. Damp shaded ground, alluvium, and wooded, calcareous slopes, throughout the state. Flowering in May–June.

4. Festuca paradoxa Desv. Fig. 17.

Generally similar to no. 3 but somewhat coarser, the panicles more compact; spikelets crowded, ovate, few-flowered, 5–7 mm long; lemmas plump, about 4.5 mm long, awnless.

Throughout the eastern United States to the Midwest, from Canada to Gulf region.

Missouri. Open woods and prairies, scattered, less commonly distributed, and occupying usually more open habitats and prairies than no. 3. Flowering in late spring and early summer.

5. Festuca rubra L. RED FESCUE. Fig. 18.

Plants forming loose tufts or sod; short rhizomes sometimes present; culms erect, sometimes decumbent near base, less than 1 m tall; foliage mostly glabrous, the lower sheaths characteristically reddish, becoming stringy, fibrous; lower blades involute or narrow, about 1 mm wide, some upper leaves flat and wider; panicles narrow, with short side branches; spikelets elongate or oblong, usually more than 5-flowered, 10–15 mm long; glumes dissimilar, the 1st narrow, sharp-pointed, the 2nd wider and longer with scarious margins; lemmas usually glabrous, sometimes pubescent, 5–6 mm long with narrow scarious edges, awnless or sometimes with an awn 1.5–3 mm long.

Plants with decumbent-spreading habit represent typical *rubra;* those with more or less upright shoots are separated as var. *commutata* Gaudin, commonly known as Chewings fescue. Both of these variants have glabrous lemmas, distinguishing them from var. *arenaria* (Osbeck) Fries, which has pubescent lemmas.

FIG. 16. **Festuca subverticillata.**
Panicle, × ½; floret, × 5.

FIG. 17. **Festuca paradoxa.** Panicle, × ½;
floret, × 5.

FIG. 18. **Festuca rubra.** Plant, × ½; spikelet and floret, × 5.

Wide-ranging, native to United States and Canada, Eurasia, and North Africa, often in the montane.

Missouri. Not well known, the several variants reported occasionally as escapes; Randolph, Boone, Pulaski, and St. Louis Counties. Flowering in spring and early summer.

6. Festuca ovina L. SHEEP'S FESCUE. Fig. 19.

Plants forming dense tufts, lacking rhizomes; culms wiry, usually not more than 50 cm tall; lower sheaths light-colored, intact, not becoming fibrous; leaf blades involute; panicles narrow, rather dense; spikelets oblong, about 6-flowered, 5–8 mm long; glumes firm, sharp-pointed; lemmas 4–5 mm long, aristate or short awned.

Northern and western United States and eastward to mid-Atlantic region, in some eastern areas occasionally self-established; introduced from Europe as a forage species.

Missouri. Rare and little known, Boone and St. Louis Counties. Flowering in June–July.

7. Festuca longifolia Thuill. HARD FESCUE

Generally similar to no. 6, but with taller culms and coarser and more indurate foliage; spikelets somewhat larger, about 7.5–10 mm long. *F. ovina* L. var. *duriuscula* (L.) Koch.

F. ovina and *F. longifolia* form a polyploid complex with $2n = 14$ and 42, respectively (McNeill and Dore, 1976).

Northern United States and adjacent Canada from Newfoundland to Minnesota southward to New York, Virginia, and west to Missouri.

Missouri. Rare and little known, Jackson and St. Louis Counties. Flowering in early summer.

11. LOLIUM L. RYEGRASS

Annuals and short-lived perennials; spikes slender, with spikelets 2-ranked on a continuous (nonfragmenting) rachis; spikelets several-flowered, one at each concavity, oriented edgewise to the rachis; spikelets separating above the single outer glume, the first glume absent, except in the terminal spikelet; lemmas awned or awnless. $x = 7$; non-Kranz.

In earlier manuals *Lolium* was placed with the traditional tribe Hordeae (Triticeae), but the genus is more closely allied with tribe Poeae, as evidenced by extensive formation of viable hybrids with *Festuca* (see discussion under *Festuca pratensis*). Reportedly, hybridization does not occur between *Lolium* and any members of the Triticeae. The ryegrasses are of European origin and have a long history of domestic use as forage.

Key to Missouri Species

a. The single glume usually shorter than tip of 1st floret; annuals, biennials, or short-lived perennials ....1. *L. perenne*

a. The single glume usually exceeding or overtopping 1st floret; annuals

    b. Lemmas blunt-tipped, awned or awnless; caryopsis oblong, plump, not more than 3 times longer than broad ....2. *L. temulentum*

    b. Lemmas variously tipped, awned or awnless; caryopsis elongated, more than 3 times longer than broad

        c. Lemmas with awns not usually exceeding 3 mm or awnless....................3. *L. rigidum*

        c. Lemmas with awns longer than 3 mm...4. *L. persicum*

1. Lolium perenne L. Ryegrass. Fig. 20a,b.

Annual or perennial; culms 50–100 cm tall; leaf blades 2–8 mm wide; auricles conspicuous or obsolete, sometimes only 1 present; spikes erect, to 20 cm long; spikelets 5–20-flowered; single glume of variable length; lower lemmas 5–8 mm long, awnless or sometimes with delicate awn.

This species intergrades with closely related *L. multiflorum* Lam., Italian ryegrass, with which it is currently joined. A continuum of forms occurs to which several epithets have been applied. Plants of annual or biennial habit, with wider leaves and more robust stature, rolled vernation (as opposed to folded), more numerous florets, and lemmas mostly awned are separated from typical *perenne* as var. *multiflorum* Thuill. ex Bast (Terrell, 1968).

Introduced in the United States from Europe as a turf and forage species, becoming self-established in some areas.

Missouri. Widespread and common, open ground, lawns, and waste areas. Flowering in spring.

2. Lolium temulentum L. Poison Darnel. Fig. 21.

Annual; culms coarse, erect, to 1.5 m tall; leaf blades mostly glabrous, 3–6 mm wide; spikes stiff, with heavy rachis, 15–20 cm long or more; spikelets 4–8-flowered, to 20 mm long, the plump florets sometimes exceeded by the rigid, acuminate glume; lemmas awned or awnless, sometimes within same spikelet, or between spikelets of common spike; awns, when present, mostly straight, attached from below apex, variable in length, to about 2 cm, but usually less; palea about the same size and shape as lemma.

Two forms are recognized: f. *temulentum* (var. *macrochaeton* (A. Braun) Junge) with conspicuous awns, and f. *arvense* (With.) Junge (var. *temulentum* sensu Steyermark), predominantly awnless, or with reduced or obscure awns. A collection labeled as var. *macrochaeton,* St. Louis County (Muehlenbach 1398 MO), is identified as *L. rigidum* Gaudin.

Fig. 19. **Festuca ovina.** Panicle, × ½; floret, × 5.

Fig. 20a. **Lolium perenne** var. **perenne,** × ½.

FIG. 20b. **Lolium perenne** var. **multiflorum.** Plant, × ½; spikelet, × 3; floret, × 5.

Fig. 21. **Lolium temulentum,** × ½.　　　Fig. 22. **Vulpia myuros.** Spikelet, × 5.

An Old World species, introduced in the United States, widely scattered as a weedy adventive.

Missouri. Not well known; reported for Platte, Jackson, and McDonald Counties as the awnless form. Flowering in early summer.

3. **Lolium rigidum** Gaudin

Annual; culms erect to decumbent-spreading, 50–70 cm tall; leaf blades to about 5 mm wide; auricles sometimes present, about 3.5 mm long; spikes to 30 cm in length, sometimes more than one-half the total height of plant; spikelets with 2–10 fertile florets; single glume of variable length, to 20 mm long, mostly less, not over-topping lemmas; lemmas usually awnless, or awns sometimes present; palea about equal in size and shape to lemma.

L. rigidum represents a polymorphic complex, intergrading with other species including the *perenne* × *multiflorum* complex.

Widely scattered as an adventive in the United States; native throughout the Mediterranean region to Afghanistan.

Missouri. Rare and little known; collected at railroad freight yards, St. Louis County (Muehlenbach 1411 MO), probably not persisting.

4. **Lolium persicum** Boiss. & Hohen. ex Boiss.

Annual; culm erect to spreading, about 0.5 m tall; leaf blades 6–7 mm wide; auricles to 2 mm long or sometimes obsolete; spikes usually less than 15 cm long, and not more than one-half the total plant height; spikelets less than 10-flowered; the single glume of variable length, but not exceeding uppermost florets; lemmas mostly awned, from below apex; palea similar to lemma, sometimes longer.

Occurring as an adventive in the northern wheat belt of the United States and Canada; an adventive from European Russia.

Missouri. Rare and little known; collected in the railroad freight terminus, St. Louis County (Muehlenbach 1176 MO), probably not persisting.

12. VULPIA K.C. Gmel.

Small annuals, ephemeral; culms fragile, with glabrous to somewhat pubescent sheaths; ligules minute; less than 1 mm long; leaf blades narrow, sometimes involute, 0.5–2.5 mm wide; spikelets 5–15-flowered, the uppermost reduced, separating above the glumes; glumes unequal, acuminate-subulate; lemmas awned or awnless; palea thin, slightly shorter than lemma. *Festuca* L. $x = 7$; non-Kranz.

Genus *Vulpia* is separated from *Festuca* by its annual habit, cleistogamous florets, and minute anthers mostly less than 0.5 mm long.

Key to Missouri Species

a. Glumes very unequal, the 1st about ⅓ or less as long as the 2nd ....1. *V. myuros*
a. Glumes more equal, the 1st about ½ or more the length of the 2nd
    b. Spikelets more than 5-flowered; lemmas mostly glabrous ....2. *V. octoflora*
    b. Spikelets mostly less than 5-flowered, lemmas glabrous or pubescent
        c. Lemmas about 3 mm long, appressed-pubescent on back ....3. *V. sciurea*
        c. Lemmas mostly larger, to 7 mm long, glabrous or scabrous ....3. *V. bromoides*

1. Vulpia myuros (L.) K.C. Gmel. var. **myuros** RAT-TAIL SIX-WEEKS GRASS. Fig. 22.

Annual; culms slight, 20–50 cm tall; somewhat geniculate near base, the foliage mostly glabrous; leaf blades narrow, with inrolled margins; panicles delicate, narrow, spikelike, 5–15 cm long, the spikelets 4–5-flowered; glumes very unequal, the 1st about 1 mm long, the 2nd 3–5 mm long; lemmas long-tapering about 5 mm long, the awn 10–15 mm long or more. *Festuca myuros* L.

Widely scattered in the United States; weedy adventive from Europe.

Missouri. Rare and little known; reported for Boone and St. Louis Counties. Flowering in May–June.

2. Vulpia octoflora (Walter) Rydb. COMMON SIX-WEEKS GRASS. Fig. 23.

Annual; culms erect, 50 cm tall or more; foliage generally glabrous, the sheaths mostly shorter than the internodes; panicles with short, ascending branches, spikelike to more open and diffuse; spikelets 6–12-flowered; glumes subequal, the 1st 2–3 mm long, the 2nd to 5 mm long; lemmas smooth to scabrous, 3 mm long, with awn 1–5 mm in length. *Festuca octoflora* Walt. var. *octoflora;* var. *glauca* (Nutt.) Fern. Incl. var. *tenella* (Willd.) Fern.

Based on differences in inflorescence and relative awn length, varietal distinctions are noted. These are weakly separable, but tendencies are noted in some Missouri specimens. Plants with more open, spreading panicles and the longer awns represent typical *octoflora,* and those with slender, compact panicles and lemmas awnless or nearly so are separated as var. *glauca* (Nutt.) Fern.

Widespread throughout the United States and adjacent parts of Canada.

Missouri. Fields and waste ground, on dry, thin soils, occurring most commonly throughout the state as var. *glauca,* with the typical variety more restricted, mainly south of a line from Vernon to Morgan and St. Louis Counties. Flowering in May–June.

FIG. 23. **Vulpia octoflora.** Plant, × ½; spikelet, × 5.

3. Vulpia sciurea (Nutt.) Henr. SQUIRREL SIX-WEEKS GRASS. Fig. 24.

Annual; culms slight, mostly less than 50 cm tall; leaf blades narrow, involute; panicles contracted; spikelets about 5-flowered with dissimilar glumes, the 1st 2 mm long, the 2nd about twice as long; lemmas pubescent, 3 mm long, with delicate awn about 10 mm in length. *Festuca sciurea* Nutt.; *Vulpia elliotea* (Raf.) Fern.

Southeastern United States and Atlantic Coast region, west to Oklahoma and Texas.

Missouri. Fields and waste ground, mostly scattered in the south; Jasper, Douglas, Stoddard, Scott, New Madrid, and Dunklin Counties. Flowering in April–May.

4. Vulpia bromoides (L.) S.F. Gray Fig. 25.

Annual; similar in general habit to no. 3; leaf blades glabrous; panicles narrow; spikelets 4–6-flowered; glumes subequal, the 1st 4–5 mm long, the 2nd to 7 mm in length; lemmas mostly glabrous, 5–6 mm long, with stiff awn 5–10 mm in length. *Festuca dertonensis* (All.) Asch. & Graebn.

Pacific coast, also Texas, an adventive from Europe.

Missouri. Recently reported, collected on open ground, Jasper County (Christ 19-3-3A MO).

13. CYNOSURUS L. DOGTAIL

Annuals and perennials; culms 30–60 cm tall; panicles compact, spikelike, linear, or subcapitate; spikelets fertile and nonfertile, mixed in the same inflorescence, the first 2–3-flowered and sessile, exceeded by the short-stalked sterile ones, both types separating above the glumes; glumes of fertile spikelet acuminate, the lemmas awned; spikelets separating above the glumes. $x = 7$; non-Kranz.

FIG. 24. **Vulpia sciurea**. Spikelet, × 5.

FIG. 25. **Vulpia bromoides.** Plant, × ½; spikelet, × 5.

1. Cynosurus echinatus L. Fig. 26.

Culms erect, to about 0.5 m tall; foliage glabrous; ligules whitish 5–10 mm long; inflorescence subcapitate panicle, 4–7 cm long, somewhat asymmetrical, bristly in general appearance; fertile spikelets 2-flowered, lemmas about 5 mm long, with straight awn 5–10 mm long; sterile spikelets consisting of several lemmas 2–3 mm long with awns about three times the length of lemma.

Sporadic; open ground and disturbed areas, widely scattered from the east coast to central region, also Pacific Coast; weedy adventive from Europe.

Missouri. Rare and little known; collected on waste ground, St. Louis County (Muehlenbach 1628 MO).

14. PUCCINELLIA Parl.

Annuals and perennials; panicles somewhat contracted to more diffuse with spreading branches in remote whorls; sheaths characteristically open; spikelets several-flowered, separating above the persistent glumes; glumes somewhat unequal, shorter than the lemmas, the 2nd glume mostly 3-nerved; lemmas faintly nerved, obtuse or merely acute, the apex thin, scarious, or sometimes lacerated, awnless. $x = 7$; non-Kranz.

1. Puccinellia distans (L.) Parl. WEEPING ALKALI GRASS. Fig. 27.

Perennial, forming tufts; culms erect to somewhat decumbent, to 1 m tall; foliage glabrous, the leaf blades about 2 mm wide, becoming involute when dried; panicles 5–15 cm long, with spreading to drooping branches; spikelets about 5-flowered, 4–5 mm long; glumes thin-margined, the 1st about 1 mm long, the 2nd

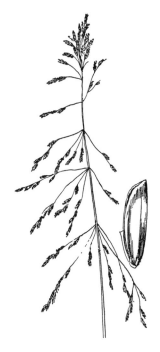

FIG. 26. **Cynosurus echinatus.** Panicle, × 1; fertile floret, × 5.

FIG. 27. **Puccinellia distans.** Panicle, × ½; floret, × 10.

somewhat longer; lemmas obscurely nerved, about 1.5–2.5 mm long, with broad apex, the margin hyaline; palea equaling lemma.

Western and northern United States and adjacent parts of Canada; also Eurasia.

Missouri. Rare and little known; collected on waste ground, St. Louis County (Muehlenbach 70 MO), also UMSL campus (McKenzie 1770 MO).

2. Puccinellia pallida (Torr.) R.T. Clausen Fig. 28.

Perennial, culms slender, somewhat decumbent, often rooting at nodes, 50–100 cm tall; leaf blades 3.5–7 mm wide; ligule thin, conspicuous, whitish, panicles with ascending to spreading branches; spikelets 4–7-flowered, 6–7 mm long; glumes subequal, 1.5–2.5 mm long; lemmas about 3 mm long, truncate, with hyaline margin. *Glyceria pallida* (Torr.) Trin.

Glyceria pallida is transferred to genus *Puccinellia* on the basis of closer agreement in sheath characteristics to the latter, venation of glumes, and basic number and size of chromosomes (Clausen, 1952).

Northeastern United States and mid-Atlantic region, west to Wisconsin and south to Missouri.

Missouri. Local, occurring in sloughs and wet woods, Scott and Butler Counties, more recently reported for Phelps County. Flowering in June–July.

15. POA L. BLUEGRASS

Annuals or perennials; leaf blades mostly keeled, V-shaped, with boat-shaped tip; panicles narrow, compact, or diffusely spreading, the branches sometimes in whorls; spikelets several-flowered, separating above the persistent glumes; glumes subequal, somewhat keeled; lemmas mostly 5-nerved, keeled, sometimes scarious at the apex, most species with web or tuft of cottony pubescence at base; palea distinctly shorter than the lemma. $x = 7$; non-Kranz.

Poa, with approximately 500 species, is a large, wide-ranging genus of cool-temperate regions and the tropical montane of both hemispheres.

FIG. 28. **Puccinellia pallida.** Plant, × 1; floret, × 10.

Key to Missouri Species
a. Plants annual, not forming sod or thick tufts, low-growing, not more than 25–30 cm tall
  b. Culms mostly upright; lemmas with cottony web at base...................1. *P. chapmaniana*
  b. Culms decumbent at base; lemmas lacking cottony web..............................2. *P. annua*
a. Plants perennial, forming tufts or sod, mostly taller
    c. Plants rhizomatous, forming loose to dense turf
      d. Culms flattened, from a loose sod ....3. *P. compressa*
      d. Culms terete, not compressed, sod mostly dense..............................4. *P. pratensis*
    c. Plants not forming rhizomes
      e. Culms with swollen base; florets replaced by minute bulblets..........5. *P. bulbosa*
      e. Culms lacking swollen base; florets not as above, bulblets lacking
        f. Panicles diffuse with slender, spreading branches; spikelets mostly sparse, distant; generally distributed woodland species
          g. Panicles elongate with numerous whorls of branches, progressively shorter upwards; spikelets about 4 mm long ....6. *P. sylvestris*
          g. Panicles loose, sparsely branched; spikelets 5–6 mm long..........7. *P. wolfii*
        f. Panicles more compact, branches short or ascending; spikelets variable; infrequent species
          h. Panicles elongate, 10–25 cm long.......................................8. *P. palustris*
          h. Panicles shorter, mostly less than 10 cm long
            i. Lower branches of panicle in distinct whorls; ligule conspicuous, to 5 mm long ....9. *P. trivialis*
            i. Lower branches not as above; ligule about 1 mm long.......................
              ....10. *P. interior*

1. Poa chapmaniana Scribn. ANNUAL BLUEGRASS. Fig. 29.

Annual, forming leafy tufts; foliage fine, glabrous, leaf blades about 1 mm wide; spikelets oblong, few-flowered, about 3.5–4 mm long, in relatively compact panicles; glumes unequal, 1–3 mm long, noticeably scarious on the margins; lemmas 3-nerved with scarious margins and dense, cottony pubescence at base.

Eastern and southern United States, west to Nebraska and Texas.

Missouri. Fallow fields, alluvial ground, and waste areas; generally distributed, but more prevalent in the south. Flowering in spring.

2. Poa annua L. ANNUAL BLUEGRASS. Fig. 30.

Annual, forming soft, leafy tufts; culms somewhat decumbent at base, 15–30 cm tall; leaf blades flat, about 3 mm wide; panicles upright with few short branches; spikelets few-flowered, ovate-oblong, 3–5 mm long; glumes unequal, 1.5–3 long; lemmas *lacking* cottony pubescence at base.

Plants in aquatic situations with creeping habit, rooting at the nodes, have been referred to var. *reptans* Haussk. These are mostly perennial. Similar forms also partly or completely submerged with greatly elongated culms and loose panicles are identified as var. *aquatica* Asch.

Widely scattered throughout the United States; adventive from Europe.

Missouri. Open ground, fields, and pastures; generally distributed as typical *annua,* the perennial aquatic forms occurring primarily in spring habitats throughout the Ozarks. Flowering in May–June.

3. Poa compressa L. CANADA BLUEGRASS. Fig. 31.

Perennial, forming loose sod, from rhizomes with extended internodes; culms 20–70 cm tall; sheaths and lower culms strongly flattened; ligule collar-shaped 1–1.5

FIG. 29. **Poa chapmaniana.** Panicle, × 1; floret, × 10.

FIG. 30. **Poa annua.** Panicle, × 1; floret, × 10.

mm long; leaf blades glabrous, 2–3 mm wide, keeled, with boat-shaped tip; panicles mostly narrow, compact, with short, ascending branches of crowded spikelets; spikelets few-flowered, 4–5 mm long; glumes 2–3 mm long; lemmas mostly glabrous, only slightly cobwebby at base, 2–2.5 mm long, with scarious apex.

Widely scattered but more common in the northern United States; introduced from Europe.

Missouri. Open ground, fields, prairie meadows and dry woods, generally distributed. Flowering in May–June.

FIG. 31. **Poa compressa.** Panicle, × 1; floret, × 10.

4. Poa pratensis L. KENTUCKY BLUEGRASS. Fig. 32.

Perennial, rhizomatous, usually forming dense sod; culms 0.5–0.8 m tall; sheaths somewhat rounded, not flattened; ligule collar-shaped, less than 1 mm long; leaf blades glabrous, 2–4 mm wide, with boat-shaped tip; panicles pyramidal, with distinct whorls of branches; spikelets ovate, few-flowered, 3.5–5 mm long; glumes unequal 2–3 mm long; lemmas distinctly 5-nerved, about 3 mm long, with conspicuous, cobwebby pubescence at base.

Widespread in the United States, less common in the South; introduced from Europe in the 1700s.

Missouri. Pastures, lawns, roadsides, and open woods; generally distributed, our most common bluegrass. Flowering in May–June.

5. Poa bulbosa L. BULBOUS BLUEGRASS. Fig. 33.

Perennial, forming tufts; culms bulbous at base, 20–50 cm tall; leaf blades about 2 mm wide, with inrolled margins; panicles somewhat contracted, with bristly appearance; spikelets in aggregate clusters, replaced by blackish bulblets about 2 mm long, subtended by narrow, tapering bracts with elongate tips.

Widely scattered in the United States, not common; introduced from eastern Europe.

Missouri. Open ground and waste areas, sporadic and not common; Adair, Boone, Camden, Carter, Christian, and Miller Counties. Flowering in April–June.

6. Poa sylvestris A. Gray Fig. 34.

Perennial, forming small, loose tufts; culms 30–80 cm tall; foliage glabrous, the leaf blades 3.5–5 mm wide, somewhat lax; ligules conspicuous; panicles diffuse, pyramid-shaped, the branches slender in several whorls; spikelets several-flowered, about 4.5 mm long; glumes 2.5–3 mm long with scarious margins; lemmas distinctly 5-nerved, 3 mm long, slightly pubescent on the back, and cobwebby at the base.

Eastern and southern United States, to Nebraska, Oklahoma, and Texas.

Missouri. Moist woods, lower slopes, and ravines, generally distributed. Flowering in May–June.

7. Poa wolfii Scribn. Fig. 35.

Perennial, forming leafy tufts; culms erect, to about 80 cm tall; leaf blades about 2 mm wide; panicles open, with few spikelets, the branches spreading, usually in pairs along the main axis; spikelets several-flowered, 4.5–6 mm long; glumes scarious-margined; lemmas 5-nerved, about 4 mm long, cobwebby at base.

This species is distinguished from no. 6 by its sparser branching and larger and fewer spikelets.

North-central United States, south to Indiana and Nebraska.

Missouri. Moist woods and ravines, generally distributed. Flowering in May–June.

8. Poa palustris L. FOWL BLUEGRASS. Fig. 36.

Perennial, forming loose tufts; culms coarse, rooting from lower nodes, to 1 m or taller; foliage glabrous, the leaf blades 2–4.5 mm wide, with conspicuous ligule 3.5–5 mm long; panicles elongate-pyramidal with whorled branches of crowded spikelets; spikelets 3–4 long; glumes somewhat purplish, 2–3 mm long; lemmas purplish, 2–3.5 mm long, with scarious margins, cobwebby at base.

Widespread in the western United States, east to New England, south to Virginia.

FIG. 32. **Poa pratensis.** Plant, × ½; spikelet, × 5; floret, × 10.

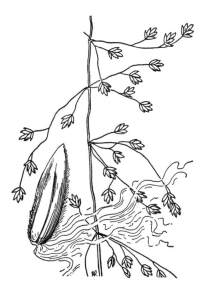

Fig. 33. **Poa bulbosa**, × 1.

Fig. 34. **Poa sylvestris**. Panicle, × 1;
floret, × 10.

Missouri. Rare and little known; reported for Jackson and St. Louis Counties. Flowering in early summer.

9. Poa trivialis L. Rough Bluegrass. Fig. 37.

Perennial, stoloniferous, forming sod; culms to 1 m tall, but usually less robust than no. 8; foliage light green, the sheaths scabrous to rough; leaf blades about 2–3 mm wide; ligules conspicuous; panicles rather small, compact, 4–10 cm long, with whorled branching, the central stalk rough; spikelets few-flowered, 3–4 mm long; glumes 2–3 mm long; lemmas purplish, about 3 mm long, scarious-margined, distinctly cobwebby at base.

This species is distinguishable generally from our other perennial forms by the distinctly rough surface of the sheaths and flowering stalk.

Widely scattered primarily in the northern United States; adventive from Europe.

Missouri. Newton County (Palmer 59826 MO) and more recently from Grindstone Park, Boone County (McKenzie 1688 MO; Brakhage s.n. UMO). Flowering in June–July.

10. Poa interior Rydb. Fig. 38.

Perennial, forming tufts; culms to 0.5 m; sheaths somewhat scabrous; the ligule minute; leaf blades about 2 mm wide; panicles compact, 5–10 cm long, with relatively short, ascending branches; spikelets 3–4-flowered; lemmas about 3 mm long, sparsely cobwebby at base. *P. nemoralis* L. ssp. *interior* (Rydb.) W.A. Weber.

Mainly western and northern United States and adjacent Canada, south to Texas.

Fig. 35. **Poa wolfii.** Panicle, × 1; floret, × 10.

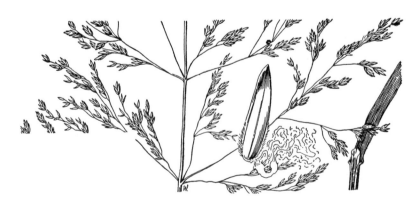

Fig. 36. **Poa palustris.** Panicle, × 1; floret, × 10.

Fig. 37. **Poa trivialis.** Panicle, × 1; floret, × 10.

Fig. 38. **Poa interior.** Panicle, × 1; floret, × 10.

Missouri. A single station, Snowball Hill Prairie, Cass County (Smith 2429 MO), a new state record. Flowering in May.

16. DACTYLIS L.

Perennials; panicles consisting of 1-sided clusters of spikelets toward the ends of branches; spikelets few-flowered, compressed-keeled, separating above the persistent glumes; glumes unequal, keeled; lemmas flattened, strongly keeled, awnless or with short, awnlike tip. $x = 7$; non-Kranz.

FIG. 39. **Dactylis glomerata.** Plant, × ½; spikelet and floret, × 5.

1. Dactylis glomerata L. Orchard Grass. Fig. 39.

Plants forming dense, leafy tufts; culms erect, to 1 m or taller; sheaths retrorsely scabrous; ligule conspicuous, thin, whitish, about 5 mm long; leaf blades as much as 10 mm wide; panicles erect, with short, somewhat stiff, ascending branches; spikelets crowded in 1-sided glomerules at the ends of the branches; glumes lanceolate, with cilia on the conspicuous keel; lemmas 5–6 mm long, flattened, the keel mostly ciliate; sharp-tipped or sometimes with a short awn 1–2 mm long.

Widely distributed in the United States, more common in the eastern sections; introduced from Europe as a forage species, consisting of numerous strains and ecotypic variations, often self-established.

Missouri. Fields, pastures, open ground, and roadsides, generally distributed throughout the state. Flowering in spring and early summer.

17. SCLEROCHLOA P. Beauv. Hardgrass

Low annuals; racemes dense, spikelike; spikelets falling entire, arranged in double row on one side of a heavy rachis, 3–4-flowered, the upper floret sterile; glumes broad, unequal, somewhat thick or firm but with thin margins, the 1st 3-nerved, the 2nd 7-nerved; lemmas broad, conspicuously nerved, awnless, exceeding glumes. $x = 7$; non-Kranz.

1. Sclerochloa dura (L.) P. Beauv. Fig. 40.

Plants forming tufts, spreading to erect; culms 3–8(–13) cm tall, branching at base; leaf blades narrow, 1–5 mm wide, glabrous; sheaths overlapping; racemes dense, to 2 cm long, about one-half as thick, somewhat exceeded by upper leaf blades; spikelets about 5–6 mm long on short, thick stalks; lemmas of fertile florets 5 mm long.

Fig. 40. **Sclerochloa dura.** Plant, × 1; spikelet and floret, × 10.

Widely scattered, Washington and Oregon to Colorado, Kansas, and Texas, also New York; introduced from Europe.

Missouri. Mostly disturbed areas and dry soils, reported for St. Louis (Sullivan s.n. MO), Dallas (Ladd 4836 DNR), and also Barry, Christian, and Laclede Counties; a new addition to the flora. Flowering in April–May.

TRIBE 7. MELICEAE

18. GLYCERIA R. Br.

Perennials; culms from creeping rootstocks or rhizomes; sheaths connate or mostly closed; panicles contracted, or open with spreading or drooping branches; spikelets several-flowered, separating above the persistent glumes; glumes unequal, shorter than the lowermost lemma, the 2nd glume usually 1-nerved; lemmas conspicuously nerved, obtuse to acute, the apex usually thin and scarious, awnless; palea nearly equal to or exceeding lemma. $x = 10$; transverse leaf anatomy; non-Kranz.

Key to Missouri Species

a. Spikelets ovate, about 3 mm long...1. *G. striata*
a. Spikelets narrow, elongate, 10–40 mm long
    b. Spikelets loosely flowered, with tapering lemmas, the palea noticeably longer, with 2-toothed apex...2. *G. acutiflora*
    b. Spikelets with overlapping florets, more compact and cylindrical; lemmas oblong, the palea shorter, with simple apex...3. *G. septentrionalis*

1. Glyceria striata (Lam.) Hitchc. Fig. 41.

Plants forming clumps; stems erect, to 1 m tall or more; foliage glabrous, the leaf blades 3.5–7 mm wide with a conspicuous, whitish ligule; panicles diffuse, with slender, drooping branches; spikelets ovoid, about 3 mm long; glumes thin, rounded, the 1st less than 1 mm long, the 2nd slightly longer; lemmas noticeably nerved, 2 mm long, rounded at apex, with thin, scarious margins; palea nearly equal to the lemma.

Widespread throughout the United States.

Missouri. Streams, springs, low woods, and meadows, generally distributed, our most common species of *Glyceria.* Flowering in June–July.

2. Glyceria acutiflora Torr. Fig. 42.

Plants with weak, decumbent stems, rooting at the nodes, to 1 m in length; foliage glabrous, the leaf blades about 5 mm wide, with prominent, whitish ligules 4–6 mm long; panicles slender with short, appressed branches; spikelets few, elongate, 2.5–4 cm long; glumes pointed, the 1st 1–2 mm long, the 2nd about twice as long; lemmas acuminate, 7.5–9 mm long; palea with conspicuous bidentate apex, much exceeding the lemma.

Northeastern United States, west to Missouri, south to Tennessee.

Missouri. Swampy meadows, sloughs, and sinks, central and southern Ozarks, north to Laclede and Dent Counties. Flowering in June–July.

3. Glyceria septentrionalis Hitchc. Floating Manna Grass. Fig. 43.

Plants generally coarser than no. 2, with weak, soft stems and decumbent habit, rooting at the nodes; foliage glabrous, the leaf blades flat, as much as 1.5 cm wide; ligule conspicuous, thin, whitish; panicles narrow, branches appressed upward; spikelets linear, 1–2.5 cm long; glumes thin-margined, obtuse, the 1st 2–3 mm long, the 2nd 3–4 mm long; lemmas mostly distinctly nerved, slightly scabrous to pubescent, 3.5–4 mm long, with a blunt, scarious apex; palea equal to or slightly longer than the lemma.

Plants with large spikelets, to 2.5 cm long, and scabrous lemmas represent typical *septentrionalis;* those with generally shorter spikelets and pubescent lemmas are separated as var. *arkansana* (Fern.) Steyerm. & Kucera. *G. arkansana* Fern.

FIG. 41. **Glyceria striata.** Plant, × ½; spikelet, × 5; floret, × 10.

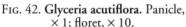

FIG. 42. **Glyceria acutiflora.** Panicle, × 1; floret, × 10.

FIG. 43. **Glyceria septentrionalis.** Panicle, × 1; floret, × 10.

Eastern United States to the Midwest, south to Texas.

Missouri. Sloughs, wet woods, upland sinks, and meadows, widely scattered, mainly in the eastern sections as the typical variety; var. *arkansana* reported for Ripley, Butler, Wayne, Stoddard, and Dunklin Counties. Flowering June–July.

19. MELICA L.

Perennials; culms characteristically with closed sheath; panicles mostly diffuse, with spreading branches; spikelets few-flowered, separating above the persistent glumes or sometimes falling entire; glumes subequal, thin-papery, scarious; lemmas several-nerved, thin-margined, awnless or with a short awn from the 2-lobed apex; upper lemmas much reduced, sterile. $x = 9$; non-Kranz.

1. Melica nitens (Scribn.) Nutt. ex Piper MELIC GRASS. Fig. 44.

Plants forming loose, sparse clumps; culms erect, 50–80 cm tall; foliage mostly glabrous, the leaf blades thin, 5–7 mm wide, long-tapering; panicles with few spreading branches, these of varying length; spikelets pendulous, 2–3-flowered, about 10 mm long; the upper florets much reduced; glumes papery, with broad apex, the 2nd glume about equal to total spikelet length; lower lemmas fertile, conspicuously nerved, with wide, scarious margins, about 7 mm long; the uppermost lemmas about

Fig. 44. **Melica nitens.** Plant, × 1; floret, × 5.

2–3 mm long, usually sterile, with rounded apex, not protruding beyond the apex of fertile lemma.

Eastern and central United States, west to Wisconsin and Texas.

Missouri. Wooded slopes and limestone ledges, generally distributed. Flowering in May–June.

TRIBE 8. AVENEAE

20. ARRHENATHERUM P. Beauv.

Perennials; panicles mostly narrow, with short, loose branches; spikelets 2-flowered, the lower floret usually staminate, the upper one perfect; glumes thin, persistent, the florets falling separately; lemmas thin, the lower dorsally awned, the upper awnless or with minute awn; rachilla extended behind 2nd floret. $x = 7$; non-Kranz.

1. Arrhenatherum elatius (L.) J. & C. Presl ssp. **elatius** TALL OATGRASS. Fig. 45.

Plants forming leafy tufts; culms erect, to 1 m tall or more; foliage glabrous, the leaf blades 5–10 mm wide; panicles shiny, 10–25 cm long, with short, spreading branches; spikelets about 8 mm long; glumes unequal, the 2nd longer, reaching upper floret; florets about 7 mm long, bearded at base, the lower one staminate, its lemma with twisted, bent awn 10 mm long or more and attached from below middle, the upper floret perfect, with minute awn attached slightly below apex or awnless.

Widely scattered in the United States; introduced as a forage species from Europe in the nineteenth century.

Missouri. Waste ground and grassy openings, uncommon; Pike, Washington, Boone, Phelps, and Jasper Counties. Flowering in June–July.

21. AVENA L. OAT

Annuals; panicles large, terminal, with spreading branches; spikelets 2–3-flowered, separating above the glumes; glumes equal, noticeably nerved, thin, papery, mostly exceeding the florets; lemmas hard, smooth or hairy, awnless, sometimes with reduced awn or with conspicuous awn attached dorsally from near or below middle; apex bidentate. $x = 7$; non-Kranz.

1. Avena fatua L. Fig. 46a,b.

Culms leafy, erect to 1 m tall; foliage mostly glabrous, the leaf blades 5–15 mm wide, long-tapering; spikelets 2.5–3 cm long, the glumes overtopping the florets.

The spikelets of wild oat, var. *fatua,* are mostly 3-flowered, the lemmas with stiff, brownish hairs and geniculate awn to 4 cm long, twisted in lower part; cultivated oat, var. *sativa* (L.) Hausskn., is characterized by spikelets generally 2-flowered, the florets glabrous, lacking awn, or sometimes with reduced simple awn. False wild oats or "fatuoids," often appearing in domestic grain, resemble var. *fatua,* varying in pubescence, awn development, spikelet fragmentation, and degree of seed dispersal, reflecting an ancestry from which var. *sativa* was derived.

Introduced from the Old World; var. *fatua* is most common in the northern and western United States, becoming invasive under certain conditions, including seasonal fires as in California; var. *sativa* is cultivated mainly in the cooler regions for grain and forage, occasionally spontaneous, not persistent.

Missouri. Casual ephemerals; open ground, fields, and waste areas; var. *fatua* reported for Jackson, Boone, and St. Louis Counties, but probably more widespread. Flowering in May–June.

22. TRISETUM Pers.

Perennial; panicles diffuse to somewhat dense; spikelets 2-flowered, separating above the persistent glumes; glumes dissimilar, thin, papery; lemmas thin, with tuft of hairs at base, awned below split apex. $x = 6, 7$; non-Kranz.

FIG. 45. **Arrhenatherum elatius.** Plant, × ½; spikelet and upper floret, × 5.

FIG. 46a. **Avena fatua** var. **fatua.** Plant, × ½; spikelet and floret, × 2.

Fig. 46b. **Avena fatua** var. **sativa.** Spikelet, × 2.

Fig. 47. **Trisetum flavescens.** Panicle, × 1; floret, × 5.

1. Trisetum flavescens (L.) P. Beauv. YELLOW OAT. Fig. 47.

Culms slender, erect to 1 m tall; foliage mostly glabrous but with lower sheaths pubescent; leaf blades 2–5 mm wide; panicles somewhat congested, with short, compact branches; spikelets 3–4-flowered, about 5 mm long, excluding awns; glumes dissimilar, the 1st narrow-lanceolate, the 2nd longer, broader, and not exceeding upper florets; lemmas 4–5 mm long with scarious margins and bent awn 8–10 mm long.

Widely scattered in the United States; adventive from Europe.

Missouri. Rare and little known, status uncertain; reported for Jackson and Pike Counties. Flowering in May–June.

23. KOELERIA Pers.

Annuals or perennials, panicles narrow, spikelike; spikelets 2- to several-flowered, separating above the persistent glumes, glumes somewhat unequal, firm, keeled, the 2nd about equal to uppermost floret; lemmas glabrous, firm, awnless; palea thin, about equal to lemma; rachilla prolonged behind the upper floret as a short stipe. $x = 7$; non-Kranz.

1. Koeleria macrantha (Ledeb.) J.A. Schultes JUNEGRASS. Fig. 48.

Perennial, forming tufts; culms erect, to 50 cm tall or more; lower sheaths pubescent, becoming glabrous above; ligule collar-shaped, less than 1 mm long; leaf blades narrow, about 2 mm wide, involute when dry; panicles spikelike, 5–10 cm long, with short, compact branches; spikelets 2-flowered, 4–5 mm long; glumes scabrous on keel, the 2nd exceeding the 1st and only slightly shorter than the closely imbricated florets; lemmas scabrous, about 3 mm long. *K. cristata* auct. p.p. non Pers.; *K. pyramidata* auct. p.p. non (Lam.) P. Beauv. (Greuter, 1968).

Widespread in the United States, but absent in the mid-Atlantic region and Southeast; native also to southern Europe and temperate Asia.

Missouri. Prairies, open woods, and glades; generally distributed. Flowering in May–June.

Fig. 48. **Koeleria macrantha.** Plant, × ½; glumes and floret, × 10.

24. SPHENOPHOLIS Scribn.

Perennials; panicles compact, spikelike, or somewhat diffuse with spreading branches; spikelets generally 2-flowered, separating *below* the glumes and falling entire; glumes strongly dissimilar, the 1st narrow or awl-shaped, the 2nd broader, mostly obovate; lemmas firm, keeled near apex, rounded below, awnless or with awn; palea thin, about equal to lemma. $x = 7$; non-Kranz. *Trisetum* Pers., in part.

Key to Missouri Species

a. Lower floret awnless, the upper floret with straight awn about 5 mm long ....
....1. *S. pensylvanica*
a. Both florets awnless
    b. Panicles somewhat compact, the branches densely flowered........................2. *S. obtusata*
    b. Panicles more diffuse, the branches sparsely flowered.....................................3. *S. nitida*

1. Sphenopholis pensylvanica (L.) Hitchc. Swamp Oat. Fig. 49.

Plants slender, erect, or somewhat decumbent near base, 50–80 cm tall; foliage mostly glabrous, the leaf blades 2–6 mm wide; panicles narrow, the short branches loosely ascending; spikelets 2-flowered, 5–7 mm long; glumes keeled, thin-textured, about 4–5 mm long, the 1st oblong, abruptly acute, the 2nd slightly longer and obovate; lemmas about 4 mm long, the lower one usually awnless, the upper one with straight awn 4–5 mm long. *Trisetum pensylvanicum* (L.) P. Beauv.

The transfer of *T. pensylvanicum* back to genus *Sphenopholis* where it had once been placed is supported by mode of disarticulation (below the glumes), and the presence of hybrids between this taxon and several species of *Sphenopholis* including no. 2 (Erdman, 1965).

Eastern United States and Gulf region to Ohio, Tennessee, and to Missouri.

Missouri. Rare and little known; collected from spring-branch on Crowley's Ridge, Stoddard County (Steyermark 78285 MO).

2. Sphenopholis obtusata (Michx.) Scribn. Prairie Wedgegrass. Fig. 50.

Plants forming small tufts; culms leafy, erect, to 1 m tall; foliage glabrous to somewhat pubescent, the leaf blades 3–4 mm wide; ligule 1.5 mm long, with lacerated margin; panicles erect, spikelike, with short lobes, or with somewhat flexuous branching; spikelets crowded, 2-flowered, 2–3 mm long; 1st glume narrow, oblong to awl-shaped, the 2nd obovate with rounded apex, almost as broad as long, or sometimes narrower and distinctly longer than broad; lower lemma 2–2.5 mm long.

Plants with lobed, compact panicles and broad 2nd glume represent typical *obtusata;* those with more open panicles and narrower glumes, the 2nd glume longer than broad, are separated as var. *major* (Torr.) Erdman (*S. intermedia* Rydb.).

Widespread throughout the United States and adjacent parts of Canada, south to Mexico.

Missouri. Prairies, woodlands, rocky slopes, and low ground, both varieties gener-

Fig. 49. **Sphenopholis pensylvanica.** Panicle, × 1; glumes and floret, × 5.

FIG. 50. **Sphenopholis obtusata.** Plant, × ½; glumes and floret, × 10.

ally distributed, with var. *major* usually found in the more moist locations. Flowering in May–June.

3. **Sphenopholis nitida** (Biehler) Scribn. Fig. 51.

Plants tufted; culms slender, erect, 40–80 cm tall; foliage somewhat pubescent, the leaf blades 2–4 mm wide; panicles diffuse, sparsely flowered, with spreading

FIG. 51. **Sphenopholis nitida.** Panicle, × 1; glumes and floret, × 10.

branches; spikelets 3.5 mm long; glumes nearly equal in length, the 1st narrow-oblong, the 2nd obovate, but longer than broad; lemmas 2.5–2.7 mm long.

Eastern United States, trans-Mississippi to Texas, local elsewhere.

Missouri. Open woods and barren slopes, on dry, rocky soils, south of a line from Barton to Texas and Jefferson Counties; also Randolph County (Conrad 8536 NEMO). Flowering in May–June.

25. HOLCUS L.

Perennials; panicles narrow, contracted; rather dense; spikelets 2-flowered, separating below the glumes and falling entire; glumes nearly equal and overtopping the florets; lower lemma perfect, awnless, the upper staminate and short-awned. $x = 7$; non-Kranz.

1. Holcus lanatus L. Velvetgrass. Fig. 52.

Plants leafy, erect to somewhat decumbent near base, rooting at the lower nodes, 50–100 cm tall; sheaths generally soft-pubescent; leaf blades to 1 cm wide; panicles contracted, spikelike, 5–15 cm long; spikelets 3.5–4 mm long; glumes overtopping the florets; lemmas about 2 mm long, the lower one awnless, the upper with short, curved awn about 1 mm long, attached below apex.

Widely scattered throughout the United States; adventive from Europe.

FIG. 52. **Holcus lanatus.** Plant, × ½; spikelet, florets, and mature fertile floret, × 5.

Missouri. Open ground and waste areas, Boone, Jackson, Vernon, Jasper, Phelps, St. Francois, Madison, and Cape Girardeau Counties. Flowering in May–June.

26. AIRA L.

Small annuals; panicles delicate, diffuse; spikelets 2-flowered, separating above the glumes, the latter exceeding florets; lemmas firm, the lower one sometimes awnless, the upper mostly awned from below the middle. $x = 7$; non-Kranz.

1. Aira caryophyllea L. Silver Hairgrass. Fig. 53.

Plants solitary, sparsely tufted, 10–25 cm tall; leaf blades narrow, 2–3 mm wide; panicles with spreading branches; spikelets clustered toward ends of branches, about 2.5 mm long; glumes exceeding the florets; both lemmas with delicate awn 3–4 mm long.

Widely scattered, Atlantic and Gulf Coast regions inland to Ohio; also Pacific Coast region.

Missouri. Open ground and dry soils; Taney County (Castaner 1085 WARM), a new record for the state; subsequently reported for Greene, Dent, Howell, and Wayne Counties. Flowering in May.

2. Aira elegantissima Schur Fig. 54.

Plants forming small tufts; culms erect, about 30 cm tall at most; foliage generally glabrous, the leaf blades narrow, 1–2 mm wide, becoming involute; panicles diffuse, delicately branched; spikelets 2–2.5 mm long, from ends of the branches; glumes exceeding the 2 florets; lemmas with minute tuft of hairs at base, the lower one awnless, the upper with bent awn 2–3 mm long. *A. elegans* Willd. ex Kunth.

Southeastern and mid-Atlantic states, to trans-Mississippi region; also Pacific Coast.

Missouri. Open ground and dry prairies, St. Louis, Dent, and Oregon Counties; more recently Barton County (Ladd 14012 MO). Flowering in May.

27. ANTHOXANTHUM L.

Annuals and perennials, with fragrant scent; panicles terminal, spikelike; spikelets with 1 fertile floret and 2 sterile lemmas below, separating above the glumes; glumes strongly unequal; lemma of the fertile floret awnless, falling with and enveloped by the larger, awned, sterile lemmas. $x = 5$; non-Kranz.

1. Anthoxanthum odoratum L. Sweet Vernalgrass. Fig. 55.

Perennial, forming clumps, culms erect, to about 50 cm tall; sheaths glabrous; ligule conspicuous, membranous; leaf blades 3–5 mm wide, glabrous or sparsely pilose, the edges ciliate toward base; panicles erect, yellowish brown, spikelike, 3–6 cm long; spikelets 7–8 mm long; glumes unequal, acuminate, the 1st about one-half as long as the 2nd, both much exceeding the florets; fertile lemma smooth, dark, about 2 mm long; the two sterile lemmas pilose, twice as long as fertile lemma, notched at apex, their awns twisted, one lemma with awn attached dorsally near base, the other with awn from near apex.

Eastern and central United States, widely scattered, also Pacific Coast region; adventive from Eurasia.

Missouri. Open ground and pastures, Jackson, Boone, Monroe, St. Louis, Jefferson, and Iron Counties. Flowering in spring.

Fig. 53. **Aira caryophyllea.** Plant, × ½; spikelet and floret, × 10.

28. PHALARIS L.

Annuals and perennials; panicles dense, spikelike; spikelets 1-flowered, separating above the persistent glumes; 2 reduced or minute sterile bracts usually present, these appressed to and falling with the fertile floret; glumes mostly equal, laterally flattened or winged on keel; lemma awnless, exceeded by the glumes. x = 6, 7; non-Kranz.

Key to Missouri Species

a. Large coarse perennial; panicles short-lobed, interrupted ....1. *P. arundinacea*

a. Annuals; panicles dense, ovoid to oblong-elliptic, more or less continuous

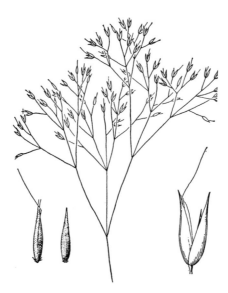

FIG. 54. **Aira elegantissima.** Panicle, × 1; spikelet and florets, × 10.

b. Panicles ovoid, about 3 cm long or less; glumes broadly winged ....2. *P. canariensis*
b. Panicles oblong-elliptic, as much as 8 cm long, usually less; glumes narrower, not broadly winged ....3. *P. caroliniana*

1. Phalaris arundinacea L. REED CANARY GRASS. Fig. 56.

Perennial, rhizomatous, forming dense sod; culms erect, to 1.5 m tall or more; foliage mostly glabrous, the leaf blades 1–2 cm wide; ligule large, white, membranous, 3–5 mm long; panicles straw-colored, narrow, spikelike, with short, appressed lobes; spikelets about 5 mm long, the glumes flattened, more or less winged, much overtopping the floret; fertile lemma ovate, 3–4.5 mm long, sparsely pilose near base; sterile bracts narrow, about 1 mm long, conspicuously villous, appressed to base of fertile lemma.

Plants distinguished by white-striped leaves and cultivated as an ornamental are designated as var. *picta* L., commonly known as ribbongrass.

Northern two-thirds of United States and adjacent Canada, and higher elevations in the West, planted extensively for soil-erosion control and to some extent as forage; also Eurasia.

Missouri. Wet embankments, sloughs, and waterways; scattered, primarily in the northern and central counties. Flowering in June–July.

2. Phalaris canariensis L. CANARY GRASS. Fig. 57.

Annual; culms erect, 50–70 cm tall; leaf blades to 1 cm wide; ligule conspicuous; panicles ovoid, compact, about 2–3 cm long, 1.5–2 cm thick; spikelets about 7 mm long, the glumes flattened, broadly winged, with abrupt tip; fertile lemma ovate, 5 mm long, appressed-pubescent, sterile bracts linear, about one-half as long as fertile lemma.

Scattered in the United States; introduced from the Mediterranean region as a pasture and forage species; also sold commercially as bird seed.

Missouri. Fields and waste ground, scattered, not common; Jackson, Johnson, Jasper, Greene, Butler, Scott, and Dunklin Counties. Flowering in June–July.

FIG. 55. **Anthoxanthum odoratum.** Plant, × ½; spikelet, sterile lemmas, and fertile floret, × 5.

Fig. 56. **Phalaris arundinacea.** Plant, × 1; glumes and floret, × 4.

P. brachystachya Link, which has more diminutive spikelets but is otherwise similar to no. 2, was reported for Missouri based on a single 1938 collection from Laclede County (initially identified as *P. canariensis*). Its current status is doubtful; no other collections are known.

3. Phalaris caroliniana Walt. Fig. 58.

Annual; culms erect to 1 m tall but mostly shorter; leaf blades 4–8 mm wide; ligule a conspicuous membrane; panicles 5–10 cm long, compact, elliptic, tapering to both ends; spikelets 4–6 mm long, the glumes compressed, acute, not noticeably winged as in no. 2; fertile lemma ovate, 3–4 mm long, somewhat pubescent, the sterile bracts linear, 1–2 mm long.

Southern United States, from Virginia to California.

Missouri. Open ground, infrequent and scattered, mainly in the western counties; also reported for Butler, Stoddard, Scott, and Dunklin Counties. Flowering in May–June.

29. AGROSTIS L.

Annuals or perennials; panicles narrow, relatively compact to diffuse, with spreading branches; spikelets 1-flowered, separating above the persistent glumes; glumes about the same length, acuminate, equaling or sometimes exceeding the floret; the 2nd glume 1-nerved; lemma awnless or with delicate awn attached just below apex; palea thin, equal to lemma or much reduced or absent; rachilla not prolonged. $x = 7$; non-Kranz.

Agrostis with over 200 species is a wide-ranging genus of the temperate and montane zones of both hemispheres; it includes several important forage and turf species.

Key to Species

a. Florets mostly awnless; palea present
    b. Ligule membranous, about 2 mm long, shorter than broad............................1. *A. tenuis*
    b. Ligule conspicuous, to 3–4 mm in length, longer than broad
        c. Culms to 1 m tall or more, spreading by rhizomes................................2. *A. gigantea*
        c. Culms mostly 0.5 m tall or less, decumbent at base, spreading by long stolons............
        ....3. *A. stolonifera* var. *palustris*

FIG. 57. **Phalaris canariensis.** Plant, × ½; spikelet and floret, × 5.

a. Florets with delicate awn or awnless; palea absent or much reduced
    d. Lemmas with delicate awn; annuals..4. *A. elliottiana*
    d. Lemmas awnless; perennials
        e. Spikelets 2 mm or less in length, aggregated toward ends of panicle branches;
        spring-flowering ....5. *A. hyemalis*
        e. Spikelets larger, usually exceeding 2 mm, more diffuse; summer-flowering.........
        ....6. *A. perennans*

1. Agrostis tenuis Sibthorp Colonial Bent. Fig. 59.

Perennial, forming tufts or sod, from rhizomes or sometimes stoloniferous; culms mostly less than 0.5 mm tall; leaf blades narrow, 2–4 mm wide; ligule membranous, 1–2 mm long, mostly shorter than broad; panicles pyramidal, diffuse, with slender, whorled branches; spikelets purplish, 2–3 mm long; glumes exceeding the florets; lemma about 2 mm long, awnless; palea shorter than lemma. *A. capillaris* L.

Plants with awned lemmas, the awns geniculate, attached near base, have been treated as var. *aristata* (Parnell) Druce.

Scattered in the northern areas of the United States, primarily in the northeast and Pacific Coast regions; introduced from Europe as a turf and forage species.

Missouri. Utilized in turf mixtures and occasionally self-established, widely scattered but not common. Flowering in June–July.

2. Agrostis gigantea Roth Redtop. Fig. 60.

Perennial, forming sod, spreading by rhizomes; culms erect, to 1 m tall or more; leaf blades 3–5 mm wide, sometimes more, with long taper; ligule membranous, 3–4 mm long, truncate; panicles erect, pyramidal, with distinct whorls of spreading branches; spikelets crowded, reddish to purplish, 2–3 mm long; glumes overtopping the lemma; lemma thin, 2 mm long or less; palea one-half as long as lemma. *A. alba* auct. non L.

Widespread in the United States, naturalizing especially in the cooler regions; introduced as a forage species from Europe.

Missouri. Fields, pastures, and waste ground, generally distributed; one of our most common species. Flowering in June.

3. Agrostis stolonifera L. var. **palustris** (Huds.) Farw. Creeping Bent. Fig. 61.

Perennial, sod-forming, spreading by stolons; culms 30–50 cm tall, decumbent at base; leaf blades 1–3 mm wide, ligule membranous, to 6 mm long; panicles somewhat compact with short branches, not verticillate as in no. 2; spikelets crowded,

Fig. 58. **Phalaris caroliniana.** Plant, × 1; glumes and floret, × 5.

Fig. 59. **Agrostis tenuis.** Panicle, × 1; glumes, floret, and ligule, × 5.

FIG. 60. **Agrostis gigantea.** Plant, × ½; 2 spikelets and floret, × 5.

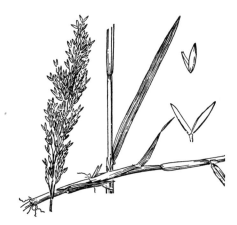

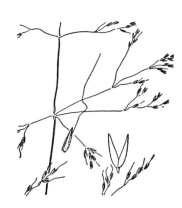

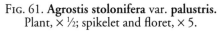

Fig. 61. **Agrostis stolonifera** var. **palustris.** Plant, × ½; spikelet and floret, × 5.

Fig. 62. **Agrostis elliottiana.** Panicle, × 1; glumes and floret, × 5.

2–2.5 mm long; glumes exceeding lemma; palea shorter than lemma. *A. alba* L. var. *palustris* (Huds.) Pers.

Northeastern United States and adjacent parts of Canada, south to Virginia and Ohio valley; also Pacific Coast states to Colorado, New Mexico, and Texas.

Missouri. Sporadic, not common; several locations questionable based on collections under earlier synonymy, these conforming more closely to typical *gigantea,* no. 2. Flowering in May–June.

4. Agrostis elliottiana J.A. Schultes Fig. 62.

Annual, forming small tufts; culms erect, mostly less than 50 cm tall; leaf blades narrow, short, about 1 mm wide; ligule conspicuous, tapering to a point, several times longer than broad; panicles diffuse, delicate, more than one-half the length of entire plant; spikelets about 2 mm long; glumes nearly equal, exceeding the floret; lemma conspicuously nerved, with threadlike awn to 10 mm long; palea absent.

Eastern and southern United States, west to Kansas and Texas.

Missouri. Glades, prairies, rocky slopes, and fields, primarily south of a line from Bates to Morgan and Pike Counties. Flowering in May–June.

5. Agrostis hyemalis (Walter) Britton, Sterns & Pogg. var. **hyemalis** Fig. 63.

Perennial, forming dense tufts; culms slender, erect, 50–100 cm tall; leaf blades narrow, 1–2 mm wide; ligule conspicuous, with lacerated margin; panicles diffuse, with delicate, spreading branches in several whorls; spikelets minute, about 1.5 mm long, crowded toward ends of the branches; glumes somewhat unequal, acuminate, exceeding the floret; lemma awnless, about 1 mm long; palea absent.

Eastern and northern United States, west to Oklahoma and Kansas.

Missouri. Fields, prairies, and open woods, generally distributed. Flowering in May–June.

6. Agrostis perennans (Walter) Tuckerman Fig. 64.

Perennial, forming sparse tufts; culms erect to weak-stemmed, decumbent, about 50 cm or taller; leaf blades lax, 1–4 mm wide; ligule blunt, 1–4 mm long; panicles diffuse, with slender, forking branches; spikelets 2–3 mm long; glumes unequal,

FIG. 63. **Agrostis hyemalis.** Plant, × ½; glumes and floret, × 5.

acuminate, the 1st somewhat longer, both exceeding the floret; lemma about 1.5–2 mm long, awnless; palea absent.

Weak-stemmed, decumbent plants with thin, lax leaf blades are separated from typical *perennans* as var. *aestivalis* Vasey, possibly a habitat form.

Eastern and central United States, west to Nebraska, Oklahoma, and Texas.

Missouri. Upland woods, shaded slopes, bottomlands, and alluvial banks, generally distributed; the decumbent form, var. *aestivalis,* occurs in damp, shaded habitats throughout. Flowering in summer.

Fig. 64. **Agrostis perennans.** Panicle, × 1; glumes and floret, × 5.

30. CALAMAGROSTIS Adans.

Perennials; panicles contracted to more open with spreading branches; spikelets 1-flowered, separating above the persistent glumes; glumes similar, acute or narrow-pointed, nearly equaling or slightly exceeding the floret; lemma with basal tuft of soft, ascending hairs, dorsally awned; palea only slightly shorter than lemma; rachilla usually extended behind the floret as a hairy bristle. $x = 7$; non-Kranz.

Key to Missouri Species

a. Panicles compact, mostly spikelike, with short branches; awn of lemma straight ....1. *C. stricta*
a. Panicles somewhat open, the branches spreading; awn of lemma straight or bent
　b. Awn straight, simple; species of damp prairies, mostly in the northern counties, infrequent southward..2. *C. canadensis*
　b. Awn bent, twisted below; uncommon species, dry sites in Ozarks region......3. *C. porteri*

1. Calamagrostis stricta (Timm) Koeler var. **brevior** Vasey Fig. 65.

Plants forming clumps, rhizomatous; culms 50–100 cm tall; sheaths glabrous; ligule conspicuous, about 5 mm long; leaf blades scabrous on the margins, about 4

Fig. 65. **Calamagrostis stricta** var. **brevior.** Panicle, × 1; glumes and floret, × 10.

mm wide; panicles narrow, compact; glumes 3–4 mm long, slightly longer than the floret; lemma inconspicuously nerved, tufted at base, with straight awn from the back. *C. inexpansa* Gray var. *brevior* (Vasey) Stebbins.

Northern and eastern United States and adjacent parts of Canada, south to Midwest region, also higher elevations in the Southwest to California. A wide-ranging and variable species, typical *stricta*, with spikelets slightly larger than those of var. *brevior*, has a more northern distribution in the United States, not reaching our area.

Missouri. Prairies and swales, infrequent and scattered, Jackson, Barton, Jasper, Texas, Ripley, and Butler Counties. Flowering in June–July.

2. Calamagrostis canadensis (Michx.) P. Beauv. BLUEJOINT. Fig. 66.

Plants spreading by rhizomes; culms erect, to 1.5 m tall or more; sheaths glabrous, somewhat keeled; ligule conspicuous, with irregular margin; leaf blades scabrous on the edges, otherwise glabrous, about 5–6 mm wide; panicles pyramidal, with flexible branches in distinct whorls; spikelets purplish, 2–4 mm long; glumes slightly longer than the floret; the lemma 2–3.5 mm long, with copious tuft of white hairs at base and slender awn from the middle of the back.

Specimens with generally smaller spikelets (2–3 mm long) are separated from typical *canadensis* as var. *macouniana* (Vasey) Stebbins.

Wide-ranging across the northern United States and adjacent Canada south to Midwest region; also higher elevations in the Southwest.

Missouri. Wet lowlands, prairie swale, and sloughs, both varieties most common north of Missouri River, typical *canadensis* reported also for St. Louis, Cape Girardeau, and Mississippi Counties. Flowering in May–July.

3. Calamagrostis porteri Gray ssp. **insperata** (Swallen) C.W. Greene Fig. 67.

Plants rhizomatous; culms about 1 m tall; sheaths glabrous; ligule conspicuous; leaf blades 4.5–8 mm wide, long-tapering; panicles with spreading branches in several whorls; spikelets about 5 mm long; glumes subequal, the 1st somewhat longer, both exceeding the floret; lemma with dense tuft of callus hairs from the sides and base, not reaching the apex, with bent, twisted awn from near base. *C. insperata* Swallen.

Rare and widely scattered as ssp. *insperata*, originally known from Jackson County, Ohio. Typical *porteri* with sheaths hairy at summit is an eastern form ranging from the mid-Atlantic region and northward, not reaching our area.

Missouri. Cherty limestone sites, Ozark and Douglas Counties (Steyermark 20043, 23350 MO), recently reported for Howell, Shannon, Texas, and Wright Counties (Summers et al. 3602, 3710, 3907, 3919 MO). Flowering in summer.

31. APERA Adans.

Annuals, sparsely tufted; ligules conspicuous, membranous; panicles somewhat compact to spreading; spikelets 1-flowered, separating above the persistent glumes; glumes subequal, acuminate, the upper 3-veined and equaling or slightly exceeding floret; lemma awned, from below tip; palea about equal to lemma, rachilla prolonged behind palea as a short bristle. $x = 7$; non-Kranz. *Agrostis* L.

1. Apera interrupta (L.) P. Beauv. Fig. 68.

Annual, forming small tufts; culms branching, about 50 cm tall; sheaths glabrous; ligule 2–3 mm long; leaf blades flat, 2–5 mm wide; panicles with short,

FIG. 66. **Calamagrostis canadensis.** Plant, × ½; glumes and floret, × 10.

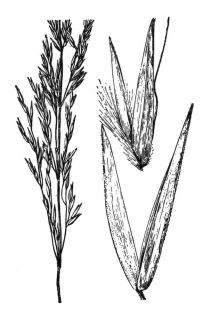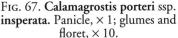

FIG. 67. **Calamagrostis porteri** ssp. **insperata.** Panicle, × 1; glumes and floret, × 10.

FIG. 68. **Apera interrupta.** Panicle, × ½; glumes and floret, × 5.

ascending branches interrupted on the central axis, floriferous to base; spikelets crowded, about 2 mm long; glumes subequal, the 2nd somewhat longer and equaling the floret; lemma with a delicate awn to 10 mm long, attached from below the apex; palea about equal to the lemma. *Agrostis interrupta* L.

Widely scattered in the United States; a weedy adventive from Europe.

Missouri. St. Louis County, based on a single collection, its status doubtful.

2. **Apera spica-venti** (L.) P. Beauv. Fig. 69.

Annual, habit similar to no. 1 but with more open, spreading panicles, floriferous at ends of secondary branching, naked below; spikelets about 2 mm long; glumes subequal, nearly equaling floret; lemma with awn about 10 mm long, attached from below apex; palea and lemma about equal. *Agrostis spica-venti* L.

Widely scattered in the United States; a weedy adventive from Europe.

Missouri. Waste ground and railroad right-of-way, St. Louis and Jackson Counties. Flowering in late spring and early summer.

32. CINNA L.

Perennials; panicles dense with somewhat spreading branches; spikelets 1-flowered, separating below the glumes, falling entire; glumes mostly equal, acuminate; floret on a short stipe; lemma with minute awn below bidentate apex; palea slightly shorter than the lemma. $x = 7$; non-Kranz.

1. **Cinna arundinacea** L. WOOD REED. Fig. 70.

Plants single or few in loose tufts; culms erect, to 1 m tall or more, from a bulbous base; ligule membranous, lacerated on the margin; leaf blades 4.5–10 mm wide, flat, mostly glabrous; panicle somewhat lax, the branches drooping, with crowded

FIG. 69. **Apera spica-venti.** Plant, × ½; glumes and floret, × 5.

Fig. 70. **Cinna arundinacea.** Plant, × ½; glumes and floret, × 10.

spikelets; spikelets compressed, 4–6 mm long; 1st glume 1-nerved, the 2nd 3-nerved; lemma 3–4 mm long with awn 1 mm long; palea 1-nerved. Incl. var. *inexpansa* Fern. & Griscom with tendency for more contracted panicle.

Eastern and central United States west to South Dakota and Texas.

Missouri. Swampy ground, alluvial woods, and moist ravines, generally distributed. Flowering in July–August.

33. ALOPECURUS L.

Annuals or perennials; panicles mostly dense, cylindrical, spikelike; spikelets 1-flowered, separating below the glumes and falling entire; glumes mostly equal, compressed; lemma with slender dorsal awn from near or below middle; palea absent. $x = 7$; non-Kranz.

Key to Missouri Species
a. Panicles elongate, spikelike, less than 5 mm thick; native perennial of aquatic habitats........ ....1. *A. aequalis*
a. Panicles spikelike, 5–10 mm thick; annuals or perennials of damp ground and open fields
    b. Panicles 5–7 mm thick; common native species ....2. *A. carolinianus*
    b. Panicles 7–10 mm thick; introduced species, not common ....3. *A. pratensis*

1. Alopecurus aequalis Sobol. SHORT-AWN FOXTAIL. Fig. 71.

Perennial; culms erect to spreading-decumbent, to 50 cm or more in length; sheaths glabrous; ligules conspicuous, papery; leaf blades 2–5 mm wide, lax, long-tapering; panicles narrow, spikelike, 3–4 mm thick; spikelets light green, about 2–5 mm long; glumes silky-pubescent, 2 mm long; lemma with straight awn, from below middle, reaching or only slightly exceeding the apex.

Northern United States, to Ohio, to Arizona.

Missouri. Sinks, ponds, and sloughs, shallow water or swampy ground, Clay, Boone, St. Louis, Shannon, Reynolds, Ripley, and Stoddard Counties. Flowering in May–June.

2. Alopecurus carolinianus Walter Fig. 72.

Annual, forming tufts; culms branching from the base, erect to somewhat decumbent, to about 50 cm tall; upper sheaths mostly inflated, or enlarged; ligule conspicuous; leaf blades 2–5 mm wide, not much longer than the sheaths; panicles cylindrical, spikelike, about 5–7 mm thick; spikelets 2–5 mm long; glumes joined at base, pubescent, nearly reaching level of floret; lemma with bent awn, from below middle, exceeding the apex about 3 mm.

Widespread, represented in most regions of the United States.

Missouri. Field, swales, and alluvial banks, on damp ground, generally distributed. Flowering in April–May.

3. Alopecurus pratensis L. MEADOW FOXTAIL. Fig. 73.

Perennial, forming loose tufts; culms erect to somewhat decumbent, to 50 cm or taller; leaf blades as much as 20 mm wide, long-tapering, panicles dense, spikelike, 7–10 mm thick; spikelets about 5 mm long; glumes joined at base, long-ciliate, about reaching level of floret; lemma with bent awn attached near base and extending beyond apex about 5 mm.

Northern and central areas of the United States; introduced as a forage species from Eurasia in the mid–nineteenth century.

FIG. 71. **Alopecurus aequalis.** Panicle, × 1; glumes and floret, × 10.

FIG. 72. **Alopecurus carolinianus.** Plant, × 1; glumes and floret, × 10.

Missouri. Infrequent and scattered, Vernon, Johnson, Adair, Boone, Callaway, and St. Louis Counties; probably more widespread. Flowering in April–May.

34. BECKMANNIA Host

Annuals and perennials; panicles stiff, spikelike, with short, crowded, lateral lobes; spikelets 1–2-flowered, strongly overlapping, separating below the glumes and falling entire; glumes equal, obovate, inflated; lemmas obscurely nerved, narrow, acuminate-tipped in contrast to broadened glumes; palea shorter than lemma. $x = 7$; non-Kranz.

1. Beckmannia syzigachne (Steud.) Fern. Fig. 74.

Plants sparsely tufted; culms to 1 m tall; foliage glabrous to scabrous, the leaf blades 4.5–8 mm wide; ligule conspicuous, 5–7 mm long, acuminate; panicles narrow, elongate, with numerous short lobes or spikes, the latter about 1–1.5 cm long; spikelets congested, overlapping, orbicular, about 3 mm long; glumes prominently nerved, wrinkled, broadened upward, and somewhat crescent-shaped, with abrupt tip; lemma narrow, the pointed, tapering apex slightly exceeding glumes.

Northern and western United States to Alaska; also parts of the Old World.

Missouri. Rare and little known, based on a single specimen, its status doubtful; Jackson County (Bush, near Courtney). Flowering in June–July.

35. PHLEUM L.

Annuals and perennials; panicles dense, cylindrical, spikelike; spikelets 1-flowered, separating above the persistent glumes; glumes equal, keeled, pointed or somewhat awnlike, exceeding the floret; lemma elliptic-ovate, awnless; palea shorter than lemma. $x = 7$; non-Kranz.

FIG. 73. **Alopecurus pratensis.** Plant, × ½; glumes and floret, × 10.

Fig. 74. **Beckmannia syzigachne.** Plant, × ½; spikelet and floret, × 5.

FIG. 75. **Phleum pratense.** Plant, × ½; glumes and floret, × 10.

1. Phleum pratense L. TIMOTHY. Fig. 75.

Perennial, forming clumps; culms erect, to 1 m tall, with bulbous bases; sheaths glabrous; ligule conspicuous, 2.5–3 mm long; leaf blades 4.5–10 mm wide; panicles spikelike, 5–8 mm thick, as much as 15 cm long; spikelets dense, 3–3.5 mm long; glumes stiffly ciliate on keel, with abrupt, awnlike tip 1 mm long; lemma thin, 1–2 mm long.

Widespread forage species naturalized in the United States; introduced from Europe.

Missouri. Fields, pastures, and waste ground, generally distributed. Flowering in late May–June.

TRIBE 9. BROMEAE

36. BROMUS L. Brome

Annuals and perennials; culms with closed sheaths; panicles terminal, with more or less spreading branches, to somewhat contracted, compact; spikelets several-flowered, large, separating above the persistent glumes; glumes unequal, acute to narrow-pointed; lemmas with bidentate apex, sometimes entire, awned from below apex, or awnless; pistil with pubescent apex, the 3 stigmas separate and subterminal, attached from below the tip; palea adhering to grain. $x = 7$; non-Kranz.

Bromus is a wide-ranging genus of temperate latitudes and the tropical montane with approximately 150 species, some with considerable forage value while others are weedy adventives.

Key to Missouri Species

a. Spikelets compressed, with thin-edged keel ....1. *B. catharticus*
a. Spikelets more rounded on the back, not distinctly flattened
  b. Spikelets awnless or nearly so..2. *B. inermis*
  b. Spikelets awned
    c. Perennials, culms to 1 m tall; native woodland species
      d. Sheaths shorter than internodes, not overlapping with sheaths above......................
      ....3. *B. pubescens*
      d. Sheaths mostly equal to or exceeding internodes, overlapping partially with sheaths above
        e. Auricles flange-like, prominent; 2nd glume 3-nerved ....4. *B. latiglumis*
        e. Auricles absent; 2nd glume 5–7-nerved ....5. *B. nottowayanus*
    c. Annuals, culms mostly shorter; adventives of waste ground, fields, and roadsides
      f. 1st glume relatively broad, 2 mm wide or more; 2nd glume 5-nerved
        g. Panicles somewhat compact, with short, ascending branches; foliage soft-pubescent...6. *B. hordeaceous*
        g. Panicles more open, with spreading branches; foliage glabrous to pubescent
          h. Lemma with inrolled margins in mature spikelets, the rachilla becoming partially visible at maturity
            i. Foliage mostly with varying pubescence.......................7. *B. japonicus*
            i. Foliage glabrous or nearly so...8. *B. secalinus*
          h. Lemma usually not inrolled, the margins mostly flat, the rachilla usually not visible
            j. Awns divergent, sometimes twisted
              k. Spikelets mostly single, on short, ascending branches.................
              ....9. *B. squarrosus*
              k. Spikelets several, on flexuous, drooping branches.......................
              ....7. *B. japonicus*
            j. Awns mostly straight, not twisted
              l. Lemmas narrow-acuminate; rare species.............10. *B. arvensis*
              l. Lemmas broadly acute, short-pointed; common adventive......
              ....11. *B. racemosus*
      f. 1st glume narrow-elongate, 1 mm wide; 2nd glume 3-nerved
            m. Awns of lemma to 1.5 cm long; common adventive..........
            ....12. *B. tectorum*
            m. Awns longer, to 4–5 cm in length; rare species
              n. Awns 2–3 cm long.....................................13. *B. sterilis*
              n. Awns 3.5–5 cm long............................14. *B. diandrus*

1. Bromus catharticus M. Vahl RESCUE GRASS. Fig. 76.

Annual; culms erect, to 1 m tall; foliage mostly glabrous except for lower sheaths; leaf blades 3.5–5 mm wide; panicles sparsely flowered, with stiffly ascending branches; spikelets sharply keeled, pale green, 2–3 cm long; glumes nearly equal, elongate; lemmas essentially glabrous, the nerves ciliate, 10–15 mm long, awnless or nearly so. *B. willdenowii* Kunth.

Widely scattered in the United States, most common in southern areas; adventive from South America.

Missouri. Rare and little known, collected on waste ground, Jackson, Jasper, Newton, Monroe, and St. Louis Counties. Flowering in May–June.

2. Bromus inermis Leyss. SMOOTH BROME. Fig. 77.

Perennial, forming a sod, spreading by rhizomes; culms erect, to 1 m tall or more; nodes and foliage mostly glabrous, the leaf blades 5–15 mm wide; panicles somewhat dense, 10–25 cm long, the branches whorled, stiffly erect at maturity; spikelets narrow, somewhat cylindrical, 2–3 cm long, becoming brownish; glumes awl-shaped, the 1st 1-nerved, the 2nd 3-nerved, both with thin, hyaline margins; lemmas glabrous or rarely pubescent, also thin-margined, about 10 mm long, awnless or sometimes with short awn to 3 mm in length; anthers conspicuous, 4–6 mm long.

Primarily northern and western United States, less common in the South; introduced from Europe as a forage species.

Missouri. Open ground, fields, and roadsides, most common in the northern counties, scattered and infrequent elsewhere. Flowering in June–July.

B. inermis and the following native species, nos. 3–5, are our only perennials (Section Bromopsis).

3. Bromus pubescens L. Muhl. ex Willd. CANADA BROME. Fig. 78.

Perennial, solitary or in small clumps; culms erect, to 1 m or more tall; sheaths mostly pubescent, sometimes glabrous, the upper ones usually *shorter* than the internodes; leaf blades pilose to smooth, thin, lax, 5–15 mm wide; panicles diffuse, with whorled, drooping branches; spikelets 1.5–3 cm long; 1st glume 1-nerved, the 2nd

FIG. 76. **Bromus catharticus,** × 1.

FIG. 77. **Bromus inermis.** Plant, × ½; spikelet, × 2 ½.

3-nerved, both with narrow, hyaline margins; lemmas pubescent or rarely smooth, 8–10 mm long, distinctly awned. *B. purgans* auct. non L.

Eastern and central United States, west to North Dakota and Texas.

Missouri. Shaded ground and rocky slopes, mostly on calcareous soils, generally distributed. Flowering in May–June.

4. Bromus latiglumis (Shear) Hitchc. Fig. 79.

Perennial, solitary or in small clumps; culms about 1 m tall, somewhat resembling no. 3; sheaths mostly pilose, rarely glabrous, with conspicuous auriculate flange at summit, usually *exceeding* the node above; panicles diffuse with drooping branches; 1st glume 1-nerved, the 2nd 3-nerved; lemmas pubescent, about 10 mm long, distinctly awned. Incl. f. *incana* (Shear) Fern., with pilose sheaths.

Northeastern United States and adjacent Canada, to North Dakota, south to Missouri and mid-Atlantic region.

Missouri. Damp, shaded ground and alluvial banks, infrequent and scattered,

Fig. 78. **Bromus pubescens.** Plant, × ¾; spikelet, × 2½.

mostly in the eastern counties. Flowering in July–August, several weeks later than no. 3.

5. Bromus nottowayanus Fern. Satin Brome. Fig. 80.

Perennial, similar to no. 4; sheaths overlapping the node above, but mostly pubescent with conspicuous tuft of hairs at summit, and lacking conspicuous auriculate flange; 1st glume 1-nerved, the 2nd 5-nerved; lemmas pubescent, 9–12 mm long, distinctly awned. A distinctive character is the bright sheen of the lower leaf surface observed in fresh specimens.

FIG. 79. **Bromus latiglumis,** × 1.

FIG. 80. **Bromus nottowayanus.** Glumes and lower floret, × 5.

Illinois to Arkansas, eastward to North Carolina and Maryland; probably more widespread.

Missouri. Shaded alluvium and stream banks, Lewis and St. Louis Counties (Ladd 13756, 13758 MOR), subsequently collected in Boone (McKenzie 1237 MO), Callaway (McKenzie 1741 MO), and Adair (Jacobs s.n. UMO) Counties, new records for the state; earlier reports (Wagnon, 1952) for Madison and Jackson Counties have not been verified, but the scattered distribution of these native populations in obligatory habitats would suggest a more widespread representation. Flowering in June–July, generally intermediate between nos. 3 and 4.

6. Bromus hordeaceous L. SOFT CHESS. Fig. 81.

Annual; culms 50–100 cm tall; foliage soft, downy-pubescent; leaf blades 3–5 mm wide; panicles somewhat contracted with short, ascending branches; spikelets 1.5–2.5 cm long; glumes unequal, the 1st 3-nerved, the 2nd 5-nerved; lemmas about 8 mm long, mostly pubescent or sometimes glabrous, with broad scarious margins, awned from a deeply 2-cleft apex. *B. mollis* auct. non L.

Plants with glabrous lemmas have been referred to ssp. *pseudothominei* (P.M. Smith) H. Scholz and are otherwise similar to typical *hordeaceous.*

Widely scattered in the United States, particularly common in the California range; adventive from Europe.

Missouri. Rare and little known, reported on waste ground for Jackson, Cole, and St. Louis Counties as typical *hordeaceous;* ssp. *pseudothominei* more recently reported for Howell, Stoddard, and Mississippi Counties (Summers MO). Flowering in May–June.

FIG. 81. **Bromus hordeaceous,** × 1.

7. Bromus japonicus Thumb. ex Murray JAPANESE CHESS. Fig. 82.

Annual; culms 50 cm tall or more; foliage pubescent; leaf blades 3–6 mm wide; panicles open, with spreading branches arranged in whorls; spikelets 2–3 cm long; glumes unequal, the 1st 3-nerved, the 2nd 5-nerved; lemmas smooth, 8–9 mm long, with slender, divergent awn, about 1 cm long; similar in general habit to no. 10, with straight awns of comparable length.

Widespread as a weed in the United States, a weedy adventive from the Old World.

Missouri. Waste areas, open ground, and fields, generally distributed. Flowering in May–June.

8. Bromus secalinus L. CHESS. Fig. 83.

Annual; culms about 50 cm tall, sometimes more; foliage glabrous or nearly so; leaf blades 3.5–9 mm wide; panicles open, with spreading branches; spikelets

FIG. 82. **Bromus japonicus,** × 1.

Fig. 83. **Bromus secalinus.** Plant, × ½; spikelet and floret, × 5.

glabrous, 1–2 cm long; glumes oblong, short-pointed; lemmas plump, 7–9 mm long, with a short awn less than 5 mm in length; margins of the mature lemmas becoming inrolled, exposing the rachilla.

Widespread in the United States; adventive from Europe.

Missouri. Waste ground and grain fields, generally distributed. Flowering in May–June.

9. Bromus squarrosus L. Fig. 84.

Annual; culms relatively short, less than 50 cm tall; leaf blades and sheaths soft-pubescent; panicles with short, ascending branches, in whorls; spikelets few, relatively large, to 2 cm in length; lemma with flat, laterally spreading, twisted awns.

Widely scattered in the United States as an adventive weed; introduced from Europe.

Missouri. Rare and little known; St. Louis and New Madrid Counties, the latter representing a more recent collection (Clement 149 SEMO).

10. Bromus arvensis L.

Annual, similar to no. 7 in general habit with only minor differences to distinguish them, including a straight, less divergent awn in *arvensis;* selected analyses including hybridization studies are required to determine the degree of intrinsic relationship between these and other close allies, nos. 6–11, all weedy annuals of Old World origin (Section Bromus = Bromium).

Missouri. Reported for St. Louis County, railroad freight yards (Muehlenbach 4192 MO), probably not persistent; since identified as *B. japonicus.*

11. Bromus racemosus L. CHESS. Fig. 85.

Annual, 0.4–1 m tall; panicles with spreading to somewhat stiff branches; foliage variably pubescent; spikelets mostly glabrous, 2–3 cm long; glumes unequal, the 1st 3-nerved, the 2nd 5-nerved; lemmas 8–10 mm long, with thin, scarious margins, the awns straight, ascending. Incl. *B. commutatus* Schrad., sometimes maintained as a separate species and distinguished on the basis of somewhat larger spikelets and more open, spreading panicles.

Pavlick (1991) separates *B. racemosus* from *B. commutatus,* but acknowledges their similarity and possible conspecificity. In view of difficulty in separating with certainty some of our material, both are provisionally included here under the older name, *B. racemosus.*

Widespread weed in the United States; introduced from Europe.

Missouri. Open ground, fields, and waste areas, generally distributed. Flowering in May–June.

12. Bromus tectorum L. DOWNY CHESS. Fig. 86.

Annual, forming tufts, sometimes becoming more extensive; culms erect, 30–50 cm tall; foliage pubescent, the leaf blades 3–5 mm wide; panicles soft, dense, silvery green, with slender, drooping branches; spikelets narrow, tapering to the base; 1st glume subulate, about 1 mm wide, 1-nerved, the 2nd glume wider with scarious margins and 3-nerved; lemmas soft-pubescent, about 10 mm long with a straight awn, 10–15 mm in length.

This species and nos. 13 and 14 are close allies of European origin (Section Genea = Eubromus), characterized by narrow, straight-awned spikelets with pointed bases, differing mainly in size of the spikelet and awn length.

Fig. 84. **Bromus squarrosus**, × 1.   Fig. 85. **Bromus racemosus**, × ½.

Widely scattered in the United States, less common or absent in the Southeast; introduced from Europe.

Missouri. Open ground, fields, and roadsides, generally distributed, one of our most common annual bromes, the seeds germinating in fall and overwintering with suitable conditions. Flowering in early May.

13. **Bromus sterilis** L. Fig. 87.

Annual; culms erect, 50 cm tall or more; lower sheaths becoming pubescent, the leaf blades mostly glabrous or nearly so; panicles diffuse, with drooping branches; spikelets about 3 cm long; glumes dissimilar, the 1st 1-nerved, the 2nd 3-nerved; lemmas smooth or scabrous, about 1.5 cm long, with straight awns 2–3 cm in length.

Widely scattered in the United States; introduced from Europe.

Missouri. Open ground and waste areas, widely scattered, mainly central and southern counties. Flowering in May–June.

14. **Bromus diandrus** Roth Ripgut Grass. Fig. 88.

Annual; culms erect, about 50 cm tall or more; foliage pubescent, the leaf blades 3–6 mm wide; panicles, with somewhat stiff branches; spikelets about 4 cm long, with sharp, tapering base; glumes dissimilar, the 1st one narrow, 1-nerved, about 1.5

Fig. 86. **Bromus tectorum.** Plant, × ½; spikelet and floret, × 5.

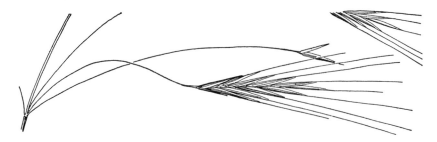

FIG. 87. **Bromus sterilis.** Spikelet, × 1.

cm long, the 2nd broader, 3-nerved, and longer; lemmas 2.5–3 cm long with straight awns 3–5 cm long. *B. rigidus* auct. non Roth var. *gussonei* (Parl.) Coss. & Durieu.

Widely scattered in the United States; introduced from Europe.

Missouri. Rare and little known, collected from waste ground, Jackson and St. Louis Counties. Flowering in May–June.

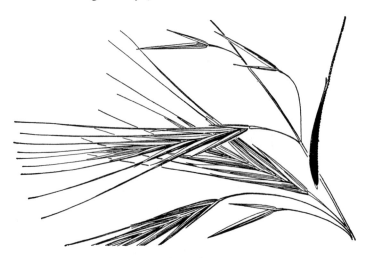

FIG. 88. **Bromus diandrus.** Spikelet, × 1.

TRIBE 10. TRITICEAE

37. ELYMUS L. WILD RYE

Annuals and perennials (our species all perennials); spikes stiff or nodding, narrow, compact to bristly, with spreading awns, the rachis continuous in most species, but sometimes fragmenting; spikelets 1- to several-flowered, sessile, 1 to several at each node of the rachis; at maturity spikelets mostly separating above the persistent glumes, but in some species falling entire; glumes ranging from well developed to narrow-lanceolate, awned or awnless, to bristlelike, or much reduced or obsolete. $x = 7$; non-Kranz.

Elymus constitutes a polymorphic assemblage including taxa that traditionally were maintained in different genera, separated mainly on morphological characters of inflorescence and spikelet. Hybridization studies in the assessment of degree of sterility between genera, and genomic analyses, prescribe the merging of *Hystrix* Moench and *Sitanion* J.G. Sm. with *Elymus* (Church, 1967). Similarly, several species of *Agropyron* Gaertn. are joined with *Elymus,* including all native North American representatives with the exception of monotypic *Pascopyrum* A. Löve (Barkworth & Dewey, 1985).

Key to Missouri Species

a. Spikelets usually single at each node, arranged flatwise to the rachis; glumes well developed
  b. Plants rhizomatous, forming a tough sod; spikelets mostly falling entire
    c. Leaf blades sometimes involute, with distinct bluish green cast.................1. *E. smithii*
    c. Leaf blades mostly flat, not bluish green.....................................2. *E. repens*
  b. Plants lacking rhizomes, forming dense tufts; spikelets mostly separating above glumes
    d. Spikelets much compressed; leaf blades inrolled; rare adventive........3. *E. elongatus*
    d. Spikelets not compressed; leaf blades flat, not inrolled; native species ....
    ....4. *E. trachycaulus*
a. Spikelets usually more than 1 at each node, not arranged flatwise to the rachis
  e. Spikes diffuse, with few, widely spaced spikelets; glumes obsolete or much reduced ....5. *E. hystrix*
  e. Spikes generally more compact, with numerous spikelets; glumes bristlelike to well developed
    f. Glumes bristlelike, at most 0.5 mm wide
      g. Lemma with several awns, the central awn to 10 times length of its lemma
      ....6. *E. elymoides*
      g. Lemma with single awn, much less than 10 times length of lemma ....
      ....7. *E. diversiglumis*
    f. Glumes broader than 0.5 mm in width
      h. Awns of mature spikelets curling and spreading..............8. *E. canadensis*
      h. Awns mostly straight, not curling, or absent
        i. Glumes noticeably bowed or curved at base, variably awned to merely subulate-tipped ....9. *E. virginicus*
        i. Glumes not distinctly bowed or curved, awned
          j. Spikelets noticeably pubescent (except in f. *arkansas*); upper side of leaf blades soft-downy................................10. *E. villosus*
          j. Spikelets glabrous; leaf blades not as above
            k. Spikes somewhat flexible and nodding; glumes distant and divergent; common species.....................................11. *E. riparius*
            k. Spikes stiff, upright; glumes close together and parallel; restricted species...12. *E. glaucus*

1. Elymus smithii (Rydb.) Gould Western Wheatgrass. Fig. 89.

Plants forming a sod, spreading by brownish rhizomes; culms to about 30 cm tall or more; foliage mostly glabrous, conspicuously bluish green; leaf blades narrow, 2–5.5 mm wide, somewhat stiff, with scabrous, inrolled margins; auricles prominent; spikes stiff, pale or bluish green, 5–15 mm long; spikelets usually more than 5-flowered, 15–20 mm long; glumes rigid, lanceolate, with long-tapering tip about 10 mm long or more; lemmas 10–15 mm long, subulate or with short awns about 1 mm long. *Agropyron smithii* Rydb.; *Pascopyrum* A. Löve *smithii* (Rydb.) A. Löve.

Wide-ranging, in the western two-thirds of the United States, east to Ohio and Kentucky.

Missouri. Open ground, fields, and prairies; generally distributed, but not abundant. Flowering in May–June.

2. Elymus repens (L.) Gould Quackgrass. Fig. 90.

Plants forming a tough sod, spreading by long, yellowish, creeping rhizomes; culms erect, to about 1 m tall; leaf blades thin, somewhat lax, 5–10 mm wide, with conspicuous midvein; auricles present; spikes erect, 5–15 cm long; spikelets 3–8-flowered, 10–20 mm long; glumes generally lanceolate, scarious-margined or margins inrolled, 8–15 mm long, subulate-tipped or merely short-awned; lemmas about 10 mm or somewhat longer, awnless or with awns usually less than 10 mm long. *Agropyron repens* (L.) P. Beauv.; *Elytrigia repens* (L.) Devs. ex B.D. Jackson.

Widely distributed, but most common in and probably native to the northern United States, absent from the Southeast and lower Mississippi valley; also Eurasia.

Missouri. Open ground, fields, and waste areas; widely scattered, but most abundant in the northern counties, frequently invasive. Flowering in May–June.

3. Elymus elongatus (Host) Runemark Tall Wheatgrass

Plants forming dense tufts; culms erect, coarse, with stiff leaf blades having inrolled margins; auricles well developed; spikes erect, with continuous rachis, the spikelets many-flowered, compressed; glumes indurate, 2–3 mm wide; with conspic-

Fig. 89. **Elymus smithii**, × 1.

FIG. 90. **Elymus repens.** Plant, × ½; spikelet and floret, × 3.

uous nerves; lemmas also hard, lanceolate-acuminate about 10 mm long or more. *Agropyron elongatum* (Host) P. Beauv.; *Elytrigia elongata* (Host) P. Beauv.

Widespread forage species introduced from Eurasia, mainly in the western states east to Iowa and Kansas.

Missouri. Rare and little known, railroad freight yards, St. Louis County (Muehlenbach 2756 MO), probably not persisting.

4. Elymus trachycaulus (Link) Gould ex Shinners SLENDER WHEATGRASS. Fig. 91.

Plants typically forming tufts, lacking rhizomes; culms to 1 m tall; leaf blades flat, mostly glabrous, 2.5–8 mm wide; auricles mostly present, or sometimes one or both absent; spikes as much as 20 cm in length; spikelets slender, becoming distant or remote on the lower rachis, usually less than 5-flowered; glumes variable in length, 7–15 mm long, long-tapering to subulate-awned; lemmas about 10 mm long, awnless or with variable awn to 10 mm in length. *Agropyron trachycaulum* (Link) Malte ex H.F. Lewis.

Rhizomatous hybrids of this species and *E. repens* have been reported.

Wide-ranging in the western and northern United States, absent in the lower Mississippi valley and southeastward.

Missouri. Fields and waste ground, infrequent and widely scattered, including Jackson, Jasper, Newton, Marion, Ralls, Pike, and St. Louis Counties. Flowering in late June–July.

5. Elymus hystrix L. BOTTLEBRUSH GRASS. Fig. 92.

Plants perennial, culms solitary or few together in sparse clumps; culms erect, 0.5–1.5 m tall; leaf blades mostly glabrous, flat, 7–15 mm wide; spikes diffuse, somewhat flexuous, 5–15 cm long, with continuous rachis; spikelets mostly 2 at each node, the awns horizontally spreading, the florets dropping readily at maturity; glumes variable, obsolete to bristlelike; lemmas typically glabrous or sometimes pubescent, about 10 mm long, with straight, scabrous awn 10–40 mm long. *Hystrix patula* Moench.

Plants with pubescent lemmas are separated from typical *hystrix* as f. *bigeloviana* (Fern.) Dore. (*Hystrix patula* f. *bigeloviana* (Fern.) Gleason).

Eastern and central United States, west to North Dakota and Kansas.

Missouri. Woods and rocky slopes, generally distributed, a most distinctive grass; plants with pubescent lemmas reported for Atchison, Holt, and Jackson Counties. Flowering in late June–July.

FIG. 91. **Elymus trachycaulus**, × 1.

Fig. 92. **Elymus hystrix.** Plant, × ½; spikelet and floret, × 3.

6. Elymus elymoides (Raf.) Swezey Squirreltail. Fig. 93.

Plants perennial, sparsely tufted; culms erect, to about 0.5 m tall; leaf blades mostly glabrous to slightly pubescent, 1–4 mm wide, occasionally involute; spikes 5–10 cm long, bristly, with usually long spreading awns, the rachis separating readily at the nodes; spikelets usually 2-flowered, 2 at each node, falling entire with the rachis joint; glumes bristlelike, less than 0.5 mm wide; lemmas scabrous, firm, about 10 mm

Fig. 93. **Elymus elymoides.** Plant, × ½; spikelet and floret, × 3.

long, several-awned, the central awn to 10 cm in length; palea equal to lemma. *Sitanion hystrix* (Nutt.) J.G. Smith; *S. longifolium* J.G. Smith.

    Western United States, east to Missouri.

    Missouri. Apparently adventive; dry waste ground, Jackson County (Bush 3907 MO). Flowering in summer.

7. Elymus diversiglumis Scribn. & C.R. Ball Fig. 94.

Plants perennial, forming narrow tufts; culms erect, about 1 m tall; principal leaf blades generally glabrous, sometimes scabrous above, 5–10 mm wide; spikes diffuse, somewhat flexuous, 5–15 cm long, the rachis joints thin, flat, about 7 mm long; glumes bristlelike, divergent; lemmas about 10 mm long, the scabrous awns horizontally spreading, several times longer than the body. *E. interruptus* Buckley.

This taxon is reportedly a vigorous F_1 hybrid of nos. 5 and 8 when the latter is the pistillate parent. All reciprocal crosses were unsuccessful (Church, 1967).

North-central United States and western Great Lakes region; also in the Southwest, to New Mexico, Texas, and Mexico; sporadic and not common.

Missouri. Scattered and infrequent; Barry, Lafayette, Gentry, and Worth Counties. Flowering in midsummer.

8. Elymus canadensis L. CANADA WILD RYE. Fig. 95.

Plants perennial, forming tufts; culms mostly stout, 1–1.5 m tall; leaf blades green to bluish green, glabrous to somewhat scabrous, 1–2 cm wide; auricles conspicuous; spikes curving or nodding, bristly, 10–25 cm long, the rachis joints elongating toward base; glumes conspicuously nerved, more than 1 mm wide, awned; lemmas 10–15 mm long, with spreading or divergent awn 20–30 mm in length; palea nearly equal to body of lemma.

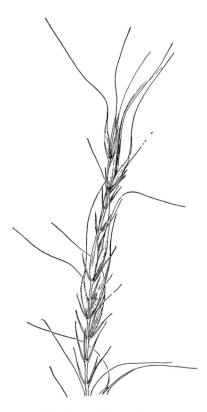

FIG. 94. **Elymus diversiglumis**, × 1.

Fig. 95. **Elymus canadensis.** Plant, × ½; spikelet and floret, × 5.

Plants usually coarse-robust, distinguished by bluish green foliage and large spikes to 20 cm long or more, have been designated variously, including f. *glaucifolius* (Muhl.) Fern. This condition is particularly distinctive in some Missouri plants. *E. canadensis* var. *robustus* (Scribn. & J.G. Smith) Mackenz. & Bush.

Widespread in the United States; absent in the Southeast from Alabama to South Carolina.

Missouri. Prairies, roadsides, swales, and limestone slopes, generally distributed. Flowering in July–August.

9. Elymus virginicus L. VIRGINIA WILD RYE. Fig. 96.

Perennial, sparsely tufted; culms erect, 0.5–1 m tall; leaf blades generally smooth to scabrous 5–15 mm wide; auricles small or imperfectly developed; spikes generally erect, 5–15 cm long, exserted or sometimes partially enclosed in the upper spathelike sheaths; glumes more than 1 mm wide, bowed and rounded at the smooth yellowish base; lemmas smooth to hirsute, with straight awns 1–3.5 cm long or awnless.

This is a most heterogeneous complex, including several varieties and forms for our area. Plants with spikes wholly or partially inserted in the upper sheaths, the spikelets awned and mostly glabrous, represent var. *virginicus* f. *virginicus;* those with hirsute tendency are referred to var. *virginicus* f. *hirsutiglumis* (Scribn.) Fern. Plants with well-exserted spikes, the spikelets awned and glabrous, are designated as var. *glabriflorus* (Vasey) Bush f. *glabriflorus;* and those with some degree of pubescence as f. *australis* (Scribn. & C.R. Ball) Fern. Plants with mostly awnless glumes and lemmas are separated as var. *submuticus* Hook.

Widespread in the United States, most common southeastward, west to Arizona and the Pacific Northwest.

Missouri. Wooded areas, prairie openings, moist banks, and stream bottoms, generally distributed, except var. *submuticus,* which is infrequent and less common. Flowering in late June–July.

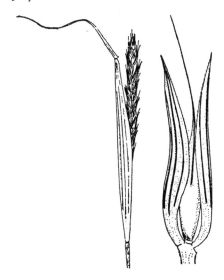

FIG. 96. **Elymus virginicus** var. **virginicus.** Panicle, × ½; spikelet, × 5.

10. Elymus villosus Muhl. ex Willd. Fig. 97.

Perennials forming small tufts; culms slender, mostly less than 1 m tall; leaf blades soft-pubescent on upper surface, 5–15 mm wide; auricles conspicuous; spikes generally nodding, 5–10 cm long; the rachis hairy, consisting of numerous short joints 2–3 mm in length; glumes setaceous, conspicuously nerved with straight awns; lemmas typically pubescent, sometimes glabrous or nearly so, about 7.5–8 mm long, with straight awn 10–30 mm in length. Incl. f. *arkansanus* Scribn. & C.R. Ball with more or less glabrous spikelets.

Eastern and central United States, west of North Dakota, Wyoming, and Texas.

Missouri. Usually rich or moist woods, low ground, creek banks, and limestone slopes, generally distributed as typical *villosus;* plants with a tendency for smooth to scabrous spikelets occur only infrequently and are integrated completely with the typical form. Flowering in midsummer.

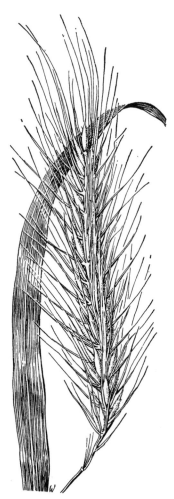

Fig. 97. **Elymus villosus,** × 1½.

11. Elymus riparius Wiegand Fig. 98.

Perennial; culms to 1 m or taller; leaf blades thin, long-tapering to fine tip, 5–15 mm wide; auricles present; spikes generally nodding, 5–20 cm long, the rachis somewhat flexuous, consisting of joints 4–5 mm long; glumes linear, conspicuously nerved, straight-awned; lemmas glabrous, about 10 mm long, exceeding the palea, the awn straight, 10–30 mm long.

Eastern and central United States, west to Nebraska and Kansas.

Missouri. Rich or moist woods, alluvial banks and north-facing limestone slopes, widely scattered; mostly absent or rare in the west-central and northwestern counties. Flowering in midsummer.

12. Elymus glaucus Buckley BLUE WILD RYE. Fig. 99.

Perennial, forming small tufts; culms to 1 m tall; leaf blades mostly smooth or soft, minutely pubescent on the upper surface, 5.5–10 mm wide; spikes long-exserted, erect, narrow, 5–10 cm long, the rachis smooth, consisting of relatively few joints, each about 5 mm long, fragmenting readily; glumes widening above the base and tapering to a short awn about one-half the length of the body, the abaxial pair close and parallel; lemmas 8–9 mm long with awn 10–20 mm in length; palea equal to the body of the lemma.

Western United States to the Midwest, to Michigan.

Missouri. Dry prairies and limestone bluffs, mainly in the southwest; Barton, Jasper, Newton, Barry, Lawrence, Stone, Taney, and Ozark Counties; also Shannon County. Flowering in June–July.

38. HORDEUM L. BARLEY

Annuals and perennials; spike bristly, the rachis mostly articulate, breaking readily at maturity (except in common barley); spikelets mostly 1-flowered usually in threes at each node of the rachis, all falling attached together with the rachis section; only the central spikelet of each group of 3 fertile and sessile, the 2 lateral spikelets sterile and pedicelled, or all spikelets sessile and fertile; glumes narrow, awned or bristlelike; perfect lemma firm, rounded on back, long-awned, lemmas of the sterile spikelets reduced; rachilla extended behind palea. $x = 7$; non-Kranz.

Hordeum includes several domesticated species, such as common barley, and a larger number of wild relatives, from temperate regions of both hemispheres.

Key to Missouri Species

a. Rachis mostly continuous, not fragmenting; all spikelets fertile, sessile, awned or awnless ... .1. *H. vulgare*
a. Rachis fragmenting at maturity; only central spikelet fertile, sessile, the 2 laterals sterile and pedicellate
   b. Annual; spikes short, somewhat strict, upright; the awns stiff, about as long as the lemmas ....2. *H. pusillum*
   b. Perennial; spikes more open, flexuous, or nodding; the awns delicate, mostly several times the length of the lemmas
      c. Awns to 3–6 cm long ....3. *H. jubatum*
      c. Awns about 1–2 cm long...4. *H.* × *caespitosum*

1. Hordeum vulgare L. COMMON BARLEY. Fig. 100.

Coarse annual with wide, flat leaves to 15 mm wide, and conspicuous, curved auricles; spikes stiff, erect, dense with continuous rachis, thus differing from the

Fig. 98. **Elymus riparius.** Panicle, × ½; floret, × 5.

Fig. 99. **Elymus glaucus.** Panicle, × ½; floret, × 5.

following Missouri taxa, nos. 2 and 3, which fragment readily; the 3 spikelets at each node sessile, well developed, producing full grains; glumes narrow, awned; lemmas with straight awn to 15 cm long.

Plants differing from typical *vulgare* having awnless spikelets, the lemmas with 3-lobed apex, are designated as var. *trifurcatum* (Schlecht.) Alef., commonly known as beardless or pearl barley.

Cultivated barley from Eurasia is occasionally spontaneous in waste ground but never persistent.

Missouri. Specimens with trifurcate lemmas have been reported.

2. Hordeum pusillum Nutt. Little Barley. Fig. 101.

Annual; culms erect, 15–40 cm tall, with sheaths glabrous to short-pilose; uppermost sheaths sometimes inflated and including the base of the spike; leaf blades scabrous, 2.5–5 mm wide; spikes erect, strict, narrow, about 1.5 cm wide, 3–7 cm long, breaking readily at maturity; spikelets in threes, the central one sessile, with fertile lemma 8–12 mm long, the awns of similar length, the 2 lateral spikelets sterile, smaller, on short stalks, also awned; outer glume of each lateral spikelet bristlelike,

Fig. 100. **Hordeum vulgare**. Plant and spike, × ½; group of spikelets, × 3; spike of beardless barley, × ½.

the inner one and those of the central spikelet broadened above the base and terminating in straight awn.

Widespread in the United States, more common westward.

Missouri. Open ground, fields, and waste areas, on dry soils; generally distributed. Flowering in May–June.

3. Hordeum jubatum L. Foxtail Barley. Fig. 102.

Perennial, forming small tufts, culms erect, 25–50 cm tall; upper sheaths spathelike, enclosing the base of the spike; leaf blades scabrous, 2–5 mm wide, tapering to
fine tip; mature spikes appearing bushy, somewhat nodding, pale green and becoming tawny, 5–10 cm long, the rachis fragmenting readily; spikelets in threes, the central one sessile, with fertile lemma 6–8 mm long, the awns to 5 cm long or more, the
2 lateral spikelets sterile, on short stalks, the lemmas much reduced but also long-
awned; glumes also narrow, with long, slender awns.

Wide-ranging, northern and central United States, common throughout the
west; absent in the southeast and mid-Atlantic region.

Missouri. Open ground, fields, and waste areas, scattered and more common in
the northern and western counties, mostly absent or infrequent in the Ozarks. Flowering in June–July.

4. Hordeum × caespitosum Scribn. Bobtail Barley

Perennial, forming tufts; culms erect to 70 cm tall or more, reported as a hybrid
of no. 3 and *H. brachyantherum* Nevski, the latter with more compact spikes and

Fig. 101. **Hordeum pusillum**, × 1.   Fig. 102. **Hordeum jubatum**, × 1.

much shorter awns; the hybrid is sterile with inflorescence and spikelet characters intermediate between the proposed parents (Mitchell & Wilton, 1964).

Hybridization occurs where both parental species have occupied a common habitat for several years, but *H. brachyantherum* heretofore has not been reported for the state. Additional study is required to document the presence of this taxon in Missouri and the proximal relationships of both parents in the vicinity of the hybrid. *H. jubatum* var. *caespitosum* (Scribn. ex Pammel) Hitchc.

Widely scattered, California and Arizona to North Dakota and Alaska; also Mexico; sometimes a contaminant in cured forage, and known to cause mechanical injury to livestock from the barbed awns.

Missouri. Open ground, north and west of a line from Buchanan to Gentry Counties, also Johnson, Henry, Saline, Pettis, Randolph, and Callaway Counties. Flowering in summer.

39. AGROPYRON Gaertn. WHEATGRASS

Annuals and perennials; spikes stiff, narrow, or occasionally bristly, the rachis mostly continuous or sometimes breaking at the joints; spikelets several-flowered, flattened, sessile, arranged singly and flatwise at each node of the rachis; at maturity, spikelets separating above the persistent glumes or falling entire with disarticulated rachis joints; glumes equal, well developed, subulate or awned; lemmas awnless or sometimes awned; palea equal to lemma. $x = 7$; non-Kranz.

Agropyron is an Old World genus. All native American species previously treated here, including *A. repens* (L.) Gould of Eurasia and wide areas of North America, are assigned to genus *Elymus* L. (Church, 1967; Estes & Tyrl, 1982).

1. Agropyron desertorum (Fisher ex Link) Schult. Fig. 103.

Perennial; culms to 1 m tall, forming tufts; sheaths mostly glabrous to somewhat pubescent, the leaf blades about 2.5–4 mm wide; spike dense, bristly, tapered

FIG. 103. **Agropyron desertorum**, × 1.

upward, with pubescent rachis; spikelets numerous, the lower ones about 1 cm long, 6–7-flowered; glumes narrow, with awn 2.5–3 mm long; lemma 4.5–6 mm long, with short awn. A. *cristatum* (L.) Gaertn. var. *desertorum* (Fisch. ex Link) Dorn.

Widespread in northern United States and adjacent Canada, south to California and Arizona; introduced from Eurasia as a forage species in the Great Plains.

Missouri. Rare and little known; Franklin (Davit s.n. MO) and St. Louis (Muehlenbach 2471 MO) Counties.

40. SECALE L. RYE

Annuals and short-lived perennials; spikes bristly, continuous or articulate; spikelets mostly 2-flowered, arranged singly and flatwise at each node of the rachis; glumes small, subulate, 1-nerved, persistent, the florets falling separately; lemmas much wider than glumes, 5-nerved, with long, ascending awn. $x = 7$; non-Kranz.

Secale, which includes both wild and cultivated species, originated under steppe conditions in southwestern Asia.

1. Secale cereale L. COMMON RYE. Fig. 104.

Annuals; culms erect, to 1 m tall or more; leaf blades flat, about 7 mm wide; spike dense, somewhat nodding; with thin, flattened rachis, differing from *Hordeum* L. by the single spikelet at each node of the rachis and from *Triticum* L. by narrow tapering glumes. Common rye occurs as an occasional volunteer, but not persisting.

41. TRITICUM L. WHEAT

Annuals; spikes jointed, the rachis fragmenting at maturity, sometimes falling entire or continuous and persistent; spikelets several-flowered, sessile, arranged singly and flatwise at each joint, or recessed in the concavity of the rachis and the rachis joint enlarged upward; glumes firm, broad, toothed at the apex; lemmas thick, broad, awned or awnless. $x = 7$; non-Kranz.

The genus *Triticum*, of Eurasian origin, includes wild and domesticated species, the primitive types characterized by weak, fragmenting spikes.

1. Triticum aestivum L. COMMON WHEAT. Fig. 105.

Plants relatively coarse, erect, to 1 m tall; leaf blades wide, flat, to 1 cm wide or more; auricles conspicuous; spikes erect, thick, continuous; spikelets plump, the lemmas awnless or with long, scabrous awns in the bearded strains and varieties.

Occasionally volunteering in open ground and along roadsides where grain is scattered, not persisting.

2. Triticum cylindricum (Host) Ces., Pass. & Gibelli JOINTED GOATGRASS. Fig. 106.

Plants forming leafy tufts; culms erect, about 50 cm tall; leaf blades 2.5–4 mm wide; spikes numerous, about 4 mm thick, 5–10 cm long or more; rachis joint broadened upward; spikelets 8–10 mm long; glumes stiff, conspicuously nerved, about 10 mm long, with keel to one side and terminating in lateral awn, sometimes bidentate at apex, the awn central; lemmas thickened, broadened toward apex, those of the upper spikelets with progressively longer awns, to 4–5 cm long. *Aegilops cylindrica* Host.

Widely distributed in the United States, occurring in wheatlands and pastures;

FIG. 104. **Secale cereale.** Plant, × ½; spikelet, × 3.

FIG. 105. **Triticum aestivum.** Plant with awned spikes (bearded wheat) and a nearly awnless spike (beardless wheat), × ½; spikelet and floret, × 3.

Fig. 106. **Triticum cylindricum,** × ½.

adventive from Europe. The long, scabrous awns may cause injury to grazing animals.

Missouri. Fields and waste areas, widely scattered, and locally abundant in some sections, including Adair, Boone, Clinton, Cole, Franklin, Howell, and Reynolds Counties. Flowering in early summer.

TRIBE 11. CENTOTHECEAE

42. CHASMANTHIUM Link

Perennials; panicles narrow, contracted, to more spreading with pendulous spikelets; spikelets several-flowered, separating between the florets and above the glumes; glumes similar, firm, narrow-acuminate; lemmas many-nerved, the lower one(s) sterile. $x = 12$; non-Kranz. *Uniola* L., in part.

1. Chasmanthium latifolium (Michx.) Yates WIDE-LEAF UNIOLA. Fig. 107.

Plants in loose clumps, or colonies from short rhizomes; culms erect, to 1 m tall; sheaths glabrous; ligule membranous, less than 1 mm long; leaf blades somewhat lax to 2 cm wide; panicles nodding, the spikelets from flexible pedicels; spikelets about 10-flowered, sharply keeled, 10–15 mm wide, 15–30 mm long, becoming brown at maturity; glumes and sterile lemma linear-lanceolate, the fertile lemmas larger, 10–12 mm long, wider, ovate-lanceolate; palea about two-thirds as long as lemma, the enclosed grain dark, ellipsoid, 4–5 mm long. *Uniola latifolia* Michx.

Southern and eastern United States to Ohio valley, to Kansas and Texas.

Missouri. Forested slopes, alluvial bottoms, and creek banks, widespread but absent north and west of a line from Platt to Mercer Counties. Flowering in summer.

2. Chasmanthium laxum (L.) Yates Fig. 108.

Plants sparsely tufted, from short rhizomes; culms erect, 0.5–1 m tall; upper part of sheaths glabrous to variably pilose; leaf blades 4.5–10 mm wide, tapering to long, fine tip; panicles narrow with short, stiff branches; spikelets about 5 mm in length, mostly sessile, not as compressed as in no. 1; glumes narrow-pointed, 1–2.5 mm long; lower lemma sterile; fertile lemmas 3.5–4 mm long with palea one-half as long. *Uniola laxa* (L.) Britton, Sterns & Pogg.; *U. sessiliflora* Poir.

Plants with glabrous sheaths represent typical *laxum;* those with pilose sheaths are separated as ssp. *sessiliflorum* (Poir.) Yates (*C. sessiliflorum* (Poir.) Yates).

Southern and eastern United States to New York, to Oklahoma and Texas.

Missouri. Rare and little known; typical *laxum* collected on damp ground, Ripley County (Steyermark 66921 MO), and ssp. *sessiliflorum,* St. Louis County (Kellog s.n. MO). Flowering in summer.

Our species of *Chasmanthium* are transferred from the genus *Uniola* on the basis of differences in leaf anatomy (non-Kranz vs. Kranz) and chromosome number (Yates, 1966). All species of *Chasmanthium* occur mainly in mesic forest sites; those retained in *Uniola* are characteristic of beach and strand environments, including sea oat (*U. paniculata* L.) of the Atlantic and Gulf coasts.

Fig. 107. **Chasmanthium latifolium.** Plant, × ½; spikelet and floret, × 3.

Fig. 108. **Chasmanthium laxum** ssp. **sessiliflorum.** Plant, × 1; floret, × 5.

TRIBE 12. ARUNDINEAE

43. ARUNDO L.

Tall, leafy-stemmed perennials, spreading by thick, coarse rhizomes; leaves distichous; panicles terminal, large, showy; spikelets several-flowered, soft-fluffy, separating above the glumes; glumes similar, elongate, about equal to upper florets, lemmas conspicuously pilose, with short awn. $x = 12$; non-Kranz.

1. Arundo donax L. GIANT REED. Fig. 109.

Plants robust, forming large clumps with numerous culms; culms 1–3 cm thick, to 5–6 m tall, with hollow internodes; leaf blades 4–5 cm wide; panicles stout, terminal, dense-woolly, to 50 cm in length; spikelets about 10 mm long with tapering glumes and elongate, hairy lemmas.

Widely planted in the southern United States as an ornamental and for erosion control along waterways and stream banks, occasionally spreading; introduced from southern Europe.

Missouri. Widely scattered as an escape on open ground; Boone, Jasper, Dunklin, and St. Louis Counties. Flowering in mid- to late summer.

44. PHRAGMITES Adans.

Tall, leafy, canelike perennials, rhizomatous; panicles terminal, showy, initially purplish, becoming lighter-colored at maturity; spikelets several-flowered, hairy, separating above the glumes; glumes dissimilar, long-pointed; lemmas *glabrous,* lanceolate, all more or less reaching the same level, the upper ones reduced; palea much shorter than its lemma; rachilla long-pilose, contributing to the hairy appearance of the spikelets. $x = 12$; non-Kranz.

1. Phragmites australis (Cav.) Trin. ex Steud. COMMON REED. Fig. 110.

Plants forming extensive colonies; culms 2–4 m tall; leaf blades numerous, elongate, 2-ranked, 2–3 cm wide or more; panicles dense, plumelike, with ascending branches; spikelets about 10 mm long; glumes much unequal; lemmas long-pointed, the lower ones to 9–10 mm in length, shorter upward; rachilla pilose, the hairs exceeding the florets. *Phragmites communis* Trin. var. *berlandieri* (Fourn.) Fern.

Worldwide, and one of the most extensively distributed of flowering plants; most of the United States except mid-Atlantic region to Kentucky and Arkansas.

Missouri. Lakes and low prairies, sloughs and riverbanks, widely scattered; mainly in the northern and western counties; also locally, in Boone and Callaway Counties and more recently in Stoddard County (Summers 3101 MO). Flowering in midsummer.

Fig. 109. **Arundo donax.** Plant, × ½; spikelet and floret, × 3.

Fig. 110. **Phragmites australis.** Plant, × ⅓; spikelet and floret, × 3.

TRIBE 13. DANTHONIEAE

45. DANTHONIA DC.

Perennials; panicles narrow, contracted to somewhat spreading; spikelets 1- to several-flowered, separating above the persistent glumes; cleistogamous spikelets from lower sheaths; glumes chartaceous, nearly equal, elongate, mostly overtopping the florets; lemmas bidentate, with geniculate awn from between the teeth, the latter sometimes extending into simple awns. $x = 6, 7$; non-Kranz, Kranz.

The transfer of *Danthonia* from the tribe Aveneae of earlier works to its present arundinoid association is based on closer agreement to the latter in several traits, including chromosome size and number, arrangement of chlorenchyma, and awn attachment, with a few species exhibiting Kranz features, in part (De Wet, 1954).

1. **Danthonia spicata** (L.) P. Beauv. ex Roemer & J.A. Schultes Poverty Oatgrass. Fig. 111.

Plants forming low basal clumps of curled leaves; flowering culms erect, to about 50 cm tall; sheaths and leaf blades glabrous to sparsely pilose, the latter narrow, 1–3 mm wide, tapering to involute tip; ligule consisting of pilose hairs; panicles narrow, sparsely flowered; glumes thin, elongate-acuminate, about 10 mm long or more, overtopping the several florets; lemmas pilose, about 2.5–3 mm long, cleft at apex, with bent awn about 5–8 mm long, twisted in lower part. Incl. var. *longipila* Scribn. & Merr.

Eastern and central United States, becoming less common westward.

Missouri. Dry woods, glades, and prairies, on thin or stony soils, generally distributed, more common in the Ozarks region. Flowering in May–June.

FIG. 111. **Danthonia spicata.** Plant, × ½; spikelet and floret, × 5.

TRIBE 14. ARISTIDEAE

46. ARISTIDA L. Triple-awn

Annuals and perennials; panicles mostly fragile, narrow to somewhat open; spikelets 1-flowered, separating above the persistent glumes; glumes elongate, acuminate; lemma hard, terete, linear-elongate, with a pointed callus at base, apex terminating in a 3-parted awn; palea tightly enclosed by lemma. $x = 11, 12$; Kranz.

Key to Missouri Species

a. Sheaths woolly-pubescent ....1. *A. lanosa*
a. Sheaths glabrous to sparsely pubescent
    b. Awns of lemma nearly equal or subequal, the laterals at least ½–¾ the length of central awn
        c. Lemmas to 2 cm long, the awns to 3 cm long, more or less equal ....2. *A. oligantha*
        c. Lemmas usually less than 1 cm long, the awns shorter, the laterals about ¾ as long as central awn
            d. Column of awn articulate at junction with lemma.........................3. *A. desmantha*
            d. Column of awn continuous with tip of lemma, not jointed
                e. First glume longer than 2nd, both exceeding floret ....4. *A. purpurascens*
                e. First glume shorter than 2nd, not exceeding floret....................5. *A. adscensionis*
    b. Awns of lemma dissimilar, the laterals less than ½ the length of central awn
            f. Central awn bent at base, but not coiled or with distinct curve ....
            ....6. *A. longespica*
            f. Central awn with distinct coil, twist, or curve at base
                g. Central awn with prominent loop or curve.....................7. *A. ramosissima*
                g. Central awn with coil-like base
                    h. Central awn 6–10 mm long, the laterals only ¼ as long ....
                    ....8. *A. dichotoma*
                    h. Central awn to 15–20 mm long, the laterals about ½ as long...............
                    ....9. *A. basiramea*

1. Aristida lanosa Muhl. ex Ell. Fig. 112.

Perennial, forming sparse tufts; culms erect, to 1 m tall; sheaths conspicuously white-woolly; leaf blades elongate, 3–4 mm wide; panicles narrow, with short, as-

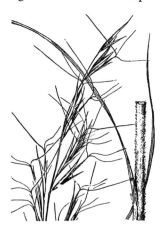

Fig. 112. **Aristida lanosa,** × 1.

cending branches; glumes about 1–1.5 cm long, unequal, the 1st slightly longer than the 2nd, both exceeding the floret; lemma about 8 mm long, with spreading awns two to three times longer, the central awn somewhat exceeding the laterals.

Southern United States and mid-Atlantic region, to New Jersey and Missouri.

Missouri. Sandy slopes of Crowley's Ridge, in Scott, Stoddard, and Dunklin Counties. Flowering in July.

2. Aristida oligantha Michx. Fig. 113.

Annual; culms slender, profusely branched, erect, to about 50 cm tall; leaf blades very narrow or stringlike, 1 mm wide; panicles loose, flexuous; glumes 2–3 cm long, subequal, acuminate, the 1st slightly shorter; lemma 1–2 cm long, the 3 awns nearly equal, spreading, not coiled at base, to 3.5–5 m long.

Eastern and central United States, west to South Dakota and Texas.

Missouri. Open ground and waste areas, on dry soils, generally distributed; one of our most common species of *Aristida*. Flowering in July–August.

3. Aristida desmantha Trin. & Rupr. Fig. 114.

Annual, forming slender tufts; culms stiff, erect, to 80–110 cm tall; leaf blades long, narrow, becoming involute; sheaths variously pilose; panicles somewhat contracted with short, ascending branches; glumes aristate, subequal, about 1 cm long, short-awned; lemmas shorter than glumes, with nearly equal awns to 2.5 cm long with deflexed tip and distinct bow at base, the column articulate; callus sharp-pointed, bearded.

Sporadic and little known, reported for Texas, Louisiana, Illinois, and Nebraska.

Missouri. Recently collected on remnant sand prairie, Scott County (McKenzie 1165 MO, 1286 UMO); new to the state. Flowering in summer.

4. Aristida purpurascens Poir. Fig. 115.

Perennial, forming narrow tufts; culms erect, about 50 cm tall; leaf blades 1–2 mm wide, involute toward tip; panicles loose, flexuous, about one-half the length of entire plant; glumes unequal, 8–10 mm long, the 1st exceeding the 2nd, both overtopping floret; lemma 5–8 mm long; central awn of lemma spreading, ascending, 1.5–3 cm long; lateral awns about three-fourths as long.

Eastern and central United States, west to Kansas and Texas.

Missouri. Open ground, dry prairies, and thin woods, on sandy or cherty soils; common in the Ozarks and southern counties; also reported for Lincoln and Montgomery Counties north of the Missouri River. Flowering in July–August.

5. Aristida adscensionis L. Fig. 116.

Annual, forming tufts; culms branching at base, erect to somewhat spreading, to about 70 cm tall; leaf blades narrow, involute; panicles flexuous, mostly dense; glumes unequal, 5–10 mm long, the 1st distinctly shorter, the 2nd about equal to floret; lemma 7–8 mm long, tufted at base; awns of lemma spreading, 8–15 mm long, the laterals only slightly shorter than the central one.

Central and South America, north to the southwestern United States, to California, Colorado, and Midwest region; also the Old World.

Missouri. Disturbed areas and waste ground; widely scattered, eastern Ozarks to St. Louis County and southwestern and western counties. Flowering in July–August.

FIG. 113. **Aristida oligantha**. Plant, × ½; glumes and floret, × 2.

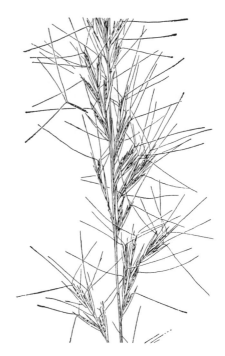

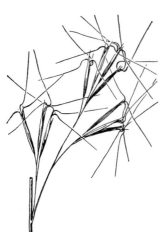

Fig. 114. **Aristida desmantha**, × 1.　　　Fig. 115. **Aristida purpurascens**, × 1.

6. Aristida longespica Poir. Fig. 117.

Annual, forming tufts; culms slender, branching; panicles narrow, flexuous, sometimes with simple branching, the single spikelets sessile or short-pedicelled, glumes 4–6 mm long, nearly equal, shorter than to slightly exceeding the lemma; central awn of the lemma 7–15 mm long, horizontally spreading, curved at the base; lateral awns straight, ascending, much shorter but variable, 1–6 mm in length.

Plants weakly separated from typical *longispica* by a tendency for longer lateral awns are designated as var. *geniculata* (Raf.) Fern. (*A. intermedia* Scribn. & C. Ball).

Eastern and central United States, west to Kansas and Texas.

Missouri. Upland prairies, fields, and dry woods, in the southern and eastern sections, absent north and west of a line from Jackson to Putnam Counties; var. *geniculata* less common than the typical variety. Flowering in July–August.

7. Aristida ramosissima Engelm. ex A. Gray Fig. 118.

Annual; culms slender, branching from the nodes, erect, to about 50 cm tall; leaf blades narrow, 1 mm wide; panicles loose, flexuous, or simply branched and racemose, the spikelets then mostly single along the main axis; glumes 1.5–2 cm long, unequal, acuminate, the 2nd longer, tapering to short awn about 3 mm long; lemma 1.5–2 cm long and together exceeding floret, the central awn as much as 2 cm in length, distinctly curved at base with quarter to nearly full turn; lateral awns much shorter, at most about 5 mm long.

Central United States, from Iowa and Indiana southward to Gulf region.

Missouri. Sandy prairies and open ground, on dry soils, scattered and not common, occurring generally south of a line from Barton to St. Louis Counties. Flowering in midsummer.

Fig. 116. **Aristida adscensionis,** × 1.

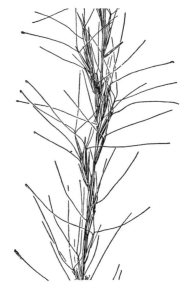

Fig. 117. **Aristida longespica,** × 1.

8. Aristida dichotoma Michx. Poverty-Grass. Fig. 119.

Annual, forming small tufts; culms branching from lower nodes, mostly erect, to about 50 cm tall; leaf blades narrow, 1 mm wide, the margins inrolled; panicles sparsely flowered; spikelets 6–12 mm long, the glumes nearly equal, or the 2nd

Fig. 118. **Aristida ramosissima,** × 1.

longer and about equal to or exceeding the floret; lemma 5–10 mm long; central awn of lemma about 6–10 mm long, coiled at base; lateral awns 2–3 mm long, not coiled.

Plants with spikelets 6–8 mm long and nearly equal glumes represent typical *dichotoma,* those with larger spikelets and glumes more dissimilar, the 2nd one exceeding floret, are separated as var. *curtisii* A. Gray (*A. curtisii* (A. Gray) Nash). These divisions are not readily separable for some Missouri specimens.

Eastern and central United States, west to Wyoming, Colorado, and Texas.

Missouri. Open ground, thin woods, and waste areas, on dry, cherty or sandy soils; typical *dichotoma* widely distributed but absent from the northwestern section; var. *curtisii* less common, occurring mainly in the central and southern counties. Flowering in July–August.

9. Aristida basiramea Engelm. ex Vasey Fig. 120.

Annual, forming thick tufts; culms branching from near the base, erect, to about 50 cm tall; leaf blades about 1 mm wide, becoming involute; panicles loose, sparsely flowered; glumes 10–15 mm long, unequal, the 1st shorter than the floret, the 2nd exceeding it; lemma about 1 cm long; central awn twisted or coiled at base, mostly longer than body of lemma; lateral awns straight, ascending, 6–10 mm long.

North-central United States, south to Oklahoma, occurring also in New England.

Missouri. Fields and waste ground, scattered and infrequent, central and southern counties, but generally excluding the Ozarks region. Flowering in July–August.

FIG. 119. **Aristida dichotoma,** × 1.   FIG. 120. **Aristida basiramea,** × 1.

TRIBE 15. ERAGROSTIDEAE

47. DISTICHLIS Raf.

Perennials, of low habit, rhizomatous, sometimes with stolons, dioecious; panicles dense, with short, compact branches; spikelets several-flowered, compressed-keeled, separating above the glumes; lemmas noticeably imbricate, acute, faintly nerved, those of the pistillate spikelets firm, mostly more indurate than the staminate ones. $x = 10$; Kranz.

1. Distichlis spicata (L.) Greene SALTGRASS. Fig. 121.

Plants rhizomatous, forming dense colonies; culms leafy, erect, 10–50 cm tall; sheaths overlapping, glabrous to pilose at the summit; leaf blades distichous, short, stiff, with inrolled margins; panicles compact, 2–6 cm long, among upper leaves; both staminate and pistillate spikelets 8–15 mm long or more, the pistillate ones 5–10-flowered, the staminate 5–15-flowered, both from short, ascending branches or nearly sessile; glumes keeled, 2–4 mm long; lemmas 3.5–7 mm long; palea nearly equal to the lemma, the keels smooth to serrulate.

Plants with relatively compact panicles, the spikelets closely imbricate, 5–10-flowered, and leaf blades with smooth margins represent typical *spicata;* those with spikelets 10–15-flowered and leaf blades with finely serrated margins are separated as var. *stricta* (Torr.) Scribn. (*D. stricta* (Torr.) Rydb.).

Coastal marshes of the United States, also western areas on alkaline soils, ranging to Minnesota, Missouri, Texas, adjacent Canada, and South America; typical *spicata* is restricted mainly to coastal areas.

Missouri. Rare and scattered, var. *stricta* reported for Buchanan, Clay, Jackson, and St. Louis Counties; var. *spicata* collected from Saline County (Steyermark 21581 MO) and Howard County (Korschgen & Porath s.n. UMO; Ladd 13299 MO). A search for var. *spicata* in Saline County site has been unsuccessful because of habitat loss. Flowering in summer.

48. TRIDENS Roemer & J.A. Schultes

Perennials, forming tufts, panicles with spreading branches, or narrow to spike-like; spikelets several-flowered, separating above the thin, mostly equal glumes; lemmas with 3 conspicuous nerves, these sometimes extending beyond apex as minute teeth or short awns, fringed on margins; palea about equal to lemma. $x = 8, 10$; Kranz.

Key to Missouri Species
a. Panicles broad, pyramidal, with spreading to ascending branches
  b. Panicles terminal, diffuse, with spreading branches; axillary panicles lacking ...1. *T. flavus*
  b. Panicles more contracted, the branches stiff, ascending; axillary panicles present............
  ....2. *T.* × *oklahomensis*
a. Panicles compact, spikelike, or narrow with short branches
  c. Panicles spikelike, with numerous spikelets ....3. *T. strictus*
  c. Panicles narrow with relatively few spikelets on short branches ....
  ....4. *T. muticus* var. *elongatus*

1. Tridens flavus (L.) Hitchc. PURPLETOP. Fig. 122.

Plants forming conspicuous tufts; culms erect, to 1 m tall or more; sheaths smooth, the basal ones compressed; leaf blades elongate, 3–8 mm wide, with promi-

FIG. 121. **Distichlis spicata** var. **stricta.** Staminate plant, × ½; staminate spikelet and floret, × 5; pistillate panicle, × 1; pistillate floret, × 5.

nent midnerve; panicles open, diffuse, the spreading branches and central axis with dark-viscid coating; spikelets several-flowered, 6–10 mm long, mostly purplish or rarely yellow; glumes scarious, less than one-half as long as entire spikelet, about 3 mm long, with short, abrupt tip; lemmas 4–5 mm long, the 3 nerves villous toward base, each terminating beyond the apex as a short tip.

Plants with depauperate panicles and tufts of hairs at base of branches are

FIG. 122. **Tridens flavus**. Plant, × ½; spikelet and floret, × 5.

separated from typical *flavus* as var. *chapmanii* (Small) Shinners (*T. chapmanii* (Small) Chase).

Eastern and southern United States, to Nebraska and Texas.

Missouri. Old fields, upland woods and roadsides, widely distributed as the typical variety; var. *chapmanii* reported for Shannon County. Flowering in late summer.

2. Tridens × oklahomensis (Feath.) Feath. ex Chase Fig. 123.

Plants robust, sometimes to 2 m tall; panicles terminal and axillary, more compact than no. 1, the stiff branches floriferous for a greater proportion of their total length, with somewhat viscid exudate; spikelets several-flowered, about 8 mm long, with dull purplish hue; glumes nearly equal, one-half the total spikelet length; lemmas 3–4 mm long, villous on the 3 nerves. This taxon is the F_1 hybrid of nos. 1 and 3 (Crooks & Kucera, 1971).

Type locality, Stillwater, Oklahoma, on open ground; since collected in Missouri and Louisiana.

Missouri. Roadsides and old fields, always in association with nos. 1 and 3, Boone (Kucera 301 UMO) and Butler Counties. Flowering in late summer but not producing developed caryopses.

Plants observed in Boone County with panicle measurements intermediate between *flavus* and × *oklahomensis,* indicate a backcross, the former serving as the staminate parent, the progeny producing viable seed (Schuckman & Kucera, 1984).

3. Tridens strictus (Nutt.) Nash. Fig. 124.

Plants forming clumps; culms erect, about 1 m tall; sheaths glabrous, compressed below; leaf blades elongate 4–8 mm wide; panicles terminal and axillary, dense, spikelike, 1–2 cm thick, 8–15 cm long; spikelets crowded, somewhat flattened, about

FIG. 123. **Tridens × oklahomensis.**
Panicle, × 1; floret, × 5.

FIG. 124. **Tridens strictus.** Panicle, × 1;
two views of floret, × 5.

5 mm long; glumes linear-elongate, equal to or sometimes exceeding upper floret; lemmas 3 mm long, the 3 nerves villous on lower part, only the central nerve protruding beyond apex as minute tip.

Southeastern United States, west to Missouri and Texas.

Missouri. Open ground, roadsides, and upland prairies, mostly in the southern counties, south of a line from Barton to Laclede Counties and eastward; observed as an adventive in Boone County where well established in several locations, more recently collected in Cole County (Raveill 2173 MO), suggesting possibly a selective movement northward into disturbed habitats. Flowering in late summer.

4. Tridens muticus (Torr.) Nash var. **elongatus** (Buckley) Shinners Fig. 125.

Plants forming clumps; culms erect, 30–80 cm tall; sheaths scabrous; leaf blades 2–4 mm wide, long-tapering; panicles slender, erect, with few, short, ascending branches; spikelets conspicuously nerved, the 1st acuminate, the 2nd less pointed, both about 6 mm long; lemmas 5–6 mm long, the 3 nerves villous on lower part and not excurrent as short awns. *T. elongatus* (Buckley) Nash.

Southwestern United States, north to Colorado, and Missouri.

Missouri. Dry prairies and limestone glades, west-central and southwestern sections. Flowering in late summer.

49. TRIPLASIS P. Beauv.

Annuals and perennials; panicles narrow, included in the sheaths, to exserted and spreading; spikelets few-flowered, separating above the persistent glumes; glumes about equal; lemmas 3-nerved, villous, with short awn between the 2-lobed apex; palea densely villous on the upper margins. $x = 10$; Kranz.

Fig. 125. **Tridens muticus** var. **elongatus.** Panicle, × 1; two views of floret, × 5.

1. Triplasis purpurea (Walter Chapman) SANDGRASS. Fig. 126.

Annual, forming small tufts; culms slender, erect, 20–80 cm tall; sheaths somewhat inflated; nodes bearded; leaf blades short, stiff, about 2 mm wide; panicles sparsely branched, partially exserted at summit of culm, some also reduced and included in lower sheaths; spikelets few-flowered, about 6 mm long, purplish, those included in sheaths cleistogamous; glumes thin, lanceolate, 2–3 mm long; lemmas 3.5–4 mm long, the 3 nerves conspicuously villous, with short awn about 1 mm long; grain brownish, elliptic, 2 mm long.

Eastern and southern coastal regions of the United States; also Great Lakes area and westward to Colorado and Texas.

Missouri. Dry sands and alluvial flats, Jackson, Osage, Clark, St. Charles, St. Louis, Jefferson, Ozark, and Dunklin Counties. Flowering in summer.

50. LEPTOCHLOA P. Beauv.

Annuals and perennials; inflorescence consisting of numerous, slender, spikelike branches or racemes, floriferous the entire length of the rachis; spikelets 2- to several-flowered, sessile or nearly so, arranged on one side of the rachis, separating above the persistent glumes; glumes mostly unequal; lemmas 3-nerved, usually awnless or merely awn-tipped; palea about equal to lemma. $x = 10$; Kranz. *Diplachne* P. Beauv. in part.

Key to Missouri Species

a. Spikelets 2–4-flowered; lemmas minute, about 1.5 mm long; annuals ....1. *L. panicea*
a. Spikelets 5–12-flowered; lemmas 2–5 mm long; annuals or perennials
    b. Lemmas awned from split, tapering apex; common annual ......2. *L. fusca* ssp. *fascicularis*
    b. Lemmas awnless; annuals or perennials; not common
        c. Annual species; lemmas variably pubescent on margins toward base
            d. Spikelets 6–9-flowered, 5–7 mm long ....2. *L. fusca* ssp. *uninervia*
            d. Spikelets 5–7-flowered, 4–5 mm long ....3. *L. panicoides*
        c. Perennial species; lemmas glabrous...4. *L. dubia*

1. Leptochloa panicea (Retz.) Ohwi. RED SPRANGLETOP. Fig. 127.

Annual; culms usually branching from base, erect, to 50 cm tall or more; sheaths sparsely pubescent; leaf blades soft, 5–10 mm wide; panicles about one-half the length of entire plant, consisting of divergent, slender, spikelike racemes; spikelets 2–4-flowered, reddish purple, 1.5–3 mm long; glumes lanceolate-subulate, 1–3 mm long, mostly shorter than the uppermost floret or sometimes exceeding it; lemmas small, 0.5–1.5 mm long, awnless. *L. filiformis* (Lam.) P. Beauv.

Plants with relatively shorter glumes not exceeding the top floret are separated as ssp. *brachiata* (Steud.) N. Snow (*L. filiformis* (Lam.) P. Beauv. var. *filiformis*); those with tapering glumes to 3 mm long usually exceeding the florets are referred to ssp. *mucronata* (Michx.) Nowack (*L. filiformis* var. *attenuata* (Nutt.) Steyermark & Kucera).

Tropical America and northward through the southern and central United States.

Missouri. Fields and open ground, on moist sands and alluvium, both subspecies equally distributed and most common south of the Missouri River, absent from the extreme northern counties. Flowering in July–August.

FIG. 126. **Triplasis purpurea.** Plant, × ½; spikelet and floret, × 5.

FIG. 127. **Leptochloa panicea.** Plant, × ½; spikelet and floret, × 10.

2. Leptochloa fusca (L.) Kunth SALT-MEADOW GRASS. Fig. 128.

Annual, forming tufts or clumps; culms branching from base, erect to somewhat decumbent, to 1 m tall; foliage glabrous, the leaf blades 1–3 mm wide, the margins sometimes inrolled; panicles narrow, the branches spikelike, crowded, appressed-ascending, partly included in the sheaths; spikelets 6–10-flowered, 5–10 mm long; glumes unequal, 1.5–3 mm long; lemmas distinctly imbricated, sparsely pubescent, 4–8 mm long, with delicate awn or awnless. *L. fascicularis* (Lam.) A. Gray, incl. var. *acuminata* (Nash) Gleason; *Diplachne fascicularis* (Lam.) P. Beauv.

Plants with awned tapering spikelets are referred to ssp. *fascicularis* (Lam.) N. Snow; those with spikelets lacking awns, the apex of lemma somewhat broadened, merely apiculate, are designated as ssp. *uninervia* (J. Presl) N. Snow (*L. uninervia* (J. Presl) Hitchc. & Chase).

Widely scattered throughout the United States, to South America.

Missouri. Wet depressions, mud flats, borders of ponds and natural sinks, widely scattered as ssp. *fascicularis;* ssp. *uninervia* reported for St. Louis freight yards, Lesperance Street (Muehlenbach 2407 MO, originally identified as *L. dubia* (Kunth) Nees), also at Loughborough Street (Muehlenbach 3910 MO), probably not persisting. Flowering in July–August.

3. Leptochloa panicoides (J. Presl) Hitchc. Fig. 129.

Annual; culms branching, erect to somewhat decumbent, to 1 m tall; foliage glabrous, the leaf blades as much as 10 mm wide; panicles with numerous short, ascending branches, giving a compact appearance; spikelets 5–7-flowered, about 4 mm long; glumes 1–2 mm long; lemmas about 2.5 mm long, with a short tip from notched apex. *Diplachne halei* Nash.

Central and lower Mississippi valley; also South America.

Missouri. Sandy banks and open ground, New Madrid County (Palmer 61658 MO), and more recently reported for Ripley, Butler, Stoddard, Scott, and Mississippi Counties (McKenzie MO). Flowering in late summer.

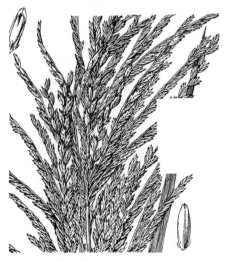

FIG. 128. **Leptochloa fusca** ssp. **fascicularis.** Panicle, × 1; two views of floret, × 10.

FIG. 129. **Leptochloa panicoides.** Panicle, × 1; two views of floret, × 10.

4. Leptochloa dubia (Kunth) Nees Green Sprangletop. Fig. 130.

Perennial; culms erect, to 1 m tall; foliage glabrous with leaf blades to 1 cm in width; panicle branches stiffly ascending; spikelets about 7–8-flowered, 5–10 mm long; lemmas with broad, emarginate apex, awnless. *Diplachne dubia* (Kunth) Scribn.

Southwestern United States, and Florida; also Mexico and South America.

Missouri. Open ground, infrequent and not well known, Crawford (Pickle 1249 UMC) and Gasconade Counties. Flowering in summer.

51. ERAGROSTIS von Wolf Lovegrass

Annuals and perennials; panicles narrow, compact, or more open with spreading or reflexed branching; ligule distinctive, consisting of hairs in most species; spikelets 2- to many-flowered, separating above the persistent glumes; glumes subequal, mostly 1-nerved; lemmas 3-nerved, sometimes keeled, acute or acuminate; palea usually persistent, mostly ciliate on margins, about equaling lemma. $x = 10$; Kranz.

Key to Missouri Species

a. Annuals, creeping or upright, mostly less than 50 cm tall
  b. Plants low, spreading, matlike, rooting from the lower nodes
    c. Plants with perfect florets (bisexual); panicles mostly longer than broad; common species ....1. *E. hypnoides*
    c. Plants dioecious, with either staminate or pistillate florets; panicles ovoid, or about as long as broad; rare species..2. *E. reptans*
  b. Plants mostly upright, to somewhat decumbent, not rooting from nodes
    d. Glands along leaf margins toward the base of leaf blades, usually also on the sheath and below nodes; spikelets elongate, imbricated, usually more than 10-flowered
      e. Spikelets elongate-linear, about 1 cm long, as thick as wide or nearly so ....3. *E. barrelieri*
      e. Spikelets somewhat flattened, the florets keeled and imbricated
        f. Spikelets as much as 3 mm wide; common species..................4. *E. cilianensis*
        f. Spikelets narrower, about 2 mm wide or less, infrequent, sporadic................. ....5. *E. minor*
    d. Glands not present; spikelets 2–10-flowered
      g. Panicles dense, narrow, elongate, to 50 cm in length; with numerous flowers from short ascending branches; little-known species in the state ....6. *E. glomerata*
      g. Panicles more or less open, not as above

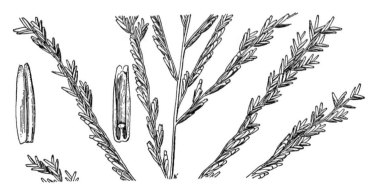

Fig. 130. **Leptochloa dubia.** Panicle, × 1; two views of floret, × 10.

  h. Spikelets loose, mostly less than 5-flowered
    i. Panicles diffuse, with delicate, spreading branches; sheaths pilose.......
     ....7. *E. capillaris*
    i. Panicles with more compact branching; sheaths mostly glabrous or
     else pilose only at summit ....8. *E. frankii*
  h. Spikelets imbricate, mostly 5- or more-flowered
    j. Axils of panicle branches long-pilose; spikelets delicate, about 1
     mm wide...9. *E. pilosa*
    j. Axils of panicle branches glabrous or nearly so; spikelets about 1.5
     mm wide
     k. Panicles open; spikelets linear, stiffly ascending; common native
      species..10. *E. pectinacea*
     k. Panicles more compact, with spikelets borne to base of branches,
      not appressed-ascending; rare adventive...........11. *E. multicaulis*
a. Perennials, mostly erect, height variable but some species to 1 m tall
    l. Spikelets 2–6-flowered, 3–5 mm long
     m. Spikelets about 1 mm wide, gray or slate-colored; sheaths
      glabrous except pilose at summit ....12. *E. intermedia*
     m. Spikelets 1–2 mm wide, not slate-colored but sometimes
      with purplish cast; sheaths variable
      n. Sheaths mostly glabrous; glumes to 3 mm long; nerves
       of lemma conspicuous..........................13. *E. trichodes*
      n. Sheaths mostly pilose or with scattered hairs; glumes
       about 2 mm long; nerves of lemma obscure.................
       ....14. *E. hirsuta*
    l. Spikelets 6–15-flowered or more, mostly more than 5 mm
     long
      o. Panicles distinctly pinkish purple, showy, with stiff,
       spreading branches, the axils conspicuously tufted,
       common native species...................15. *E. spectabilis*
      o. Panicles not as above
       p. Plants tall, mostly to 1 m or more; panicles tawny,
        with drooping branches..................16. *E. curvula*
       p. Plants mostly shorter; without drooping branches;
        q. Panicles diffuse, the branches slender, sparse;
         spikelets with elongate pedicels...17. *E. elliottii*
        q. Panicles not as above, more compact or
         densely branched
         r. Spikelets aggregated, noticeably keeled,
          10–15 mm long, in compact panicles with
          short, stiff branches..........18. *E. secundiflora*
         r. Spikelets not as above, 3–6 mm long, in
          open panicles with spreading branches ....
          ....19. *E. curtipedicellata*

1. Eragrostis hypnoides (Lam.) Britton, Sterns & Pogg. Fig. 131.

  Annual; culms low, creeping, rooting at the nodes; foliage glabrous to sparsely pubescent, the leaf blades short, about 2 mm wide; panicles diffuse to somewhat compact, 2.5–5 cm long; spikelets linear-oblong, mostly many-flowered (10 or more florets), 5–10 mm long; lemmas prominently 3-nerved, glabrous, thin, about 1.5 mm long.

  Widely scattered throughout the United States and southern Canada.

FIG. 131. **Eragrostis hypnoides.** Plant, × ½; floret, × 10.

Missouri. Alluvial banks, fields, and low ground, on sandy soils, generally distributed. Flowering in July–August.

2. **Eragrostis reptans** (Michx.) Nees Fig. 132.

Annual, with creeping habit, similar to no. 1; plants dioecious; pistillate panicles ovoid, composed of capitate clusters, the staminate ones less dense, 1–2 cm long; pistillate spikelets narrow, linear, somewhat curving; staminate spikelets broader, elliptic, compressed; lemmas prominently 3-nerved, sparsely pubescent, thin, 2–3 mm long.

Central United States, from South Dakota to Kentucky, to Texas, Louisiana, and northern Florida.

Missouri. Sandy ground, rare and little known, Jackson, Cass, and Livingston Counties. Flowering in July–August.

3. **Eragrostis barrelieri** Daveau Fig. 133.

Annual; culms erect to somewhat decumbent, to 50 cm tall, branching from basal nodes; leaf blades 2–4 mm wide, the sheaths sparsely pilose at summit; panicles with short, stiff branches, the axils glabrous; spikelets linear, more than 10-flowered, 1 cm long, much exceeding length of pedicel; lemmas about 2 mm long.

California to Missouri south to Texas, Arizona, and Mexico; introduced from southern Europe.

Missouri. Rare adventive, railroad freight yards, St. Louis County (Muehlenbach 2732 MO), probably not persistent. Flowering in summer.

FIG. 132. **Eragrostis reptans.** Pistillate and staminate plants, × ½; floret, × 10.

FIG. 133. **Eragrostis barrelieri.** Panicle, × 1; floret, × 10.

4.   **Eragrostis cilianensis** (All.) Vignolo. ex Janch. STINKGRASS. Fig. 134.

Annual, forming leafy tufts, decumbent near base; culms mostly less than 50 cm tall; leaf blades 2.5–6 mm wide, pilose at summit of sheath; foliage with glandular dots usually along lower margins of leaf blades, also on sheaths and nodes; panicles somewhat compact, oblong, upright, 5–15 cm long; spikelets linear-oblong, flattened, mostly more than 10-flowered; florets sharply keeled, imbricate; lemmas with 3 conspicuous nerves, thin, 2–2.5 mm long; grain roundish, loose within the floret. *E. megastachya* Link.

Widespread in the United States, introduced from the Old World.

Missouri. Open ground, fields, and waste areas, generally distributed; one of our most common adventives. Flowering in June–July.

Fig. 134. **Eragrostis cilianensis.** Plant, × ½; spikelet, × 5; floret, × 10.

5. Eragrostis minor Host Fig. 135.

Annual, generally similar to no. 3 but with slighter habit, more delicate leaves, and narrower panicles; glandular dots usually present on lower margins of leaves, sometimes sparingly so, also on keels of lemmas; spikelets linear, about 2 mm wide or less, 5–10 mm long; lemmas thin, about 1.5–2 mm long; grain round, loose within the floret. *E. poaeoides* P. Beauv. ex Roemer & J.A. Schultes.

Eastern and central United States, west to Kansas and Texas; adventive from Europe.

Missouri. Open ground, fields, and waste areas, infrequent and scattered, reported for Clay, Jackson, Christian, Stone, and Howell Counties. Flowering in June–July.

6. Eragrostis glomerata (Walter) L.H. Dewey Fig. 136.

Annual; culms erect to 1 m or more; foliage glabrous, the leaf blades 4–8 mm wide with long taper; ligule *membranous,* not hairy; panicles dense, narrow, elongate, with numerous short-ascending branches; spikelets 2–3 mm long, 6–8-flowered, on reduced pedicels to base of branches; lemmas thin, 1–1.5 mm long.

South-central United States to South Carolina and Florida, also South America.

Missouri. Representation in the state based originally on a single specimen, but location not defined; more recently reported on wet ground for Dunklin County (Toney 139 MO), also intersection of County Road 343 and Union Pacific Railroad, Butler County (Hudson 936 MO). Flowering in midsummer.

7. Eragrostis capillaris (L.) Nees Lacegrass. Fig. 137.

Annual, forming tufts; culms usually simple, unbranched, erect, 20–60 cm tall; sheaths sparsely long-pilose; leaf blades 2–3 mm wide; panicles broad, diffuse, more than one-half the length of entire plant; spikelets 2–3-flowered, 2 mm long, from delicate, long-spreading pedicels; glumes pointed, about 1 mm long; grain plump, with a readily visible longitudinal groove.

Eastern and central United States, west to Kansas, Oklahoma, and Texas.

Missouri. Fields, waste areas, and open woods, on dry or sandy soils, generally distributed. Flowering in July–August.

8. Eragrostis frankii C. A. Mey. ex Steud. var. **frankii** Sandbar Lovegrass. Fig. 138.

Annual, forming tufts; culms branching at the nodes, somewhat decumbent below; sheaths mostly glabrous, long-pilose at summit; leaves 1–3 mm wide, panicles elliptic, less than one-half the length of entire plant; spikelets 2–5-flowered, 2–3 mm long, from short pedicels; glumes pointed, about 1–1.5 mm long; lemmas indis-

Fig. 135. **Eragrostis minor.** Panicle, × 1; floret, × 10.

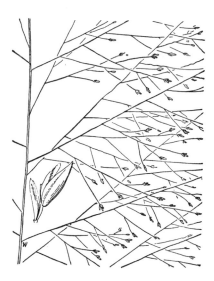

FIG. 137. **Eragrostis capillaris.** Panicle,
× 1; floret, × 10.

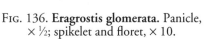

FIG. 136. **Eragrostis glomerata.** Panicle,
× ½; spikelet and floret, × 10.

FIG. 138. **Eragrostis frankii** var. **frankii.**
Panicle, × 1; floret, × 10.

tinctly nerved, glabrous, slate-colored, usually more than 1 mm long; grain plump, not grooved.

Eastern and central United States, west to Kansas and Oklahoma.

Missouri. Fields, waste areas, and sandy alluvium, generally distributed, less frequent north of Missouri River. Flowering in summer.

9. Eragrostis pilosa (L.) P. Beauv var. **pilosa** Fig. 139.

Annual, forming tufts; culms to 50 cm tall, branching from lower nodes, somewhat decumbent near base; leaf blades and sheaths mostly glabrous, the latter with

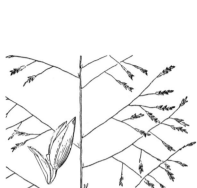
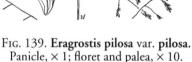

Fig. 139. **Eragrostis pilosa** var. **pilosa.** Panicle, × 1; floret and palea, × 10.

Fig. 140. **Eragrostis pectinacea.** Panicle, × 1; floret, × 10.

sparse hairs at summit; panicles diffuse, with spreading branches, the axils sparsely pilose, spikelets linear-elongate, 5–10-flowered; about 1 mm wide; pedicels somewhat flexuous, not stiff, mostly longer than the spikelet; lemmas 1.5 mm long, the nerves obscure.

Eastern and south-central United States; introduced from Europe.

Missouri. Open ground and waste areas, widely scattered, not common. Flowering in July–August.

10. Eragrostis pectinacea (Michx.) Nees Fig. 140.

Annual, forming dense tufts; culms to about 50 cm tall, branching from lower nodes, spreading to decumbent, the axils glabrous to somewhat pilose; sheaths long-pilose at the summit; leaf blades glabrous, 2 mm wide; panicles open, one-half or less the height of entire plant, the pedicels of the spikelets appressed to branches, to somewhat divergent; spikelets linear-oblong, 5–15-flowered, 5–10 mm long, 1–2 mm wide; lemmas thin, drab, sometimes with purplish cast, 1.5–1.8 mm long, the nerves more or less distinct.

Plants with appressed pedicels, the spikelets 5–7.5 mm long, and panicle branches having glabrous axils represent typical *pectinacea;* those with larger spikelets to 10 mm long, divergent pedicels, and lower panicle branches having pilose axils are separated as var. *miserrima* (Fourn.) J. Reeder (*E. arida* Hitchc.). The original description of *E. arida* by Hitchcock (1933) was for an annual species with a southwestern U.S. distribution. Missouri collections labeled as *E. arida* were difficult to separate from the more common *pectinacea* and were included with the latter (Kucera, 1961). Reeder (1986) treats both taxa throughout their range as a single species, with *E. arida* reduced to varietal rank.

Eastern and central United States, to California and Mexico.

Missouri. Open ground and waste areas, generally distributed. Flowering in July–August.

11. Eragrostis multicaulis Steud.

Annual; culms branching at base, to about 20–30 cm tall, erect to decumbent-spreading; leaf blades narrow, 1–2 mm wide; panicles somewhat open, the branches mostly floriferous to base or nearly so, the axils glabrous; spikelets 4–8-flowered, about 4 mm long; lemmas about 1.5 mm long, with visible nerves. *E. pilosa* P. Beauv.

Sporadic, New England to Virginia, also Great Lakes region, Oregon, and Missouri; introduced from Eurasia.

Missouri. Collected from railroad freight yards, St. Louis County (Muehlenbach 3723 MO), probably not persistent.

12. Eragrostis intermedia Hitchc. Fig. 141.

Perennial, forming coarse tufts with hard bases; culms wiry, 30–70 cm or more tall; sheaths long-pilose at summit; leaf blades glabrous or with few scattered hairs, narrow, with inrolled margins; panicles mostly diffuse, the branches whorled, spreading, sparsely hairy in the axils; spikelets 4–8-flowered, slate-colored, glabrous, about 2 mm long; grain oblong.

Scattered, south-central and southern United States, to Central America.

Missouri. Fields and open ground, infrequent, Jackson, Jasper, Newton, Christian, and Texas Counties. Flowering in midsummer.

13. Eragrostis trichodes (Nutt.) A. Wood Fig. 142.

Perennial, sparsely tufted; culms to 1 m tall or more; sheaths mostly glabrous; leaf blades long, stringlike; panicles with mostly purplish hue, sometimes straw-colored, about one-half the total plant height, diffuse, with spreading branches, slightly pilose in axils; spikelets 5–15-flowered, 5–12 mm long; lemma thin, glabrous, 2–3 mm long, conspicuously nerved; grain round-elliptic, dark-colored.

Plants with light-colored spikelets in the upper size range, 8–12 mm long, and 10–15-flowered, are separated from typical *trichodes* as var. *pilifera* (Scheele) Fern. (*E. pilifera* Scheele).

Fig. 141. **Eragrostis intermedia.** Panicle, × 1; floret, × 10.

FIG. 142. **Eragrostis trichodes.** Panicle, × 1; floret, × 10.

Central region of the United States from Illinois, Iowa, Nebraska, and Colorado to Arkansas and Texas.

Missouri. Open ground and dry, sandy areas, sporadic and infrequent, Jasper, Dade, Ozark, Dent, St. Francois, Ste. Genevieve, St. Louis, Carrol, and Jackson Counties as var. *trichodes;* var. *pilifera* recently collected from lead tailings, St. Francois County (McKenzie 1170 MO). Flowering in late summer.

14. Eragrostis hirsuta (Michx.) Nees var. **hirsuta** Fig. 143.

Perennial, coarsely tufted with hard, coarse bases; culms to 1 m or more tall; sheaths hirsute, sometimes nearly glabrous but pilose at summit; leaf blades 4–8 mm wide, the margins becoming inrolled with long, stringlike tips; panicles large, one-half the total height of plant, coarsely branched, spreading, pilose in the axils; spikelets 2–5-flowered, about 3–4 mm long, 1–2 mm wide; lemmas glabrous, 2 mm long, obscurely nerved; grain oblong. Plants with nearly glabrous sheaths are weakly separated from typical *hirsuta* as var. *laevivaginata* Fern.

Eastern United States from Maine to Florida, south-central region to Oklahoma and Texas, to Central America.

Missouri. Open ground and waste areas, sandy or stony soils, south of a line from Barton to Scott Counties, also Franklin and St. Louis Counties. Flowering in mid-summer.

15. Eragrostis spectabilis (Pursh) Steud. Purple Lovegrass. Fig. 144.

Perennial, forming dense tufts, from short rhizomes; culms 30–60 cm tall; sheaths mostly glabrous, sometimes sparsely hirsute, long-pilose at the summit; leaf

FIG. 143. **Eragrostis hirsuta** var. **hirsuta.** Panicle, × 1; floret, × 10.

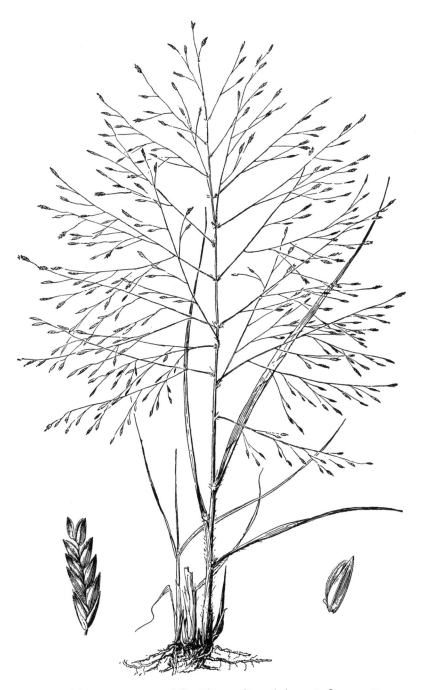

FIG. 144. **Eragrostis spectabilis.** Plant, × ½; spikelet, × 5; floret, × 10.

blades ascending, 3–5 mm wide; panicles pink-purplish, with stiffly spreading branches noticeably pilose in the axils, separating at maturity to form a tumbleweed; spikelets oblong, imbricate, 6–12-flowered, 5–6 mm long; lemmas 1.5–2 mm long, noticeably nerved; palea ciliate on the edges; grain roundish.

Widely distributed, eastern United States, to Minnesota, Nebraska, and Colorado, through the Southwest to Mexico.

Missouri. Open ground, old fields, and prairies, generally distributed; one of our most colorful grasses at maturity. Flowering in July–September.

16. Eragrostis curvula (Schrad.) Nees. WEEPING LOVEGRASS. Fig. 145.

Perennial, forming dense clumps with arching leaves, culms to 1 m or more tall; leaf blades narrow, inrolled, tapering to long stringlike tips; panicles with ascending to somewhat nodding branches, pilose in the axils; spikelets appressed along the branches, linear, 6–10-flowered, about 1 cm long; glumes deciduous; lemmas thin, conspicuously nerved, light green, 2.5–3 mm long.

Scattered in the southern United States; introduced from South Africa as a forage species.

Missouri. Roadsides, on sandy ground, Howell (Kucera 501 UMO) and Carter Counties; also railroad freight yards, St. Louis County (Muehlenbach 2955 MO), probably not persistent. Flowering in July–August.

17. Eragrostis elliottii S. Watson Fig. 146.

Perennial, forming slight tufts; culm less than 1 m in height; sheaths mostly glabrous but pilose at the summit; leaf blades glabrous, narrow, about 3 mm wide; panicles very open, diffuse, equal to one-half or more of the total plant height; spikelets from conspicuously extended, spreading pedicels, 8- or more-flowered, about 5–10 cm long and to 2 mm wide; florets imbricate, the lemmas about 2 mm long; grain ovoid. *E. campestris* Trin.

Native, low, wet areas, on the Coastal Plain from North Carolina to Texas, also Caribbean region and eastern Mexico.

Missouri. Collected from railroad freight yards, St. Louis County (Muehlenbach 3183 MO), probably not persistent.

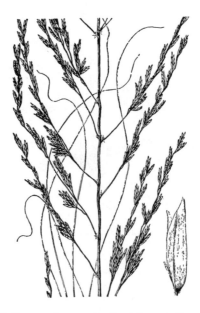

FIG. 145. **Eragrostis curvula.** Panicle, × 1; floret, × 10.

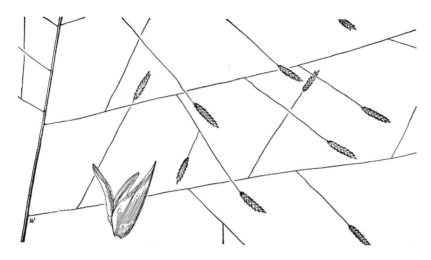

FIG. 146. **Eragrostis elliottii.** Panicle, × 1; floret, × 10.

18. Eragrostis secundiflora C. Presl ssp. **oxylepis** (Torr.) S.D. Koch RED LOVEGRASS. Fig. 147.

Perennial, somewhat tufted, about 50 cm tall; sheaths glabrous except for pilose hairs at summit; leaf blades glabrous, narrow, becoming inrolled and stringlike; panicles russet-colored, densely flowered, with short, stiffly ascending branches; spikelets with numerous florets, compressed or keeled, 10–15 mm long; lemmas strongly overlapping, with prominent nerves; grain oblong, about 1 mm long. *E. oxylepis* (Torr.) Torr.

The taxon previously known as *E. oxylepis* of the southeastern United States and

FIG. 147. **Eragrostis secundiflora** ssp. **oxylepis.** Panicle, × 1; floret, × 10.

eastern Mexico and *E. secundiflora* are elements of the same species (Koch, 1978). The latter, as ssp. *secundiflora,* is more southern, not reaching Missouri and is distinguished from ssp. *oxylepis* by its distinctly pubescent sheaths and leaf blades, and smaller, more ovoid grain.

South-central United States from Florida to Colorado, to California and eastern Mexico.

Missouri. Collected from railroad freight yards, St. Louis County (Muehlenbach 1931 MO), probably not persistent.

19. Eragrostis curtipedicellata Buckley GUMMY LOVEGRASS. Fig. 148.
Perennial, tufted; culms mostly less than 40–50 cm tall; sheaths mostly glabrous, with pilose hairs at summit and along margins; leaf blades glabrous, narrow, 2–3 mm wide; panicles mostly open, the branches spreading, typically viscid or oily on the surface, with sparse hairs in the axils; spikelets 5–10-flowered, about 5 mm long, 1.5 mm wide; lemmas thin, with prominent nerves; grain large, elliptic-oblong, 1 mm long.

South-central United States to northeastern Mexico.

Missouri. Collected from railroad freight terminus, St. Louis County (Muehlenbach 1993 MO), probably not persistent.

52. ELEUSINE Gaertn.

Annuals; inflorescence consisting of several broad spikes more or less digitately arranged at the summit of the flowering axis; spikelets several-flowered, sessile, in 2 rows on 1 side of the rachis, separating above the persistent glumes; glumes unequal; lemmas compressed, awnless. $x = 9$; Kranz.

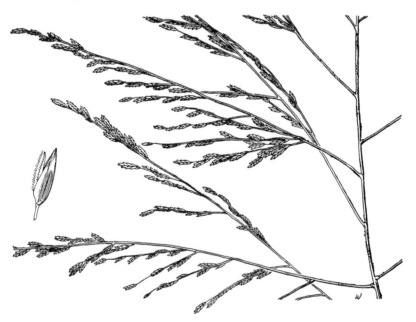

FIG. 148. **Eragrostis curtipedicellata.** Panicle, × 1; floret, × 10.

1. Eleusine indica (L.) Gaertn. YARDGRASS. Fig. 149.

Plants tufted, the culms branching near the base, erect to somewhat decumbent, 35–50 cm tall; sheaths flattened, glabrous or nearly so; leaf blades about 5 mm wide; spikes 5–15 cm long, 3 or more from summit of central stalk; spikelets 4–6-flowered, strongly compressed, arranged on 1 side of the broad, smooth rachis; glumes unequal, the 1st about one-half as long as the 2nd; lemmas conspicuously 3-nerved, 3.5–4 mm long; grain dark, furrowed, becoming loose within the floret.

Widespread throughout the United States, occasionally a troublesome plant in lawns; adventive from the tropical regions.

Missouri. Open ground, lawns, and cultivated areas, generally distributed. Flowering in July–August.

A collection previously identified as *E. indica* from St. Louis County, Highway 61 at Meramec River bridge (Peterson s.n., 1938 MO) has been verified as *E. trichastya* (Lam.) Lam., an introduction from Argentina. It is an annual with densely imbricate spikelike heads 1–3 cm long and 10–15 mm in width, readily distinguishable from *E. indica*. No other collections of *E. trichastya* are known from Missouri.

53. SPOROBOLUS R. Br. DROPSEED

Annuals and perennials; panicles narrow, spikelike, inserted in the sheath, or exserted with spreading to ascending branches; spikelets 1-flowered, separating above the persistent glumes; glumes usually unequal; lemma awnless; palea nearly equal to the lemma or sometimes exceeding it; grain somewhat spheroid or oblong, usually falling free from the floret. $x = 9, 10$; Kranz.

Key to Missouri Species

a. Panicles, mostly exserted, with spreading branches, sometimes partially enclosed in the sheath as in no. 3; perennials
  b. Spikelets 3 mm long or more; glumes sharp-acuminate, with an awnlike apex ....
    ....1. *S. heterolepis*
  b. Spikelets shorter, mostly 1.5–2.5 mm long; glumes acute, but not awn-tipped
    c. Spikelets few, toward the ends of somewhat stiffly spreading branches.....2. *S. airoides*
    c. Spikelets mostly aggregated, the panicle branches spreading or drooping, sometimes partially included in the sheath
      d. Spikelets about 2 mm long or more, the 1st glume about ½ as long as the 2nd.......
      ....3. *S. cryptandrus*
      d. Spikelets about 1.5 mm long, the 1st glume small, inconspicuous, and much shorter than 2nd glume ....4. *S. pyramidatus*
a. Panicles narrow, strict, not spreading even when exserted, frequently enclosed or partly so in the inflated sheath; annuals or perennials
    e. Glumes subequal; annual species
      f. Spikelets plump, the lemma and palea ovate to acute, glabrous....5. *S. neglectus*
      f. Spikelets narrow, the lemma and palea linear-elongate, pubescent ....
      ....6. *S. vaginiflorus*
    e. Glumes dissimilar; perennial species
      g. Panicles usually long-exserted; spikelets 2 mm long at most .....7. *S. indicus*
      g. Panicles usually partly inserted; spikelets 3–4 mm long or more
        h. Lemma obtuse, noticeably plump toward base, about equal to palea ......
        ....8. *S. asper*
        h. Lemma sharp-tapering, slender, the palea usually exceeding it ....
        ....9. *S. clandestinus*

Fig. 149. **Eleusine indica.** Plant, × ½; spikelet and floret, × 5.

1. Sporobolus heterolepis (A. Gray) A. Gray PRAIRIE DROPSEED. Fig. 150.

Perennial, densely tufted, with conspicuous basal foliage of arching leaves; flower stalks erect, to 1 m tall; leaf blades stringlike, involute toward tip; panicles erect, longer than broad, with spreading branches; spikelets 4–6 mm long; glumes unequal, acuminate, the 1st shorter than the floret, the 2nd exceeding it; lemma obtuse, somewhat shorter than palea; grain spherical.

Midcontinent, from Canada to Texas to Colorado, infrequent through Ohio and Pennsylvania, absent southward.

Missouri. Prairies, barrens, and limestone bluffs, generally distributed. Flowering in July–August.

2. Sporobolus airoides (Torr.) Torr. ALKALI SACATON. Fig. 151.

Perennial, forming dense tufts; culms erect to 1 m tall; sheaths sparsely pilose toward the summit; leaf blades narrow, involute; panicles diffuse, with broadly spreading branches; spikelets about 2 mm long; glumes unequal, the 1st shorter, the 2nd about equal to the floret; lemma and palea similar in size and texture.

Throughout the western United States, east to Missouri.

Missouri. Loessal-hill prairies, Atchison County; also Jackson County, as an adventive. Flowering in midsummer.

3. Sporobolus cryptandrus (Torr.) A. Gray SAND DROPSEED. Fig. 152.

Perennial, sparsely tufted; culms erect, to 1 m tall; sheaths densely pilose toward the summit, somewhat overlapping on the lower part of the culm; ligule consisting of hairs, about 0.5 mm long; leaf blades mostly involute, becoming stringlike toward the tip; panicles usually narrow, with short, floriferous branches, sometimes partially included in the sheath; spikelets 2–3 mm long; glumes thin, unequal, the 1st about one-half as long as the 2nd, the latter about equal to floret; lemma and palea thin, nearly equal.

Widespread in the United States, less common or absent toward the southeast.

Missouri. Loessal bluffs, dry prairies, and sandy embankments, widely scattered, but more prevalent in counties along the Missouri and Mississippi Rivers; also Jasper, Texas, and Moniteau Counties. Flowering in July–August.

4. Sporobolus pyramidatus (Lam.) Hitchc. WHORLED DROPSEED. Fig. 153.

Perennial, forming tufts; culms spreading or decumbent, to about 50 cm tall; panicles spreading, the branches whorled; spikelets small, 1.5 mm long; glumes strongly unequal, the 1st much shorter, the 2nd about equaling the floret. *S. argutus* (Nees) Kunth.

Southern and western United States, to Mexico, Central America, and southward.

Missouri. Rare and little known; collected from Jackson County (Bush 510 MO), probably not extant.

5. Sporobolus neglectus Nash BALDGRASS. Fig. 154.

Annual, forming loose tufts; culms decumbent and branching from base, to 50 cm tall; sheaths inflated; leaf blades mostly glabrous to somewhat hairy, involute; panicles congested, 2.5–4 cm long, inserted in sheaths; spikelets 2.5–4.5 mm long, glumes about equal, shorter than the floret; lemma plump, glabrous; palea similar, split at maturity, exposing the ovoid grain.

Plants generally glabrous or nearly so, with spikelets 2.5–4.0 mm long, represent

FIG. 150. **Sporobolus heterolepis.** Plant, × 1; spikelet, and floret with caryopsis and split palea, × 10.

FIG. 151. **Sporobolus airoides.** Plant, × ½; glumes and floret, × 10.

FIG. 152. **Sporobolus cryptandrus.** Plant, × ½; glumes and floret, × 10.

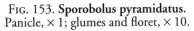

Fig. 153. **Sporobolus pyramidatus.** Panicle, × 1; glumes and floret, × 10.

Fig. 154. **Sporobolus neglectus.** Plant, × 1; spikelet and floret, × 10.

typical *neglectus;* those with pubescent sheaths and spikelets to 5 mm long are separated as var. *ozarkanus* (Fern.) Steyerm. & Kucera (*S. ozarkanus* Fern.). Specific rank for *ozarkanus* is maintained by some authors as originally described by Fernald, who separated it from *S. neglectus* on the basis of increased foliage pubescence and slightly larger spikelets (Steyermark & Kucera, 1961).

Widespread in the eastern and central United States, scattered westward.

Missouri. Limestone glades, dry woods, sandbars, and waste ground, generally distributed, known locally as "bald grass." Pubescent forms are most prevalent in the Ozarks region. Flowering in July–August.

6. Sporobolus vaginiflorus (Torr. ex A. Gray) A. Wood Fig. 155.

Annual, forming loose tufts; culms spreading to decumbent near the base, branching, similar in general habit to no. 5; panicles narrow, usually included in the inflated sheaths, differing mainly in the longer, more attenuate spikelets, 3–5 mm long, and distinctly pubescent lemma; palea about equal to the lemma, or sometimes exceeding it, as in var. *inaequalis* Fern.

Eastern and central United States, west to Nebraska, Kansas, Oklahoma, and Arizona.

Missouri. Prairie glades, dry woods, and open ground, generally distributed as typical *vaginiflorus;* var. *inaequalis* scattered and less frequent. Flowering in July–August.

7. Sporobolus indicus (L.) R. Br. Smutgrass. Fig. 156.

Perennial, forming sparse tufts, culms erect, to 1 m tall; leaf blades 2–4 mm wide, long-tapering; panicles mostly dense, slender, much elongated, with short, ascending branches; spikelets crowded, about 2 mm long; glumes shorter than the

Fig. 155. **Sporobolus vaginiflorus.** Plant, × 1; glumes and floret, × 10.

Fig. 156. **Sporobolus indicus.** Plant, × ½; spikelet and floret, × 10.

floret; lemma and palea acute, nearly equal; grain oblong-elliptic, reportedly infested by a fungus. *S. poiretii* (Roemer & J.A. Schultes) Hitchc.

Southeastern United States and mid-Atlantic region, west to Oklahoma, Texas, and Latin America; introduced from tropical Asia.

Missouri. Rare and little known; collected in cotton fields, Dunklin County (Bush 1907 MO), also in lawns, Poplar Bluff, Butler County (Hudson 594 MO).

8. Sporobolus asper (Michx.) Kunth Fig. 157.

Perennial, mostly tufted, rarely with short, knotty rhizomes; culms erect, to 1 m tall or more; upper sheaths glabrous to somewhat pubescent, inflated; leaf blades glabrous, elongate, 2–3 mm wide, becoming involute toward the tip; panicles light-colored to purplish, spikelike, exserted to partially enclosed in subtending sheath; spikelets oblong, plump, 3.5–7 mm long; glumes unequal, obtuse, both shorter than the floret; lemma glabrous, 4–6 mm long, keeled toward the apex; palea nearly equal to the lemma and similarly keeled, splitting near the base as grain matures. *S. asper* var. *hookeri* (Trin.) Vasey; *S. asper* var. *pilosus* (Vasey) Hitchc.; *S. drummondii* (Trin.) Vasey; *S. macer* (Trin.) Hitchc.; *S. compositus* (Poir.) Merr. var. *compositus; S. compositus* var. *drummondii* (Trin.) Kartesz & Gandhi; *S. compositus* var. *macer* (Trin.) Kartesz & Gandhi.

Plants with more attenuate panicles, with spikelets in the smaller size range, 3–5 mm long, are separated from typical *asper* as var. *drummondii* (Trin.) Vasey; plants bearing rhizomes are referred to var. *macer* (Trin.) Shinners.

Widespread in the United States, but absent in the Southeast and Far West.

Missouri. Prairies, glades, dry woods, and waste ground, typical *asper* and var. *drummondii* widely distributed but absent from lower Ozarks and the southeastern lowlands; var. *macer* recorded for Newton County (McGregor 38589 UK). An earlier collection by Palmer (Jasper County) labeled *S. asper* was reevaluated as var. *macer* by George Yatskievych. Flowering in late summer.

9. Sporobolus clandestinus (Bieler) Hitchc. Fig. 158.

Perennial, mostly tufted; culms erect, to 1 m tall; sheaths glabrous or sparsely pilose; leaf blades elongate, involute, with a stringlike tip; panicles narrow, inserted or partly so; spikelets 5–7 mm long; glumes subequal, acute, shorter than the floret; both lemma and palea pubescent, elongate, nearly equal, or the latter conspicuously longer, this species differing from no. 8 by less robust habit, elongate-pointed spikelets, and pubescent lemmas. Incl. *S. canovirens* Nash.

Eastern and central United States, west to Kansas and Texas.

Missouri. Prairies and dry woods, on cherty or sandy soils, predominantly in the southern and eastern counties and throughout the Ozarks, infrequent north of the Missouri River, where reported for Boone, Montgomery, Lincoln, and Clark Counties. Flowering in late summer.

54. CRYPSIS Aiton

Annuals; panicles dense, cylindrical, spikelike; spikelets 1-flowered, separating above the persistent glumes; glumes flattened, about equal, shorter than the floret; lemma awnless; palea present, similar to lemma. $x = 8, 9$; Kranz.

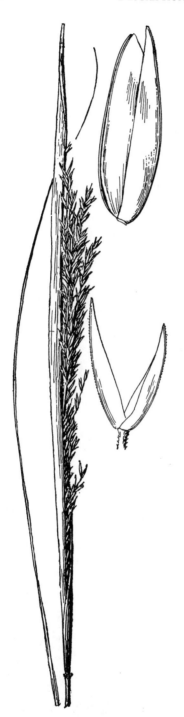

Fig. 157. **Sporobolus asper.** Plant, × 1; glumes and floret, × 10.

Fig. 158. **Sporobolus clandestinus.** Plant, × 1; glumes and floret, × 10.

1. Crypsis schoenoides (L.) Lam. Fig. 159.

Plants tufted; culms leafy, decumbent near base, 15–40 cm tall; sheaths enlarged, partially including the spikelike panicles; spikelets about 2.5–3 mm long; glumes scabrous on keel; lemma 1-nerved, awnless; palea only slightly shorter than lemma; grain dark, obconical, about 1.5 mm long. *Heleochloa schoenoides* (L.) Host.

Sporadically distributed in the United States; adventive from Europe.

Missouri. Rare and little known; waste ground, St. Louis (Muehlenbach 668 MO) and Franklin Counties. Flowering in July–August.

FIG. 159. **Crypsis schoenoides.** Plant, × ½; spikelet and floret, × 5.

55. CALAMOVILFA (A. Gray) Hack. ex Scribn. & Southworth

Perennials; panicles with close ascending branches to somewhat spreading; spikelets 1-flowered, separating above the unequal, persistent glumes; lemmas with tuft of straight hairs at the base, awnless; palea about equal to lemma; rachilla not extended behind the floret. $x = 10$; Kranz.

1. Calamovilfa longifolia (Hook). Scribn. Sand Reedgrass. Fig. 160.

Plants forming clumps or mats, spreading by rhizomes; culms leafy, erect to 1.5 m tall; sheaths glabrous except for pilose hairs at summit, overlapping on the lower culm; ligule consisting of hairs 1–2 mm long; leaf blades elongate, 3.5–7 mm wide, involute toward tip; panicles somewhat stiff, with ascending branches; spikelets about 5–7.5 mm long; glumes somewhat dissimilar, the 1st ovate, 4–6 mm long, the 2nd longer, acuminate, about level with top of the floret; lemma acute, awnless, with dense tufts of hairs; palea nearly equaling lemma.

North-central United States and adjacent parts of Canada, south to Colorado and Missouri.

Missouri. Infrequent, sandy open ground; Clay, Jackson, Jefferson, and St. Louis Counties. Flowering in midsummer.

56. MUHLENBERGIA Schreb.

Annuals or perennials; panicles condensed or spikelike to broad, diffuse with spreading branches; spikelets small, 1-flowered, separating above the persistent glumes; glumes keeled, variable, from minute or lacking to overtopping the floret, awned or awnless; lemma 3-nerved, awned from the apex or awnless; palea well developed, about equal to lemma. $x = 10$; Kranz.

Key to Missouri Species

a. Panicles broad, diffuse, with spreading branches, mostly sparsely flowered
   b. Rhizomes present; lemmas awnless ....1. *M. asperifolia*
   b. Rhizomes lacking; lemmas long-awned ....2. *M. capillaris*
a. Panicles narrow with closely ascending branches, sometimes compact, or dense
     c. Glumes minute, at most about 1.5 mm long, or obsolete, much shorter than lemma
       d. Rhizomes absent; glumes lacking central vein, the 1st sometimes obsolete.............
       ....3. *M. schreberi*
       d. Rhizomes present; glumes subequal, with central vein.................4. *M.* × *curtisetosa*
     c. Glumes conspicuous, at least ½ as long as lemma, sometimes equaling or exceeding lemma
       e. Plants with bulblike bases, lacking rhizomes, occurring in open, xeric habitats...
       ....5. *M. cuspidata*
       e. Plants with scaly rhizomes, occurring in woodland habitats or low ground
          f. Glumes about equal, both much exceeding floret; panicles dense, thickly lobed ....6. *M. racemosa*
          f. Glumes not as above, neither exceeding floret; panicles narrow, not thickly lobed
            g. Glumes with abrupt taper above the middle, the apex an awnlike projection of the midnerve
              h. Lemmas mostly awnless, sometimes with short awn 1–2 mm long.........
              ....7. *M. sobolifera*
              h. Lemmas with conspicuous, slender awn 5–10 mm long.......................
              ....8. *M. tenuiflora*

Fig. 160. **Calamovilfa longifolia.** Plant, × ½; spikelet and floret, × 5.

g. Glumes with gradual taper from base to apex
    i. Florets completely glabrous ....9. *M. glabrifloris*
    i. Florets with pilose hairs at base
        j. Culms solitary to sparsely tufted, erect, with few branches..........10. *M. sylvatica*
        j. Culms tufted, branching from upper nodes, sometimes bushy, reclining or decumbent
            k. Internodes puberulent, in upper part (below the node)........11. *M. mexicana*
            k. Internodes smooth, shiny
                l. Spikelets 2–3 mm long, the glumes nearly equal ....12. *M. frondosa*
                l. Spikelets 3–4 mm long, the glumes strongly unequal ....13. *M. bushii*

1. Muhlenbergia asperifolia (Nees & Meyen ex Trin.) Parodi SCRATCHGRASS. Fig. 161.

Plants with slender rhizomes; culms branching from the base, erect to somewhat decumbent, to 50 cm tall; sheaths crowded, flattened; leaf blades harsh, narrow, 1–2 mm wide; panicles open, with slender, spreading branches, at maturity separating as a tumbleweed; spikelets about 2 mm long, sometimes 2-flowered; glumes similar, narrow, shorter than to about equal to the floret; lemma 1–1.5 mm long, awnless.

Widespread in the western United States and adjacent parts of Canada, east to Minnesota, Wisconsin, and Indiana, to Texas, Mexico, and South America.

Missouri. Moist ground, sporadic and infrequent; Holt, Jackson, and St. Louis Counties. Flowering in late summer.

2. Muhlenbergia capillaris (Lam.) Trin. HAIRGRASS. Fig. 162.

Plants tufted, lacking rhizomes; culms stiff, erect, to 1 m tall; leaf blades 1.5–4 mm wide, becoming involute; ligule membranous, pointed, 3–5 mm long; panicles showy, broad, purplish, with fine, spreading branches, to one-half the height of plant; spikelets delicate, narrow-lanceolate, about 4 mm long; glumes subequal, both acute, the 2nd short-awned; lemma 3–4 mm long, with delicate awn several times as long.

Eastern and southern United States, west to Kansas and Texas.

Missouri. Cherty slopes, bluffs, and sandy prairies, widely scattered south of the

FIG. 161. **Muhlenbergia asperifolia**. Plant, × 1; glumes and floret, × 10.

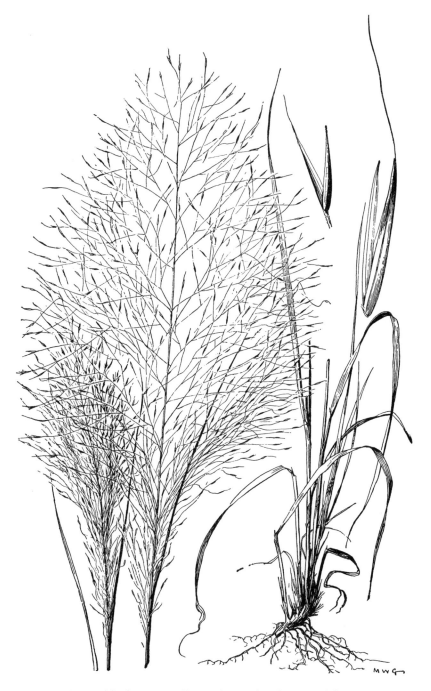

Fig. 162. **Muhlenbergia capillaris.** Plant, × ½; glumes and floret, × 10.

Missouri River, mainly western Ozarks and southwestern counties. Flowering in July–August.

3. Muhlenbergia schreberi J.F. Gmel. NIMBLE WILL. Fig. 163.

Plants, becoming matlike, lacking rhizomes; culms slender, delicate, much branched, decumbent, rooting at the lower nodes, at most about 50 cm tall; sheaths

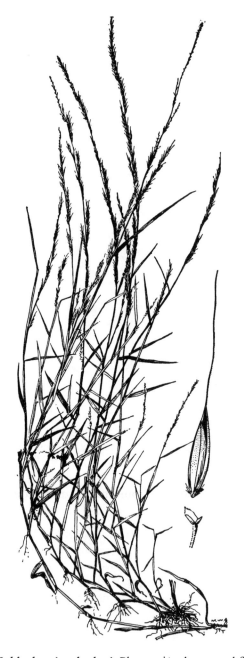

FIG. 163. **Muhlenbergia schreberi.** Plant, × ½; glumes and floret, × 10.

compressed; leaf blades short, spreading, flaglike, 3–4 mm wide; panicles slender, flexuous; glumes whitish, lacking midvein, truncate, minute, to 1.5 mm long, the 1st sometimes absent; lemma 2–3 mm long, with a delicate awn about 3 mm in length.

Eastern and central United States, to Nebraska, Texas, and eastern Mexico.

Missouri. Alluvial woods, gravel bars, and shaded lawns, on damp ground, generally distributed; one of our most common species. Flowering in midsummer to fall.

4. Muhlenbergia × curtisetosa (Scrib.) Bush Fig. 164.

Plants rhizomatous, with somewhat coarser habit than no. 3; culms not rooting at lower nodes; spikelets somewhat larger, the glumes both present with midvein. *M. curtisetosa* (Scribn.) Bush; *M. schreberi* Gmel. var. *curtisetosa* (Scribn.) Steyerm. & Kucera.

This rare and little-known taxon is a hybrid of no. 3 and one of several rhizome-bearing species (Pohl, 1969). It is reported for several widely scattered localities, including Pennsylvania, Indiana, Iowa, Missouri, and Arkansas; all specimens are pollen-sterile.

Missouri. Known only from Barry, St. Clair, Hickory, and Holt Counties. Flowering in late summer.

5. Muhlenbergia cuspidata (Torr. ex Hook.) Rydb. Fig. 165.

Plants distinctly tufted, lacking rhizomes; culms with small, hard, bulblike base, stiffly erect, 25–50 cm tall; sheaths usually pilose; leaf blades narrow, 1–2 mm wide, with involute margins; panicles slender with short, ascending branches; spikelets 2.5–3 mm long; glumes awn-tipped, shorter than the floret; lemma awnless, narrowing to minute, cuspidate apex.

North-central United States, south to Kentucky, Oklahoma, and New Mexico.

Missouri. Loessal prairies, glades, and bluffs, widely scattered, north-central Ozarks and western sections including McDonald, Vernon, Henry, Buchanan, Holt, and Atchison Counties; also Carter (Summers 3778 MO) and Adair (Conrad 10494 NEMO) Counties. Flowering in July–August.

6. Muhlenbergia racemosa (Michx.) Britton, Stearns & Pogg. Fig. 166.

Plants rhizomatous; culms stiff, erect, branching, to 1 m tall; sheaths keeled; leaf blades 2–6 mm wide, long-tapering; panicles dense, spikelike, lobed; spikelets 4.5–7 mm long; glumes nearly equal, linear, with long-tapering apex, much exceeding the lemma; lemma tufted at base, awnless; palea similar.

Widespread, northern United States and adjacent parts of Canada, south to Maryland, Oklahoma, and New Mexico.

Missouri. Sloughs and alluvial bottoms, mostly damp soils, generally distributed. Flowering in late summer.

7. Muhlenbergia sobolifera (Muhl. ex Willd.) Trin. Fig. 167.

Plants forming sparse tufts, rhizomatous; culms slender, erect, sparsely branched, 30–90 cm tall; leaf blades few, spreading, glabrous, 3–7 mm wide; panicles narrow, with short, appressed branches exserted on slender peduncles; spikelets pale green, about 2 mm long from short pedicels; glumes somewhat unequal, pale whitish, with green midrib, shorter than the lemma; lemma about 2 mm long, typically awnless, as f. *sobolifera;* or with minute awn 1–2 mm long, as f. *setigera* (Scribn.) Deam.

Northeastern United States and mid-Atlantic region, west to Nebraska and Texas.

FIG. 164. **Muhlenbergia** ×
curtisetosa. Glumes and
floret, × 10.

FIG. 165. **Muhlenbergia
cuspidata.** Plant, × 1;
glumes and floret, × 10.

FIG. 166. **Muhlenbergia
racemosa.** Panicle, × 1;
glumes and floret, × 10.

FIG. 167. **Muhlenbergia sobolifera**. Plant, × 1; glumes and floret, × 10.

Missouri. Dry woods and rocky slopes, generally distributed, as the typical form, one of our most common woodland muhlenbergias; the short-awned form reported for Christian County (Palmer 58256 MO). Flowering in late summer.

8. Muhlenbergia tenuiflora (Willd.) Britton, Sterns & Pogg. var. **tenuiflora** Fig. 168.

Plants rhizomatous, taller and coarser than no. 7; leaf blades few, spreading, 5–9 mm wide; panicles narrow, with slender, appressed branches, on extended peduncles; spikelets 3–4 mm long; glumes equal, sharp-pointed, shorter than the lemma; lemma averaging about 3 mm long, with a slender awn, 5–10 mm long.

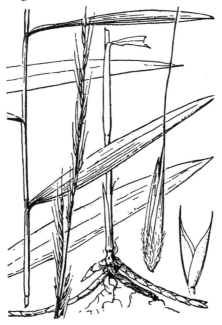

FIG. 168. **Muhlenbergia tenuiflora**. Plant, × 1; glumes and floret, × 10.

Eastern United States, west to Iowa, Oklahoma, and Texas.

Missouri. Dry woods, calcareous slopes, and infrequently on lower ground; widely scattered, generally south of the Missouri River. Flowering in late summer.

9. Muhlenbergia glabrifloris Scribn. Fig. 169.

Plants rhizomatous; culms much branched with bushy appearance, 50–100 cm tall; leaf blades glabrous about 2–4 mm wide; panicles dense, both terminal and from lower sheaths; spikelets 2–3 mm long; lemma glabrous, awnless.

This species resembles no. 12 in general habit. Further study of live plants may suggest joining it with that species (Pohl, 1969).

Widely scattered, mid-Atlantic and Gulf regions to Iowa, Arkansas, and Texas.

Missouri. Low ground, damp soils, scattered and infrequent; Cass, Barton, Jasper, Newton, Laclede, Phelps, Monroe, St. Louis, and Pemiscot Counties.

10. Muhlenbergia sylvatica (Torr.) ex A. Gray. Fig. 170.

Plants solitary to somewhat tufted, short-rhizomatous; culms sparsely branched, erect, to 1 m tall; leaf blades thin, 2–7 mm wide; ligule conspicuous, lacerate, about 2 mm long; panicles delicate, narrow, with closely ascending branches, from extended peduncles, the axillary ones not exserted; spikelets about 3 mm long; glumes nearly equal, with scarious margins, tapering from near the base to an acute or awnlike apex; lemma 2.5–3 mm long, pilose near the base, with a straight awn, 5–10 mm long, as f. *sylvatica,* or occasionally awnless, as f. *attenuata* Palmer & Steyerm.

Fig. 169. **Muhlenbergia glabrifloris.** Glumes and floret, × 10.

Fig. 170. **Muhlenbergia sylvatica.** Plant, × 1; glumes and floret, × 10.

Eastern and central United States, west to South Dakota and Texas.

Missouri. Moist ravines, calcareous slopes, and creek bottoms, widely distributed as the awned form but apparently absent from southeastern lowlands; f. *attenuata* scattered and infrequent. Flowering in July–August.

11. Muhlenbergia mexicana (L.) Trin. Fig. 171.

Plants rhizomatous, similar to no. 12 but less branched and sprawling, the internodes also somewhat puberulent in the upper part (below the node); panicles thick, compact with short appressed branches, the axillary or lateral ones, if present, on extended peduncles, not inserted; spikelets 2–4 mm long; glumes nearly equal, linear-attenuate, about equal to the floret; lemma pilose at base, awnless, as f. *mexicana,* or sometimes with awns 5–10 mm long, as f. *ambigua* (Torr.) Fern.

Widespread throughout the United States and adjacent parts of Canada, absent from the Southeast to Texas.

Missouri. Moist woods and prairies, low ground, generally distributed as typical *mexicana,* the awned form sporadic and less common. Flowering in late summer and early fall.

12. Muhlenbergia frondosa (Poir.) Fern. Fig. 172.

Plants rhizomatous; culms profusely branched, mostly from the upper nodes, top-heavy, eventually reclining or sprawling, to 1 m long, internodes usually glabrous in the upper part (below the node); leaf blades numerous, usually short, 2.5–6 mm wide; panicles numerous, narrow, condensed, with short, ascending branches, some terminal, others axillary and included in the leaf sheaths; spikelets mostly 2–3 mm long, occasionally to 4 mm; glumes nearly equal, awn-tipped; lemma pilose near the base, awnless, as f. *frondosa,* or with an awn to 10 mm long, as f. *commutata* (Scribn.) Fern.

Eastern and central United States to North Dakota and Texas, absent in the Southeast.

Missouri. Low woods and alluvium, mostly moist areas, generally distributed and common, the awnless forms occurring more frequently than awned plants. Flowering in late summer.

13. Muhlenbergia bushii Pohl. Fig. 173.

Plants rhizomatous; culms erect, 50–90 cm tall, with numerous branches; sheaths glabrous, overlapping, keeled, with prominent midrib; leaf blades glabrous, numerous, 2–5 mm wide; ligule mostly less than 0.5 mm long; panicles narrow,

FIG. 171. **Muhlenbergia mexicana.** Plant, × 1; glumes and floret, × 10.

FIG. 172. **Muhlenbergia frondosa.** Plant, × 1; glumes and floret, × 10.

FIG. 173. **Muhlenbergia bushii.** Plant, × 1; glumes and floret, × 10.

sparsely flowered, with short, ascending branches, both terminal and axillary; spikelets 3–4 mm long; glumes unequal, mostly shorter than the lemma, with awnlike tip; lemma 2.5–3 mm long, with pilose hairs at base, awned or awnless. *M. brachyphylla* Bush.

Central United States from Iowa and Indiana to Texas.

Missouri. Open woodlands, prairie transitions and rocky slopes, also low ground and wet areas, widely scattered. Flowering in late summer.

Earlier manuals indicate a wider distribution for *M. brachyphylla* than presently recognized by Pohl (1969) for the new combination, *M. bushii,* the latter with a mid-continental emphasis, to the exclusion of more eastern locales. This restriction, together with a habitat description that includes less mesic sites than usually ascribed to our specimens of *brachyphylla,* suggests a need to reexamine the ecogeographic relationships of this taxon and its close allies.

TRIBE 16. CYNODONTEAE

57. CHLORIS Sw.

Annuals and perennials; inflorescence consisting of slender, spreading spikes at or near summit of flowering stalk; spikelets sessile, in 2 rows on one side of the rachis, 2- to several-flowered, separating above the persistent glumes; only lower (or lowermost) floret fertile, the upper one(s) reduced, sterile; glumes mostly unequal, acuminate, shorter than the florets; fertile lemma awned from below apex, the sterile lemmas progressively reduced in size, awnless or short-awned. $x = 10$; Kranz.

1. Chloris verticillata Nutt. WINDMILL GRASS. Fig. 174.

Perennial, forming leafy clumps; culms occasionally rooting from lower nodes, erect to somewhat decumbent, 15–30 cm tall; sheaths noticeably flattened; leaf blades about 3 mm wide; inflorescence terminal, the spikelike racemes horizontally spreading, 5–15 cm long, the whole readily breaking away at maturity as a tumbleweed; spikelets about 3 mm long, excluding awn; glumes elongate, with tapering apex, the 1st about 2 mm long, the 2nd somewhat longer; fertile lemma conspicuously pubescent on nerves, about 2.5 mm long, the delicate awn straight, several times longer; sterile lemma broadened upward, truncate, also awned.

Southwestern United States from California to Louisiana, north to Colorado and trans-Mississippi, sporadic eastward where introduced.

Missouri. Lawns, fields, and waste ground, on dry soils, generally common, mostly in the central and western sections, also St. Louis and St. Francois Counties. Flowering in summer.

2. Chloris virgata Sw. FEATHER FINGERGRASS. Fig 175.

Annual, usually more robust than no. 1; upper sheaths enlarged; leaf blades 5–6 mm wide; spikes terminal, erect-ascending, with distinctive silky appearance; spikelets crowded, about 3–3.5 mm long; 1st glume 1.5 mm long, about one-half as long as the 2nd; fertile lemma ciliate near base and toward apex, about 3 mm long, the awn as much as 10 mm long; sterile lemma reduced, obovate, similarly awned.

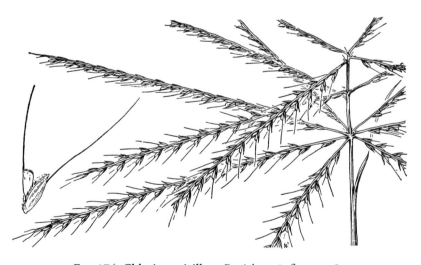

FIG. 174. **Chloris verticillata.** Panicle, × 1; floret, × 5.

Fig. 175. **Chloris virgata.** Plant, × ½; glumes and florets, × 5.

Widespread across the United States; adventive from tropical America.

Missouri. Open ground and waste areas, scattered and infrequent; Cass, Clay, Jackson, St. Louis, and Oregon Counties. Flowering in summer.

58. SCHEDONNARDUS Steud.

Perennials; inflorescence consisting of a few narrow spreading spikes along the main axis; spikelets 1-flowered, sessile, arranged on two sides of a triangular rachis, separating above the persistent glumes; glumes somewhat unequal, narrow-lanceolate; lemma 3-nerved, also narrow, pointed; palea shorter than lemma. $x = 10$; Kranz.

1. Schedonnardus paniculatus (Nutt.) Trel. TUMBLEGRASS. Fig. 176.
Plants tufted, leafy toward base; culms erect, flowering stalks to 50 cm tall; leaf blades narrow, 1–2 mm wide, 5 cm long; ligule conspicuous, 2–3 mm long; inflorescence relatively large, about one-half as long as entire plant, eventually breaking away as a tumbleweed; individual spikes of the inflorescence variable in length, to 10 cm long; spikelets 4–5 mm long, appressed along 2 sides of the 3-cornered rachis; glumes rigid, pointed, the 1st about 3 mm long, the 2nd longer, and slightly exceeding floret; lemma firm, scabrous above, enveloping palea.

Wide-ranging through the midcontinent, from Canada to Louisiana and Arizona, to South America.

Missouri. Open ground and prairies, scattered and infrequent, on dry soils, mostly in the central and western counties. Flowering in summer.

59. GYMNOPOGON P. Beauv.

Perennials; inflorescence broad, relatively large, consisting of divergent, narrow-elongate spikes along the main axis; spikelets few, mostly 1-flowered, separating above the persistent glumes; glumes narrow, tapering, both exceeding the floret; lemma narrow, with straight awn; rachilla extended behind palea as a short stipe with rudimentary floret. $x = 10$; Kranz.

1. Gymnopogon ambiguus (Michx.) Britton, Stearns & Pogg. Fig. 177.
Plants sparsely tufted, rhizomatous; culms leafy near base, erect, about 50 cm tall; leaf blades glabrous, somewhat stiff, with rounded or cordate bases, 5–10 mm wide, less than 10 cm long; panicles large, as much as one-half the length of entire plant, consisting of slender, spreading spikes 10–15 cm long; spikelets appressed along rachis, few near base, becoming more numerous toward tip; glumes linear-lanceolate, 4–6 mm long; lemma shorter than glumes, about 4 mm long, pilose, the awn straight, 5–10 mm long; rachilla terminating in short awn or sterile bract.

Southeastern United States and Coastal Plain, north to Ohio and Pennsylvania, west to Kansas and Texas.

Missouri. Dry wooded slopes and sandy open ground, scattered, south of line from Barton to St. Charles Counties. Flowering in July–August.

60. CYNODON L.C. Rich.

Perennials; inflorescence consisting of several narrow spikes arranged digitately at summit of flowering stalk; spikelets 1-flowered, sessile, on one side of rachis, separating above the persistent glumes; glumes about equal; lemma flattened, awnless; palea

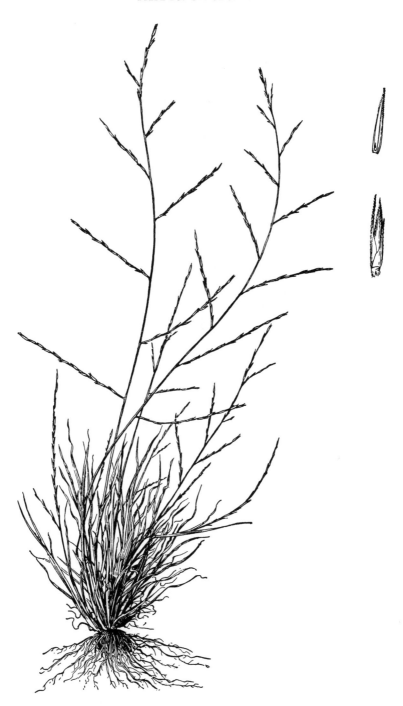

FIG. 176. **Schedonnardus paniculatus.** Plant, × ½; spikelet and floret, × 5.

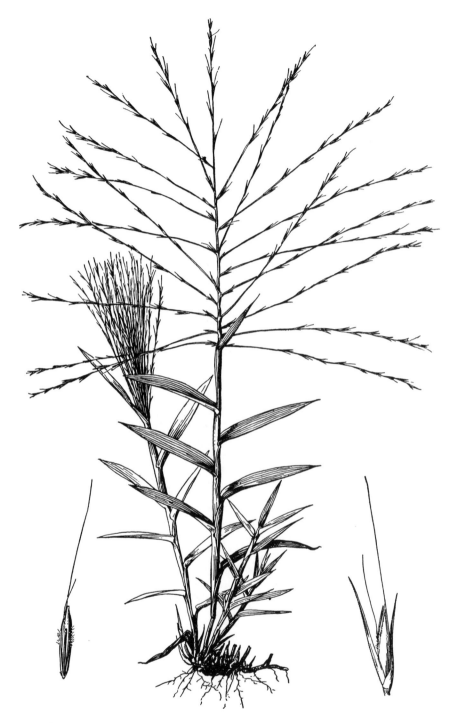

FIG. 177. **Gymnopogon ambiguus.** Plant, × ½; spikelet and floret, × 5.

about equal to lemma; rachilla extended behind palea as a noticeable stalklike projection. x = 9, 10; Kranz.

1. Cynodon dactylon (L.) Pers. BERMUDA GRASS. Fig. 178.

Plants forming thick mats, spreading by tough runners on the surface or sometimes just below it; culms leafy, 10–25 cm tall; leaf blades short, thin, 3–4 mm wide; ligule a fringe of white hairs; inflorescence consisting of 4–6 short, narrow spikes, about 5 cm long, digitate; spikelets about 2.5 mm long, flattened, overlapping along the rachis; 1st glume curved, the 2nd straight, both shorter than the floret; lemma pubescent on keel.

Widespread in the United States, absent north-central region; a warm-season

FIG. 178. **Cynodon dactylon.** Plant, × ½; spikelet and two views of floret, × 5.

species known from both hemispheres, introduced as a forage and turf grass in the South, frequently spreading.

Missouri. Lawns, gardens, and waste ground, most common south of the Missouri River, sporadic northward. Flowering in summer.

61. SPARTINA Schreb.

Perennials; inflorescence consisting of ascending or somewhat spreading 1-sided spikes arranged along the main axis; spikelets 1-flowered, sessile, crowded, conspicuously flattened, separating below the glumes and falling entire; glumes unequal, narrow-acuminate to awned; lemma firm, flattened, awnless; palea equal to lemma or slightly longer. $x = 7, 10$; Kranz.

1. Spartina pectinata Link SLOUGHGRASS. Fig 179.

Plants coarse, sometimes forming dense stands, spreading by tough, scaly rhizomes; flowering culms erect, 1–2 m tall; leaf blades sharp-edged, scabrous, about 1 cm wide or more, becoming involute when dried; ligule consisting mostly of hairs, 1–2 mm long; spikes to 10 cm long, from short stalks; spikelets about 10 mm long, closely appressed and imbricated in 2 rows on one side of the rachis; glumes scabrous on keel, attenuate to long-pointed, unequal, the 2nd much longer, with awnlike apex overtopping the floret; palea slightly longer than lemma.

Widespread in the United States, absent in the Southeast and Far West.

Missouri. Marshes, sloughs, and prairie swales, generally distributed. Flowering in late summer.

62. BOUTELOUA Lag. GRAMA

Perennials and a few annuals; inflorescence consisting of short, flaglike spikes along the main axis; spikelets 2- to several-flowered, sessile, crowded on one side of the rachis, separating above the persistent glumes; lower floret fertile, the upper ones sterile, reduced; glumes unequal, narrow-acuminate; fertile lemma 3-nerved, short-awned or mucronate-tipped; sterile lemmas with 3 minute awns. $x = 10$; Kranz.

Key to Missouri Species
a. Spikes 1–1.5 cm long, numerous, usually 15–20 or more on main flower stalk ....
....1. *B. curtipendula*
a. Spikes 3–5 cm long, not more than 3 on flower stalk
  b. Uppermost spikelets of each spike terminating the end of rachis ....2. *B. gracilis*
  b. Uppermost spikelets exceeded by the pointed tip of the rachis, the latter visible.............
....3. *B. hirsuta*

1. Bouteloua curtipendula (Michx.) Torr. SIDEOATS GRAMA. Fig. 180.

Perennial, forming dense tufts, rhizomatous; culms erect, to 80 cm tall; leaf blades 3–4 mm wide, becoming involute when dried; spikes numerous, 10–15 mm long, suspended from minute peduncles twisted to one side on the flowering stalk; spikelets 4–7 per spike, each 5–7.5 mm long; glumes dissimilar, the 1st subulate, 4 mm long, the 2nd lanceolate and longer; fertile lemma with 3 short awns or mucronate tips; sterile lemma with conspicuous central awn, the 2 lateral awns much shorter.

Widespread in the United States, absent in the Southeast, extending into Mexico and southward.

FIG. 179. **Spartina pectinata.** Plant, × ½; spikelet and floret, × 5.

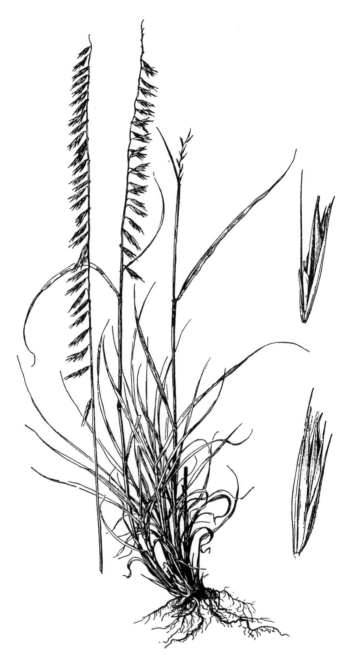

FIG. 180. **Bouteloua curtipendula**. Plant, × ½; spikelet and floret, × 5.

Missouri. Prairies, limestone glades, and dry bluffs, generally distributed. Flowering in early summer.

2. Bouteloua gracilis (Kunth) Lag. ex. Steud. BLUE GRAMA. Fig. 181.
Perennial, forming dense, leafy tufts; culms erect, to about 50 cm tall; leaf blades 1–2 mm wide, involute and curling; spikes 1–2 on each flowering stalk, 3–5 cm long;

FIG. 181. **Bouteloua gracilis.** Plant, × ½; glumes and floret, × 5.

spikelets about 5 mm long, imbricate; glumes narrow, the 1st 2–3 mm long, the 2nd 4–5 mm long; fertile lemma villous, 3-awned; sterile lemma on short stipe, conspicuously villous, with 3 slender awns.

Continental interior, from the Mississippi valley westward. Blue grama is a valuable range species of the high plains, occurring with buffalo grass over wide areas.

Missouri. Loessal-hill prairies, Atchison and Holt Counties, an adventive in Jackson and St. Louis Counties. Flowering in July–August.

3. Bouteloua hirsuta Lag. HAIRY GRAMA. Fig. 182.

Perennial, densely tufted, resembling no. 2 in general habit; sheaths hairy; leaf blades narrow, involute; spikes 1–3 on each flowering stalk, 3–4 cm long, the rachis extending about 5 mm beyond the terminal spikelet; spikelets 4–5 mm long, numerous and closely imbricated; glumes dissimilar, the 1st subulate, the 2nd lanceolate, somewhat longer, with black papillose hairs on middle nerve; fertile lemma awned, the sterile lemma 3-awned, on slender stipe.

Widespread from the Midwest through the Central Plains to California and Mexico, adventive elsewhere.

Missouri. Loessal-hill prairies, Atchison and Holt Counties, also sandy ground along Des Moines River, Clark County. Flowering in July–August.

63. BUCHLOE Engelm. BUFFALO GRASS

Perennial, the plants dioecious; staminate spikelets 2-flowered, closely imbricated, from short, 1-sided spikes above the basal foliage; pistillate spikelets 1-flowered, several aggregated in small, capitate clusters on short peduncles, exceeded by the leaves; staminate spikelets separating above the persistent glumes; pistillate spikelets falling together as an aggregate. $x = 10$; Kranz.

1. Buchloe dactyloides (Nutt.) Engelm. Fig 183.

Plants sod-forming, spreading by stolons; culms short, 15–25 cm tall; leaf blades narrow, curling, 1–2 mm wide, usually not exceeding 10 cm in length; staminate spikes about 1 cm long, the spikelets 4–5 mm in length with unequal glumes and 3-nerved, awnless lemmas; pistillate heads consisting of 4–5 spikelets; spikelets each 5–6 mm long, with thick, rounded, 3-lobed 2nd glume oriented away from floral axis and exceeding the floret; 1st or inner glume obscure, thin, or obsolete; lemma indurate, 3-lobed, awnless, enveloped by the 2nd glume.

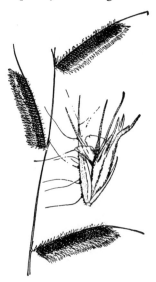

FIG. 182. **Bouteloua hirsuta.** Panicle, × 1; spikelet, × 5.

Fig. 183. **Buchloe dactyloides.** Pistillate and staminate plants, × ½; pistillate spike and floret, × 5; staminate spikelet, × 5.

Plains of the midcontinent, from lower Canada to Mexico; an important forage species occurring over the high plains as a natural associate of blue grama.

Missouri. Loessal-hill prairies bordering the Missouri River; Atchison and Holt Counties; also reported as an adventive, Boone, Cooper, and St. Louis Counties; used increasingly as a lawn grass in dry, sunny locations. Flowering in June–July.

TRIBE 17. PANICEAE

64. PANICUM L.

Annuals and perennials, the latter sometimes with basal rosettes; inflorescence usually an exserted panicle, the branches contracted to spreading; axillary panicles sometimes also developing regularly later as an autumnal phase from fascicled lower sheaths, these reduced and partially to mostly enclosed (in Subgenus *Dicanthelium*); spikelets 2-flowered, only the upper floret perfect; spikelets awnless, ovate-lanceolate to broadly elliptic, pedicellate to subsessile, at maturity disarticulating below the glumes and falling entire; 1st glume mostly triangular-ovate, shorter than 2nd glume, one-fourth to one-half as long; 2nd glume and sterile lemma (lower floret) equal or nearly so, both similarly thin-textured, conspicuously 7–9-nerved; fertile lemma smooth, indurate, with inrolled margins, the apex acute to obtuse or rounded. $x = 7$, 9, 10; non-Kranz and Kranz, generally characterizing Subgenus *Dichanthelium* and Subgenus *Panicum*, respectively.

Panicum is widely distributed and is most abundantly represented in the warm latitudes. It is the largest genus of the family, with an estimated 600 species, many of which are indigenous to the New World tropics. In Missouri, the panicums comprise the largest group, with 30 species, some with subspecific representation. Subgenus *Dicanthelium* is split from genus *Panicum* and elevated to generic status by some authors, including Gould and C.A. Clark (1978). The advocacy for this change is based on several criteria including differences in leaf anatomy as exemplified in the non-Kranz syndrome. For retention of *Panicum* as the status quo, development of basal rosettes ascribed to *Dicanthelium* is not universally manifest, particularly in the warm latitudes (Pohl 1980). In the present work, genus *Panicum* in the broad sense is maintained, following the treatment of Lelong (1984).

Key to Missouri Subgenera

a. Spikelets produced in vernal panicles, and later in summer and autumn from reduced branchlets of middle and lower culm; perennials, developing rosettes of basal leaves in our area, mostly wintergreen..A. Subgenus *Dicanthelium*
a. Spikelets produced in open, mostly terminal panicles as a seasonal flowering phase; annuals and perennials, not developing basal rosettes ....B. Subgenus *Panicum*

A. Key to Species, Subgenus *Dicanthelium*

a. Leaf blades narrow-elongate, 5 mm wide or less, at least 15–20 times as long, forming close-ascending tufts from compacted lower nodes
    b. Spikelets with obtuse apex, 2–3.5 mm long
        c. Spikelets 2–2.5 mm long..1. *P. linearifolium*
        c. Spikelets usually larger, to 3 mm long or more....................................2. *P. perlongum*
    b. Spikelets distinctly beaked or pointed, about 3.5 mm long...............3. *P. depauperatum*
a. Leaf blades varying in width but less than 15–20 times as long
        d. Some leaf blades of the main culm 2–3 cm wide, no more than 5 times longer than broad
            e. Sheaths conspicuously papillose-hispid; coarse leafy plants of low ground ....
            ....4. *P. clandestinum*
            e. Sheaths glabrous to soft-pubescent, not papillose-hispid; slender plants mostly of wooded uplands
                f. Nodes conspicuously bearded...5. *P. boscii*
                f. Nodes glabrous or nearly so ....6. *P. latifolium*

d. Most leaf blades narrower than 2 cm, 5 times longer than broad (sometimes wider in *P. sphaerocarpon* var. *isophyllum*)

    g. Ligule a conspicuous tuft of soft hairs, 2–5 mm long

        h. Spikelets large, to 4 mm long ....7. *P. ravenelii*

        h. Spikelets 1.5–2.5 mm long

          i. Leaf blades glabrous to variably pubescent on upper surface, mostly appressed-pubescent to puberulent below

            j. Sheaths and leaf blades mostly glabrous ....

                ....8a. *P. acuminatum* var. *lindheimeri*

            j. Sheaths and leaf blades variably pubescent

              k. Upper surface of leaf blades nearly glabrous, sparsely ciliate, to short-pubescent; sheaths variably pubescent ....

                ....8b. *P. acuminatum* var. *fasciculatum*

              k. Upper surface of leaf blades mostly pilose with hairs to 4–5 mm long; sheaths pilose.................................8c. *P. acuminatum* var. *implicatum*

          i. Leaf blades conspicuously pilose on *both* surfaces, the hairs sometimes to 5 mm long

            l. Spikelets less than 2 mm long.....................................9. *P. praecocius*

            l. Spikelets about 2.5 mm long ....10. *P. ovale*

    g. Ligule minute or obsolete

            m. Spikelets ovoid to roundish, about 1.5 mm long; leaf blades somewhat stiff, firm, cordate at base ....11. *P. sphaerocarpon*

            m. Spikelets elliptic-oblong, mostly more than 2 mm long; if less, leaf blades tapering to base, not cordate

              n. Leaf blades of primary culm mostly more than 1.5 cm wide

                o. Sheaths generally glabrous

                  p. Nodes conspicuously tufted ....5. *P. boscii*

                  p. Nodes glabrous...6. *P. latifolium*

                o. Sheaths hispid to soft-pubescent

                  q. Sheaths harsh, papillose-hispid ....4. *P. clandestinum*

                  q. Sheaths with conspicuous velvety pubescence.............

                  ....12. *P. scoparium*

              n. Leaf blades narrower

                r. Spikelets 3–4 mm long, mostly turgid

                  s. Foliage and culms soft-pubescent, the nodes tufted ....13. *P. malacophyllum*

                  s. Foliage and culms glabrous to hispid, not soft-pubescent

                    t. Leaf blades mostly glabrous above, puberulent below; spikelets smooth or nearly so ....

                    ....14. *P. oligosanthes*

                    t. Leaf blades papillose-hispid, spikelets pubescent ....15. *P. leibergii*

                r. Spikelets mostly less than 3 mm long, not especially turgid

                  u. Leaf blades stiff, cordate, sometimes with purplish tinge................16. *P. commutatum*

                  u. Leaf blades narrowing to base, not cordate, lacking purplish tinge

v. Spikelets 1.5–2 mm long; autumnal foliage sometimes bushy, reclining or spreading, with numerous short-acuminate leaves.............................
.........................17. *P. dichotomum*

v. Spikelets 2–3 mm long; autumnal foliage not distinctly sprawling

  w. Spikelets 2.5–3 mm long; leaf blades ascending, elongate, to 15 cm long, tapering toward base ...
.........................18. *P. bicknellii*

  w. Spikelets about 2 mm long; leaf blades not elongate nor tapering to base ....19. *P. laxiflorum*

B. Key to Species, Subgenus *Panicum*

a. Annuals

  b. Foliage typically glabrous; culms relatively coarse, erect to spreading-decumbent; native species ....20. *P. dichotomiflorum*

  b. Foliage variably pubescent; culms fine to coarse

    c. Panicles heavy, nodding; culms coarse; spikelets 4–5 mm long; introduced species .....
....21. *P. miliaceum*

    c. Panicles slender-elongate with delicate branches; spikelets 2–3.5 mm long; native species

      d. Panicles slender-elongate with delicate branches; spikelets narrow-acuminate, pointed, 3–3.5 mm long ....22. *P. flexile*

      d. Panicles ellipsoid to rhombic, or broad as long; spikelets elliptic-acuminate, 2–2.5 mm long

        e. Panicles ⅓–½ or more of total plant height, partially inserted in sheath before maturing; leaf blades to 1 cm wide or more ....23. *P. capillare*

        e. Panicles ⅓ or less of total height; leaf blades mostly less than 1 cm wide

          f. Leaf blades 3–6 mm wide; spikelets mostly in twos and threes, at end of branch ....24. *P. philadelphicum*

          f. Leaf blades coarser, sometimes to 1 cm wide; spikelets numerous, along the branch ....25. *P. gattingeri*

a. Perennials

    g. Panicles narrow, the short spikelike branches close-ascending....................
....26. *P. obtusum*

    g. Panicles more open, with spreading branches

      h. Plants rhizomatous; spikelets 3–4 mm long or more

        i. Spikelets falcate, sessile or nearly so, crowded along the branches ....
....27. *P. anceps*

        i. Spikelets ovate-lanceolate, on extended pedicels, not crowded............
....28. *P. virgatum*

      h. Plants lacking rhizomes; spikelets about 2–2.5 mm long

        j. Spikelets elliptic-oblong, clustered toward ends of branches; palea of sterile floret conspicuous, slightly exceeding sterile lemma and expanding the spikelet ....29. *P. hians*

        j. Spikelets ovate-lanceolate, usually arranged along one side of the branch; sterile palea absent ....30. *P. rigidulum*

A. Subgenus Dicanthelium

1. Panicum linearifolium Scribn. ex Nash Fig. 184.

Perennial, forming tufts with slender culms 15–40 cm tall; foliage variably pubescent to somewhat glabrous or with scattered hairs, the leaf blades narrow-elongate, close-ascending, 20–50 mm wide, 20 times as long or more; vernal panicles long-exserted, the autumnal panicles obscured or partially concealed in lower sheaths; spikelets ovate, 2–2.5 mm long, obtuse. Incl. var. *werneri* (Scribn.) Fern.; *Dicanthelium linearifolium* (Scribn. ex Nash) Gould.

Eastern and central United States to Kansas and Texas.

Missouri. Upland woods and glades, on dry soils, widely distributed but generally absent north and west of a line from Putnam to Barton Counties, absent also from

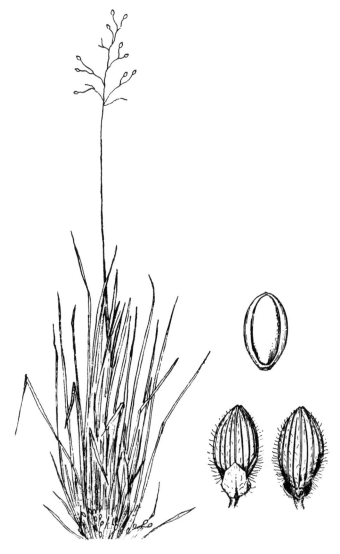

Fig. 184. **Panicum linearifolium.** Plant, × ½; two views of spikelet, and floret, × 10.

southeastern lowlands. Flowering in May–June and from axillary panicles in August–October.

2. Panicum perlongum Nash Fig. 185.

Perennial, narrow-tufted, with leafy culms to 40–50 cm tall; foliage variably papillose-pilose, the leaf blades elongate-ascending, 2–5 mm wide; vernal panicles long exserted, few-flowered, exceeding culm leaves; spikelets on relatively short pedicels, broadly ovoid, obtuse, about 3 mm long. *Dicanthelium linearifolium* (Scribn. ex Nash) Gould, in part.

Upper Midwest and adjacent Canada to Texas.

Missouri. Glades, prairies, and sparse woodlands, widely scattered, except southeastern lowlands. Flowering in May–June, and from axillary panicles in August––October.

Missouri specimens labeled *P. perlongum* are more frequent in prairie-type habitats, compared to no. 1, which is more common in woodland habitats.

3. Panicum depauperatum Muhl. Fig. 186.

Perennial, tufted, similar to no. 2 in general habit; foliage variably pilose to nearly glabrous; leaf blades narrow-ascending, 2–5 mm wide; vernal panicles exserted, sparsely flowered, the secondary or autumnal panicles much reduced, developing from basal sheaths; spikelets mostly smooth, ellipsoid, about 3.5 mm long, acute-pointed; apex of 2nd glume and sterile lemma exceeding the fertile floret. *Dicanthelium depauperatum* (Muhl.) Gould.

Eastern and central United States to Minnesota, Kansas, and Texas.

Missouri. Open woods and glades, on dry or stony ground, southern and east-

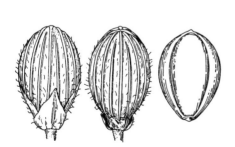

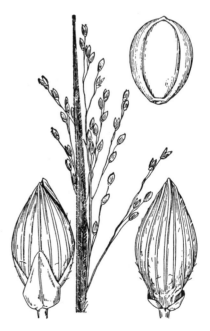

FIG. 185. **Panicum perlongum.** Two views of spikelet, and floret, × 10.

FIG. 186. **Panicum depauperatum.** Panicle, × 1; two views of spikelet, and floret, × 10.

central sections of the Ozarks region, absent from southeastern lowlands. Flowering in May–June and from axillary panicles in summer and fall.

4. Panicum clandestinum L. Fig. 187.

Perennial, forming clumps, sometimes rhizomatous, developing loose mats or colonies; culms coarse, erect or reclining, 1 m tall or more; upper sheaths mostly bristly-hispid or rough; leaf blades glabrous, stiff-ciliate on the margins, especially near the cordate base, to 1.5 cm wide or more; terminal panicles broad, with spreading branches, the axillary panicles narrow, partly enclosed in the inflated, overlapping sheaths; spikelets sparsely pilose, obtuse, averaging 3 mm long. *Dicanthelium clandestinum* (L.) Gould.

Eastern and central United States to Kansas, Oklahoma, and Texas.

Missouri. Low ground, creek banks, and sandy alluvium, generally widespread and probably in every county. Flowering in May–June and from axillary panicles in summer and fall.

5. Panicum boscii Poir. Fig. 188.

Perennial, sparsely tufted or solitary; culms slender, erect to somewhat bent at lower nodes, 30–70 cm tall, much branched and reclining in the autumnal phase; sheaths mostly glabrous to sparsely pubescent; nodes conspicuously bearded with retrorse hairs 2–3 mm long; leaf blades glabrous or nearly so, 2.5 cm wide or more, with scattered cilia near the cordate base; terminal panicles few-flowered, with spreading branches, the axillary panicles reduced or narrow, partially included; spikelets short-pubescent, elliptic-oblong, large, 3.5–4.5 mm long; 2nd glume slightly shorter than sterile lemma, both obtuse or broadly pointed. *Dicanthelium boscii* (Poir.) Gould & C.A. Clark.

Plants with glabrous sheaths and leaf blades represent typical *boscii;* those with villous condition of the lower sheaths and underside of blades are separated as var. *molle* (Vasey) Hitchc. and Chase (*Dicanthelium boscii* (Poir.) Gould & C.A. Clark).

Eastern and central United States to Oklahoma and Texas.

Missouri. Upland woods, mainly occurs in eastern and southern sections as typical *boscii;* var. *molle* less frequent and widely scattered. Generally absent in the northern counties. Flowering in May–June and from axillary panicles in August–October.

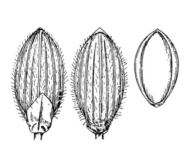

FIG. 187. **Panicum clandestinum.** Two views of spikelet, and floret, × 10.

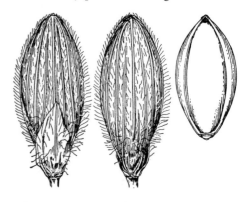

FIG. 188. **Panicum boscii.** Two views of spikelet, and floret, × 10.

6. Panicum latifolium L. Fig. 189.

Perennial, forming tufts, the culms erect, somewhat coarser than no. 5, with smooth nodes; foliage generally glabrous, or sparsely ciliate; leaf blades cordate, 2.5–3 cm wide; vernal panicles few-flowered, with ascending branches, the autumnal panicles reduced, partly included in lower sheaths; spikelets with slight pubescence, about 3.5 mm long; fertile floret slightly exceeding 2nd glume and sterile lemma. *Dicanthelium latifolium* (L.) Gould & C.A. Clark.

Eastern and central United States to Minnesota, Kansas, and Arkansas.

Missouri. Upland woods and protected slopes, widely distributed. Flowering in May–June and from axillary panicles in late summer and fall.

7. Panicum ravenelii Scribn. and Merr. Fig. 190.

Perennial, sparsely tufted; culms erect, becoming branched and somewhat spreading in the autumnal phase, to 50 cm tall or more; sheaths stiff-hirsute; nodes conspicuously bearded; ligule conspicuous, a tuft of hairs 3–4 mm long; leaf blades glabrous or nearly so on upper surface, soft-downy below, with ciliate margins, cordate, to 2 cm wide; vernal panicles with short, spreading branches, few-flowered, the

FIG. 189. **Panicum latifolium.** Plant, × 1; spikelet and floret, × 10.

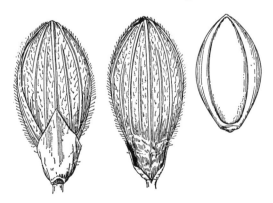

FIG. 190. **Panicum ravenelii.** Two views of spikelet, and floret, × 10.

axillary panicles reduced, from middle and upper sheaths; spikelets large, 3.5–4 mm long. *Dicanthelium ravenelii* (Scribn. and Merrill) Gould.

Southern United States and mid-Atlantic region to Missouri, Oklahoma, and Texas.

Missouri. Upland woods and glades, on dry, cherty or sandy ground, widely scattered throughout the Ozarks region, east to Crowley's Ridge. Flowering in early June and from axillary panicles in late summer and fall.

8. Panicum acuminatum Sw. Fig. 191a,b,c.

Perennials, variably tufted; culms erect, to 70 cm tall, becoming branched and somewhat sprawling or reclining in the autumnal phase; sheaths and nodes pubescent to nearly glabrous; ligule conspicuously tufted; leaf blades variably pubescent to nearly glabrous, sometimes with scattered cilia near base and along margins; blades of principal culm 3–12 mm wide, the fascicled leaves of the autumnal phase mostly narrower and not as long; vernal panicles usually long-exserted, smooth to somewhat puberulent, the axillary panicles simple and much reduced, from lower sheaths; spikelets variably pubescent, ovate-elliptic, 1.5–2 mm long. *Dicanthelium acuminatum* (Sw.) Gould & C.A. Clark.

Three varieties are recognized for Missouri:

a. Specimens with mostly glabrous foliage, the lower sheaths sometimes sparsely pubescent, ligules to 5 mm long, and spikelets small, about 1.5 mm in length, are referred to var. *lindheimeri* (Nash) Beetle (*P. lindheimeri* Nash; *P. lanuginosum* Elliott var. *lindheimeri* (Nash) Fern.; *Dicanthelium lindheimeri* (Nash) Gould; *D. lanuginosum* var. *lindheimeri* Freckmann; *D. acuminatum* (Sw.) Gould & C.A. Clark var. *lindheimeri* Gould & C.A. Clark). (Fig. 191a.) A collection with glabrous foliage and somewhat smaller spikelets labeled *P. longiligulatum* Nash from Newton County (Palmer 63506 MO), but otherwise similar to var. *lindheimeri,* is included here. No other collections to date have been observed.

A collection labeled *P. columbianum* Scribn. from Johnson's Shut-Ins State Park, Reynolds County, T33N, R2E, Sect. 16, SW ¼, NE ¼ (Nelson 341 DNR) appears more similar to *P. acuminatum* var. *lindheimeri* based on a combination of characters including conspicuous ligule length and mostly glabrous foliage. Lelong (1984) reduced *P. columbianum* to varietal status under *P. acuminatum,* indicating, however, wide integration with vars. *implicatum* and *lindheimeri.* Considering its uncertain status, *P. columbianum* is not included in the flora. (*Dicanthelium sabulorum* (Lam.) Gould & C.A. Clark var. *thinium* (Hitchc. & Chase) Gould & C.A. Clark.)

b. Specimens with sheaths variously pubescent, from sparsely hairy to papillose-hirsute, the leaf blades mostly glabrous to puberulent above with scattered cilia on margins and near base, and with short pubescence on lower surface, are segregated as var. *fasciculatum* (Torr.) Lelong (*P. lanuginosum* Elliott var. *fasciculatum* (Torr.) Fern.; *P. tennesseense* Ashe; *P. huachucae* Ashe; *Dicanthelium lanuginosum* Elliott. var. *fasciculatum* Spellen.; *D. acuminatum* Sw. var. *fasciculatum* (Torr.) Freckmann). (Fig. 191b.)

c. Specimens with papillose-pilose sheaths, and leaf blades with long-pilose hairs above, mostly appressed-pubescent below, are separated as var. *implicatum* (Scribn.) Beetle (*P. implicatum* Scribn.; *P. unciphyllum* Trinius var. *thinium* Hitchc. & Chase; *P. lanuginosum* Elliott var. *implicatum* (Scribn.) Fern.; *Dicanthelium acuminatum* Sw. var. *implicatum* Gould & C.A. Clark). (Fig. 191c.)

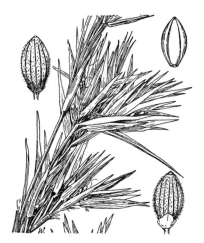

FIG. 191a. **Panicum acuminatum** var. **lindheimeri.** Plant, × 1; two views of spikelet, and floret, × 10.

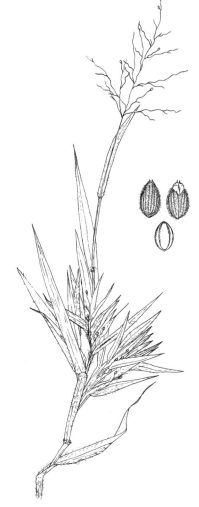

FIG. 191b. **Panicum acuminatum** var. **fasciculatum.** Plant, × ½; two views of spikelet; and floret, × 10.

FIG. 191c. **Panicum acuminatum** var. **implicatum.** Two views of spikelet, and floret, × 10.

Wide-ranging as a polymorphic complex, *P. acuminatum* is concentrated in the eastern and southeastern United States, extending westward to Montana, Nevada, and southern California as var. *fasciculatum,* the most widespread taxon. Typical *acuminatum,* characterized by uniformly villous culms, sheaths, and leaf blades, is mainly a Coastal Plain element, reported inland to Arkansas. No specimens are known from Missouri. *P. lanuginosum* Elliott var. *lanuginosum.*

Missouri. Woodlands, prairies, swales, and stream banks, with var. *fasciculatum* most ubiquitous and generally distributed, the other taxa absent from the west-central and northwestern sections, var. *lindheimeri* generally found on the more moist sites. Flowering in May–June and from axillary panicles in August–October.

9. Panicum praecocius Hitchc. & Chase Fig. 192.

Perennial, forming tufts; culms simple, erect, to 40 cm tall, soon becoming much branched and decumbent; sheaths mostly pilose with spreading hairs; ligule a conspicuous tuft 3–4 mm long; leaf blades averaging about 5 mm in width, long-pilose on both surfaces, with whitish hairs 3–5 mm long; terminal panicles ovoid, not much longer than broad, the axis pilose-pubescent; axillary or secondary panicles reduced, appearing relatively early in the season, mostly included in lower sheaths; spikelets with pilose hairs, ovoid-elliptic, 1.5–2 mm long. *Dicanthelium acuminatum* (Sw.) Gould & C.A. Clark var. *villosum* (A. Gray) Gould & C.A. Clark.

P. praecocius is distinguishable from no. 8c (*P. acuminatum* var. *implicatum*) by its earlier development of secondary branching, and pilose-pubescence on *both* sides of the leaf blades.

North-central United States, Michigan, and North Dakota, to Texas.

Missouri. Upland woods, prairies, and open ground, on mostly dry soils, generally distributed. Flowering in May–June and later from secondary panicles.

10. Panicum ovale Elliott Fig. 193.

Perennial, forming tufts; culms erect, to somewhat spreading-decumbent variably branched in the autumnal phase, to 50 cm tall; sheaths mostly pilose with spreading hairs to 5 mm long or sometimes sparsely so; ligule a conspicuous brush 3–5 mm long; leaf blades stiffly ascending, variably papillose-pilose on both surfaces, 5–10 mm wide; terminal panicles oval with spreading branches, the axis somewhat pilose to nearly smooth; axillary panicles reduced, from fascicled sheaths of the mid-culm; spikelets broad-elliptic, 2–3 mm long. *P. villosissimum* Nash; *P. villosissimum* var. *pseudopubescens* (Nash) Fern.; *P. commonsianum* Ashe; *Dicanthelium acuminatum* (Sw.) Gould & C.A. Clark var. *villosum* (A. Gray) Gould & C.A. Clark; *D. ovale* Gould & C.A. Clark var. *addisonii* (Nash) Gould & C.A. Clark.

Two varieties are reported for Missouri. Plants with mostly abundant, long, pi-

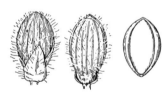

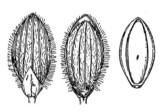

FIG. 192. **Panicum praecocious.** Two views of spikelet, and floret, × 10.

FIG. 193. **Panicum ovale.** Two views of spikelet, and floret, × 10.

lose hairs, and spikelets 2–2.5 mm long, are referred to var. *villosum* (A. Gray) Le-long; those with less marked pilosity, sometimes with only a few scattered hairs, but spikelets similar, are separated as var. *pseudopubescens* (Nash) Lelong.

Eastern and central United States to Kansas and Texas; var. *villosum* extending to Central America. Typical *P. ovale*, with larger spikelets 2.5–3 mm long, is mainly Coastal Plain in range and has not been reported for Missouri.

Missouri. Upland woods on dry, stony, or sandy soils, primarily in the Ozarks region as var. *villosum*, reported also north of the Missouri River in St. Louis and Montgomery Counties; only one collection is known for var. *pseudopubescens* (Steyermark 20685 MO), from Miller County. Flowering in May–June, the secondary panicles developing soon afterwards.

11. Panicum sphaerocarpon Elliott Fig. 194.

Perennial forming tufts; culms generally coarse; erect, decumbent-spreading in the autumnal phase, 30–70 cm tall; foliage mostly glabrous or nearly so, the leaf blades firm, ascending, sparsely ciliate toward cordate base, 0.5–2.5 cm wide, narrower on upper culm; ligule obsolete; vernal panicles ovoid to elliptic, with viscid branches; spikelets minutely pubescent, spherical, 1.5 mm long.

Two varieties are recognized for Missouri. Specimens with leaf blades 5–15 mm wide are referred to var. *sphaerocarpon* (incl. var. *inflatum* (Scribn. & Smith) Hitchc. & Chase; *Dicanthelium sphaerocarpon* (Elliott) Gould var. *sphaerocarpon*). Specimens with distinctly wider leaf blades to 2.5 cm wide, not noticeably reduced on upper culm, are separated as var. *isophyllum* (Scrib.) R. Angelo. (*P. polyanthes* J.A. Schultes; *Dicanthelium sphaerocarpon* (Elliott) Gould var. *isophyllum* (Scribn.) Gould & C.A. Clark).

Eastern and southern United States to Michigan, Kansas, Oklahoma, and Texas; var. *sphaerocarpon* extending to South America.

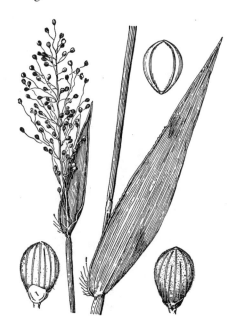

FIG. 194. **Panicum sphaerocarpon.** Plant, × 1; two views of spikelet, and floret, × 10.

Missouri. Upland woods and open ground, widely distributed, mostly south of the line from Jackson to Linn and Ralls Counties, as var. *sphaerocarpon;* var. *isophyllum* occurring on low ground and creek banks, scattered, from eastern Ozarks to Boone and Lincoln Counties. Flowering in May–June and from axillary panicles in late summer and fall.

12. Panicum scoparium Lam. Fig. 195.

Perennial, sparsely tufted; culms robust, branching from upper nodes in the autumnal phase, to 1 m tall or more; sheaths and culms conspicuously soft-villous, the latter glabrous immediately below the bearded nodes; ligule 1 mm long or less; leaf blades downy-pubescent, rounded at base, 1–1.5 cm wide, vernal panicles pubescent with viscid branches, few-flowered, the axillary panicles reduced, mostly included in the upper sheaths; spikelets hairy, obovoid, averaging 2.5 mm long. *Dicanthelium scoparium* (Lam.) Gould.

Southern and eastern United States, from New England to Kentucky, Oklahoma, and Texas.

Missouri. Low ground and prairie swales, on moist soils, central and southern sections, widely scattered, north to Henry and Phelps Counties. Flowering in May–June and later in late summer from axillary panicles.

13. Panicum malacophyllum Nash Fig. 196.

Perennial, forming narrow tufts; culms conspicuously villous with bearded nodes, erect, to about 50 cm tall, becoming bushy-reclining in the autumnal phase; sheaths villous with retrorse-spreading hairs; ligule about 1 mm long; leaf blades soft-pubescent, somewhat lax, cordate, 7–15 mm wide, those of the autumnal phase considerably reduced in size; vernal panicles villous, few-flowered; axillary panicles reduced, more or less included in middle to upper sheaths; spikelets pubescent, ellipsoid, somewhat pointed, 2.5–3 mm long. *Dicanthelium malacophyllum* (Nash) Gould.

South-central United States from Tennessee to Kansas and Texas.

Fig. 195. **Panicum scoparium.** Plant, × 1; two views of spikelet, and floret, × 10.

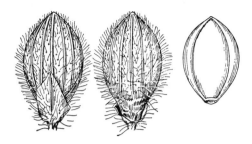

Fig. 196. **Panicum malacophyllum.** Two views of spikelet, and floret, × 10.

Missouri. Open woods and fields, on dry soils, limited mainly to the southwestern section and, locally, Johnson, Shannon, and New Madrid Counties. Flowering in May–June and from axillary panicles in late summer and fall.

14. Panicum oligosanthes J.A. Schultes Fig. 197.

Perennial, with tufts; culms erect, becoming much branched, 30–70 cm tall; sheaths glabrous to variably short-pubescent; ligule nearly obsolete to about 1 mm long; leaf blades mostly glabrous above, appressed-pubescent to puberulent below with occasional cilia along margins near base, somewhat stiff, erect-ascending, 5–10 mm wide; vernal panicles broadly ovate, stiffly branched, the autumnal panicles reduced, sparsely flowered, from aggregated upper sheaths; spikelets glabrous to sparsely pubescent, turgid, broadly elliptic, 2.5–4 mm long. *Dicanthelium oligosanthes* (J.A. Schultes) Gould.

Two varieties are recognized for Missouri. Specimens with spikelets 3.5–4 mm long and appressed-pubescent foliage, the leaf blades somewhat narrowing to base, represent typical *oligosanthes* (*Dicanthelium oligosanthes* (J.A. Schultes) Gould var.

Fig. 197. **Panicum oligosanthes** var. **scribnerianum.** Plant, × 1; two views of spikelet, and floret, × 10.

oligosanthes). Specimens with smaller spikelets averaging 3 mm in length and leaf blades glabrous to puberulent and rounded at the base are separated as var. *scribnerianum* (Nash) Fern. (*P. scribnerianum* Nash; *P. helleri* Nash; *Dicanthelium oliganthes* (J.A. Schultes) Gould var. *scribnerianum* (Nash) Gould).

Eastern and southern United States with var. *scribnerianum* extending to Pacific Coast region.

Missouri. Open woods, prairies, and waste ground, dry to relatively moist soils, most common and generally distributed throughout the state as var. *scribnerianum*, with var. *oligosanthes* occurring widely scattered, reported for Dade, Green, Taney, New Madrid, Scott, Mississippi, DeKalb, and Ray Counties. Flowering in May–June and from axillary panicles in late summer and fall.

15. Panicum leibergii (Vasey) Scribn. Fig. 198.

Perennial, sparsely tufted; culms erect to geniculate at lower nodes, to 70 cm tall; sheaths variably papillose-pubescent, not reaching the above node; ligule obsolete; leaf blades glabrous to sparsely pubescent on upper surface, papillose-pubescent below, usually ciliate on margins, 8–15 mm wide, with rounded to cordate base; vernal panicles few-flowered with short, ascending branches, at first partially included, becoming exserted; axillary panicles reduced, few-flowered, from sparsely branched middle and lower culms; spikelets distinctly papillose-pubescent, elliptic 3.5–4 mm long. *Dicanthelium leibergii* (Vasey) Freckmann.

North-central and eastern United States from North Dakota to New York, to Illinois, Kansas, and Texas.

Missouri. Open woods, prairies, and bottomlands, infrequent and widely scattered, not common. Flowering in spring and early summer and from the axillary panicles later in the season.

16. Panicum commutatum J.A. Schultes Fig. 199.

Perennial, sparsely tufted; culms simple, sparingly branched in the autumnal phase, mostly erect 20–60 cm tall; sheaths usually glabrous to sparsely pubescent; nodes smooth; leaf blades glabrous or with few cilia near the cordate base, 0.7–2 cm wide; terminal panicles exserted, with spreading branches; axillary panicles reduced, simple, partly included in the sheaths of middle culm; spikelets with slight pubescence, elliptic-oblong, 2.2–2.8 mm long. *Dichanthelium commutatum* (J.A. Schultes) Gould; incl. var *ashei* (Pearson ex Ashe) Mohlenbr.

Specimens with slightly smaller spikelets than typical *commutatum,* and stiff,

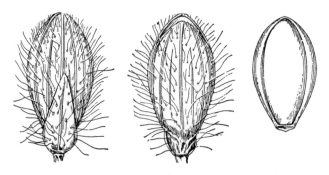

FIG. 198. **Panicum leibergii.** Two views of spikelet, and floret, × 10.

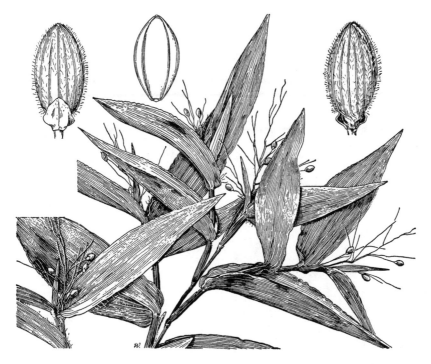

FIG. 199. **Panicum commutatum.** Plant, × 1; two views of spikelet, and floret, × 10.

narrower purplish leaf blades to 1 cm wide, are referred to var. *ashei* (Pearson) Fern., our specimens sometimes distinctive (*P. ashei* Pearson ex Ashe).

Eastern and southern United States, west to Oklahoma and Texas.

Missouri. Oak-pine woods, creek banks, and bottomlands, widely scattered through the Ozarks region and southern counties, typical *commutatum* usually occurring on moister sites than var. *ashei.* Flowering in May–June and later in summer and fall from axillary panicles.

17. **Panicum dichotomum** L. Fig. 200a,b,c.

Perennials, forming tufts or mats; culms slender, erect, 30–100 cm tall, becoming branched above, bushy-sprawling to reclining in the autumnal phase; nodes variably pubescent, from nearly glabrous to conspicuously bearded; sheaths and leaf blades glabrous or nearly so to sparsely pubescent with few cilia on the margins; ligule mostly a minute fringe less than 1 mm long; leaf blades 5–15 mm wide, those of the autumnal branches narrower, reduced in length; vernal panicles with spreading branches, ovoid, long-exserted, the axillary panicles much reduced, few-flowered from crowded upper sheaths; spikelets mostly glabrous or minutely pubescent, broadly elliptic, obtuse to somewhat acute, 1.5–2 mm long or slightly more in some specimens. *Dicanthelium dichotomum* (L.) Gould.

P. dichotomum constitutes a polymorphic complex of intergrading forms in which three varieties are recognized for Missouri:

a. Specimens with narrow leaf blades less than 7.5 mm wide and spikelets broadly elliptic, obtuse, averaging 2 mm in length are referred to typical *dichotomum* (*P. barbulatum* Michx.; *P. dichotomum* var. *barbulatum* (Michx.) Wood; *Dicanthelium dichotomum* (L.) Gould var. *dichotomum*). (Fig. 200a.)

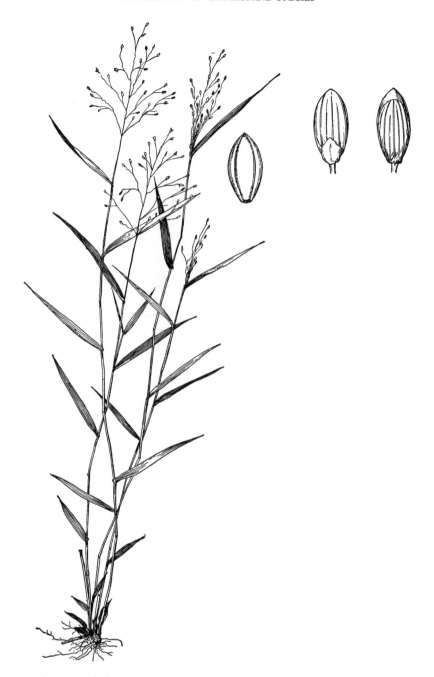

FIG. 200a. **Panicum dichotomum** var. **dichotomum.** Plant, × ½; two views of spikelet, and floret, × 10.

b. Specimens with wider leaf blades to 1 cm in width, conspicuously bearded nodes, and smaller spikelets averaging 1.5 mm long are distinguished as var. *ramulosum* (Torr.) Lelong (*P. microcarpon* Muhl. ex Elliott; *P. nitidum* Lam; *P. nitidum* Lam. var. *ramulosum* Torr.; *Dicanthelium microcarpon* (Muhl. ex Elliott) Mohlenbr.; *D. nitidum* (Lam.) Mohlenbr.). (Fig. 200b.)

c. Specimens with more or less glabrous to sparsely pubescent nodes and pointed spikelets mostly exceeding 2 mm in length are separated as var. *yadkinense* (Ashe) Lelong (*P. yadkinense* Ashe). (Fig. 200c.)

Eastern and south-central United States to Oklahoma and Texas.

Missouri. Upland woods to low ground and creek banks, mainly southern and east-central sections, not common north of Missouri River, but reported for Callaway, Warren, and Lincoln Counties and recently for Mercer County (Yatskievych 88–106 MO); typical *dichotomum* is more characteristic of thin or dry soils; var. *ramulosum* occurs more frequently in damp sites and on low ground; and var. *yadkinense* is new to the state on floodplain terrace sites in Reynolds County (Heumann 21 MO). Flowering from the terminal panicles in May–June and from axillary panicles in late summer and fall.

18. Panicum bicknellii Nash Fig. 201.

Perennials, developing slender tufts, the culms erect to 50 cm tall or more; sheaths usually glabrous, sparsely ciliate at summit; ligule wanting or obsolete; leaf blades mostly glabrous with scattered cilia at base, elongate-ascending, narrowing

FIG. 200b. **Panicum dichotomum** var. **ramulosum.** Plant, × 1; two views of spikelet, and floret, × 10.

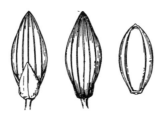

FIG. 200c. **Panicum dichotomum** var. **yadkinense.** Two views of spikelet, and floret, × 10.

from midsection to the tapered or somewhat rounded base; foliage of autumnal branches mostly similar to primary culm leaves, not much reduced; vernal panicles narrow, with short branches, few-flowered, axillary panicles reduced, from middle and upper sheaths; spikelets sparsely hairy to nearly glabrous, elliptic, 2.5–3.0 mm long, from elongated pedicels. *Dicanthelium boreale* (Nash) Freckmann.

Two varieties are recognized for Missouri. Specimens with narrowing leaf bases and spikelets averaging 2.5 mm in length are referred to typical *bicknellii;* those with a more rounded base and somewhat larger spikelets to 3 mm long are separated as var. *calliphyllum* (Ashe) Gleason (*P. calliphyllum* Ashe).

Southern New England to Georgia to central region from Michigan to Oklahoma.

Missouri. Upland woods and dry slopes, on thin soils, infrequent and scattered in southern sections as typical *bicknellii;* var. *calliphyllum* reported for Callaway and Ripley Counties. Flowering in May–June and later in season from axillary panicles.

19. Panicum laxiflorum Lam. Fig. 202.

Perennial, forming spreading tufts or loose mats; culms simple, to 50–60 cm tall, becoming much branched from base in the autumnal phase; sheaths pilose; nodes sparsely bearded with soft hairs; ligule minute or obsolete; leaf blades mostly

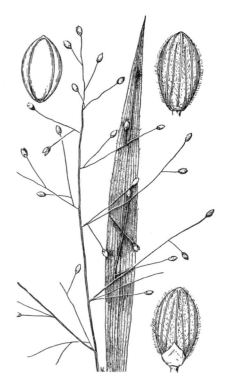

Fig. 201. **Panicum bicknellii** var. **bicknellii.** Plant, × 1; two views of spikelet, and floret, × 10.

Fig. 202. **Panicum laxiflorum.** Panicle, × ½; two views of spikelet, and floret, × 10.

glabrous, with ciliate margins, soft, to 1 cm wide, those near base generally similar in size to blades of upper culm; vernal panicles long-exserted, the branches pilose, somewhat lax, and spreading; axillary panicles much reduced, few-flowered, mostly obscured by basal leaves; spikelets papillose-pubescent, broad-elliptic, to 2.0 mm long or slightly more. *Dicanthelium laxiflorum* (Lam.) Gould.

Mid-Atlantic and Gulf regions to Missouri, Arkansas, and Texas, to Mexico and Central America.

Missouri. Dry woods, glades, and prairies east and south of a line from MacDonald to Boone to St. Louis Counties, most common in the Ozarks region. Flowering in May–June, and in summer and fall from axillary panicles.

B. Subgenus Panicum

20. Panicum dichotomiflorum Michx. Fig. 203.

Annual; culms coarse, smooth, to 1 m tall or more, erect to reclining, the lower nodes sometimes geniculate; foliage glabrous, the elongate leaf blades 4–15 mm wide, scabrous on the margins, with prominent midvein; ligule consisting of whitish hairs to 2 mm long; panicles with more or less spreading to ascending branches, glabrous, exserted to partially included; spikelets glabrous, 2.5–3 mm long, oblong, with pointed apex. Incl. var. *geniculatum* (Wood) Fern.

Eastern and central United States to Nebraska and Texas, sporadic westward.

Missouri. Fields and waste areas, low or damp ground, generally distributed; one of our most common annual panicums. Flowering in September–October.

21. Panicum miliaceum L. BROOM-CORN MILLET. Fig. 204.

Annual; culms coarse, to 1 m tall; sheaths hirsute; leaf blades glabrous to variously pubescent, elongate, to 2 cm wide; panicles dense, many-flowered, heavy at maturity, with short branches, partially included at the base; spikelets mostly smooth, conspicuously nerved, 4–5 mm long, with acute apex; caryopsis shiny, yellowish brown.

Forage and grain species introduced in the United States, mostly northern and eastern regions, occasionally a volunteer on waste ground.

Missouri. Sporadic and not common, Chariton, Morgan, Jackson, Clay, and St. Louis Counties; sometimes sown as a food plant for waterfowl in refuge areas. Flowering in July–September.

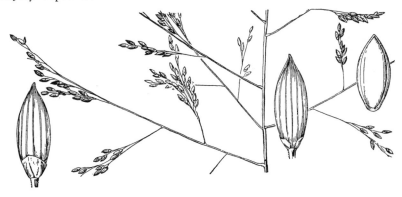

FIG. 203. **Panicum dichotomiflorum.** Panicle, × 1; two views of spikelet, and floret, × 10.

22. Panicum flexile (Gattinger) Scribn. Fig. 205.

Annual, culms slender, becoming branched, to about 50 cm tall; sheaths papillose-hairy; lower nodes pubescent; leaf blades glabrous to appressed-pubescent, sparsely ciliate on the margins toward base, 3.5–7 mm wide; panicles diffuse, with delicate branches, longer than broad, few-flowered; spikelets glabrous, lanceolate-acuminate 3–3.5 mm long.

Eastern United States and adjacent parts of Canada to North Dakota to Texas, probably introduced elsewhere.

Missouri. Upland woods, glades, and waste ground, generally distributed, except absent from the northernmost counties. Flowering in July–September.

23. Panicum capillare L. WITCH-GRASS. Fig. 206.

Annual, developing tufts; culms branching from near base, erect to decumbent-spreading, often rooting at the lower nodes, to 70 cm tall; sheaths hispid-pubescent; leaf blades soft-pubescent, 5–10 mm wide or more; terminal panicles diffuse, broadly spreading, exserted to partially included, becoming one-half or more of total culm height, at maturity sometimes breaking away as a tumbleweed; axillary panicles also present, partly included in lower sheaths; spikelets glabrous, 2–3 mm long, ovate-acuminate, on firm, slender pedicels.

Two varieties are recognized for Missouri. Specimens with relatively large, broad panicles, partially inserted in upper sheaths, and spikelets 2–2.5 mm long represent typical *capillare* (incl. var. *agreste* Gattinger). Specimens with the larger spikelets to 3 mm long and conspicuously hirsute pulvini are separated as var. *occidentale* Rydb. (*P. barbipulinatum* Nash).

Eastern and central United States; var. *occidentale* extending farther west.

Missouri. Cultivated areas, old fields, and sandbars, generally distributed as typical *capillare;* var. *occidentale* less common, absent from the Ozarks region. Flowering in July–September.

24. Panicum philadelphicum Trin. Fig. 207.

Annual; culms slender to 50 cm tall; sheaths pubescent, the hairs sometimes papillose; leaf blades mostly glabrous to sparsely hairy, 3–6 mm wide; panicles diffuse,

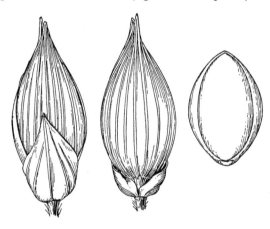

FIG. 204. **Panicum miliaceum.** Two views of spikelet, and floret, × 10.

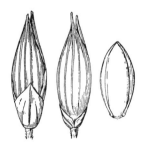

FIG. 205. **Panicum flexile.** Two views of spikelet, and floret, × 10.

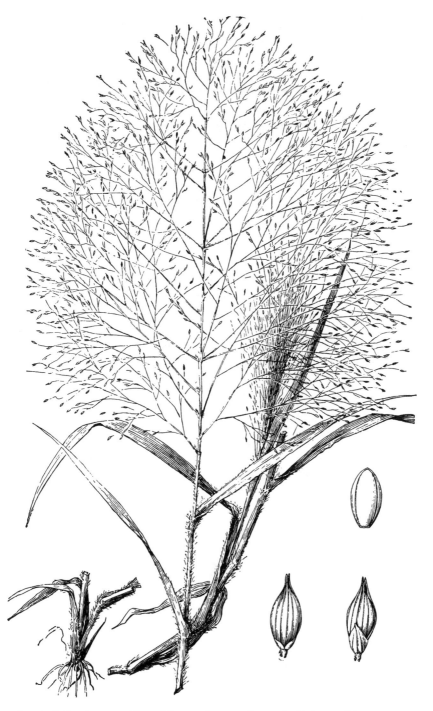

FIG. 206. **Panicum capillare.** Plant, × ½; two views of spikelet, and floret, × 10.

sparsely flowered, delicately branched, the pulvini mostly hairy, sometimes glabrous; spikelets smooth or nearly so, averaging about 2 mm long, mostly in pairs at end of panicle branches.

Specimens with glabrous pulvini and multiple spikelets are separated from typical *philadelphicum* as var. *tuckermani* (Fern.) Steyermark & Schmoll (*P. tuckermani* Fern.).

Eastern and central United States, from Minnesota to Texas.

Missouri. Open woods, glades, waste ground, and fields, on dry soils, mostly south of a line from Barton to Ralls Counties as typical *philadephicum;* var. *tuckermani* reported for Washington County (Steyermark 77796 MO).

25. Panicum gattingeri Nash Fig. 208.

Annual; culms relatively coarse, freely branching, erect to decumbent-spreading, rooting at the lower nodes; sheaths usually papillose-pubescent; leaf blades variably pubescent to nearly glabrous, 5–10 mm wide; panicles becoming numerous, with glabrous pulvini; spikelets glabrous, averaging 2 mm in length, broad-elliptic, abruptly pointed. *P. capillare* L. var. *campestre* Gattinger.

East-central United States from New York to Minnesota and adjacent parts of Canada to Arkansas, Tennessee, and mid-Atlantic region.

Missouri. Glades, fields, waste ground, and alluvium, widely scattered, mostly in central and southern sections. Flowering in late summer and fall.

26. Panicum obtusum Kunth Vine Mesquite. Fig. 209.

Perennial; culms wiry, stiffly erect, to 1 m tall, forming slender tufts from extensive, creeping runners or stolons with swollen, conspicuously bearded nodes; foliage mostly glabrous, the leaf blades relatively narrow, 3–6 mm wide, elongate-ascending; panicles strict, narrow, with few, short, ascending branches; spikelets smooth, obovoid, obtuse, averaging 3.5 mm in length; 1st glume about *same* length as 2nd glume and sterile lemma.

Centered in the southwestern United States and Mexico, to Utah, Colorado, Kansas, and Missouri.

Missouri. Rare and little known; collected from Jackson County (Bush 1832, 3107). No other collections are known.

27. Panicum anceps Michx. var. anceps Fig. 210.

Perennial, with well-developed rhizomes; culms coarse, erect to about 1 m tall; sheaths glabrous, becoming pubescent on lower culm; leaf blades glabrous or nearly so, elongate, 5–10 mm wide; panicles open, the branches stiffly spreading or ascending; spikelets smooth, lanceolate-falcate, sessile, 3–4 mm long, arranged on one side of the rachis.

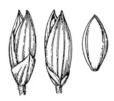

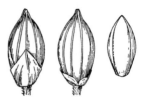

Fig. 207. **Panicum philadelphicum.** Two views of spikelet, and floret, × 10.

Fig. 208. **Panicum gattingeri.** Two views of spikelet, and floret, × 10.

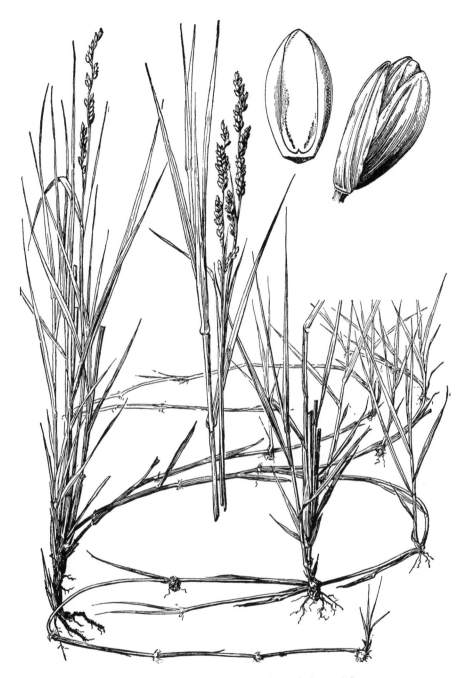

FIG. 209. **Panicum obtusum.** Panicle, × ½; spikelet and floret, × 10.

FIG. 210. **Panicum anceps** var. **anceps.** Spikelet and floret, × 10.

Mid-Atlantic and Gulf regions ranging to Ohio, to Oklahoma and Texas.

Missouri. Swales and spring branches, moist sandy ground, south of a line from Barton to St. Louis Counties. Flowering in July–August.

Var. *rhizomatum* (Hitch. & Chase) Fern., with contracted panicles and smaller spikelets than typical *anceps,* reaches inland to Tennessee from the Coastal Plain but has not been reported for Missouri.

28. Panicum virgatum L. var. **virgatum** SWITCHGRASS. Fig. 211.

Perennial, rhizomatous, forming dense stands or clumps; culms of variable height, sometimes to 1.5 mm tall or more; sheaths glabrous; ligule a fringe of hairs about 2.5 mm long; leaf blades mostly glabrous, sparsely pilose near base, elongate 5–10 mm wide; panicles smooth, with somewhat stiff, spreading or ascending branches; spikelets smooth, plump, 3.5–4 mm long, acuminate; 2nd glume long-pointed, slightly exceeding the sterile lemma.

Widespread from eastern United States to North Dakota, Nevada, and Arizona, to Mexico and Central America.

Missouri. Prairie swales, glades, sand flats, and low ground, generally distributed. Flowering in July–September.

Var. *cubense* Griseb., with smaller spikelets averaging 2.5–3 mm long and with less robust habit than typical *virgatum,* occurs to the east and south of Missouri.

29. Panicum hians Elliott Fig. 212.

Perennial, forming small tufts; culms slender, to 50 cm tall, occasionally becoming decumbent near base; sheaths glabrous, somewhat compressed or keeled; leaf blades smooth, elongate, 1.5–5 mm wide; panicles diffuse, the branches delicate, spreading or nodding; spikelets smooth, sessile or nearly so, averaging 2 mm long, clustered toward ends of the panicle branches; sterile palea present, indurate, enlarged, slightly longer than the sterile lemma, and distending the spikelet at maturity.

Coastal Plain region from Virginia to Texas and inland to Missouri.

Missouri. In spring branches, swampy areas, and low woods; reported for Ripley, Butler, Stoddard, New Madrid, and Dunklin Counties. Flowering in July–August.

30. Panicum rigidulum Bosc ex Nees Fig. 213.

Perennial, forming dense tufts; culms coarse, to 1 m tall or more; sheaths glabrous, compressed-keeled, crowded toward base of culm; leaf blades glabrous, to 1 cm wide, becoming shorter and more numerous from basal sheaths; panicles with stiff, divaricate branching, the crowded spikelets sessile, arranged mostly on one side of the branchlets; spikelets smooth, narrow-ovoid, pointed, 2–2.5 mm long; 2nd

FIG. 211. **Panicum virgatum** var. **virgatum.** Plant, × ½; two views of spikelet, and floret, × 10.

FIG. 212. **Panicum hians.** Spikelet and floret, × 10.

FIG. 213. **Panicum rigidulum.** Panicle, × 1; two views of spikelet, and floret, × 10.

glume and sterile lemma exceeding the fertile floret. *P. agrostoides* Spreng.; *P. stipitatum* Nash.

Eastern and central United States to Kansas, Oklahoma, and Texas.

Missouri. Prairie swales, swampy ground, and alluvium, mainly central and southern sections. Flowering in late summer.

65. SACCIOLEPIS Nash

Annuals and perennials; inflorescence mostly a contracted spikelike panicle; spikelets narrow-oblong, awnless, with 1 perfect floret; 1st glume much shorter than the 2nd, the latter saccate or inflated with numerous prominent nerves; sterile lemma more or less flat, not saccate, with fewer nerves; both 2nd glume and sterile lemma of equal length, much exceeding fertile floret, its lemma short-stipitate, indurate, with slightly inrolled margins. $x = 9$; non-Kranz.

1. Sacciolepis striata (L.) Nash CUPSCALE. Fig. 214.

Perennial; culms mostly coarse, erect to somewhat decumbent, rooting from lower nodes, 1–2 m tall; sheaths mostly glabrous or sparsely hirsute at summit; ligule a fringe of minute hairs; leaf blades 5–15 mm wide, to long, tapering point; panicles narrow-elongate, dense, to 25–30 cm long; spikelets ovate-lanceolate, with asymmetrical base, short-pedicellate; 1st glume ovate, about 1 mm long, the 2nd glume and sterile lemma equal, 3–5 mm long; fertile lemma glossy, indurate, 1.5–2 mm long.

Wet habitats and low ground, eastern and southern United States from New Jersey to Florida, to Texas and Oklahoma.

Missouri. Wet ground and ditches, Oregon County (Yatskievych & Summers 90-404 MO), a new record for the state; also Mississippi County (McKenzie 1640 MO). Flowering in summer.

66. ECHINOCHLOA P. Beauv.

Annuals and perennials, panicles generally bristly, with spikelets variably crowded, on short, ascending to spreading branches or racemes, sometimes from one side of the rachis; spikelets with 1 perfect floret, plano-convex, broadly elliptic, vari-

FIG. 214. **Sacciolepis striata.** Plant, × ½; two views of spikelet, and floret, × 10.

ably awned, cuspidate, or awnless, separating below the glumes and falling entire; 1st glume ovate-pointed or triangular, about one-third the length of usually cuspidate 2nd glume, the latter and sterile lemma nearly equal, both mostly hispid, sometimes with papillae at base of hairs; sterile lemma often prominently awned; fertile lemma, smooth, shiny, indurate, with inrolled margins enclosing palea except at its apex. $x = 9$; Kranz.

Key to Missouri Species

a. Panicles narrow, with short, somewhat distant, ascending or appressed simple branches; spikelets awnless ....1. *E. colona*

a. Panicles with congested or compact branches; spikelets awned or awnless

    b. Panicles heavy, dense, the spikelets uniformly crowded on the rachis, awnless; rare species ....2. *E. utilis*

    b. Panicles variably compact, the spikelets sometimes arrayed on one side of rachis; awned or awnless; generally distributed

        c. Sheaths hispid to papillose-hirsute; spikelets mostly with long straight awns; rare species ....3. *E. walteri*

        c. Sheaths mostly glabrous; spikelets awned or awnless; common species

            d. Fertile lemma with ring of minute, stiff hairs below thin, shriveled apex................ ....4. *E. crus-galli*

            d. Fertile lemma lacking ring of hairs, the apex mostly firm, not shriveled ....5. *E. muricata*

1. Echinochloa colona (L.) Link Jungle-rice. Fig. 215.

Annual; culms erect to geniculate-spreading, rooting at lower nodes, 20–50 cm tall; sheaths glabrous, keeled on back; ligule absent or obsolete; leaf blades glabrous, lax, 3–5 mm wide; racemes ascending, few, remote, 1–2 cm long; spikelets broadly elliptic, about 2.5 mm long, slightly pubescent, the hairs lacking papillae; 2nd glume and sterile lemma awnless or cuspidate. *E. colonum* (L.) Link.

Widespread, mainly the southern United States and mid-Atlantic region to New Jersey; introduced from the Old World tropics.

Missouri. Moist ground, sporadic and infrequent, Jackson, St. Louis, Mississippi, and Pemiscot Counties. Flowering in summer.

An early collection (1920) previously identified as *E. colonum* from open ground, Sheffield, Jackson County (Bush 9228 MO) has been verified as *E. crus-pavonis* (Kunth) P.J. Schultes var. *macera* (Wiegand) Gould. This adventive annual, ranging from the southern United States to South America, differs from typical *crus-pavonis* by the absence of the sterile palea. Both varieties have more compact, rebranching panicles than *E. colona,* but share with it the traits of the withered tip of the fertile lemma and the absence of pustular setae. *E. crus-pavonis* differs from *E. crus-galli,* no. 4, by having generally more open panicles and greater frequency of awned spikelets (Gould, Ali & Fairbrothers, 1972). No other collections of *E. crus-pavonis* are known from Missouri; however, field studies may reveal additional locations since the nearest known collection sites include Tennessee, Arkansas, and Kansas.

2. Echinochloa utilis Ohwi & Yab. Fig. 216.

Annual; culms mostly erect, stout, to 1 m tall; sheaths glabrous, keeled, sometimes exceeding the nodes; ligule absent; leaf blades coarse, to 2 cm wide; panicles dense, with crowded, ascending racemes of purplish brown to black spikelets, the central axis striate-grooved with light-colored hairs at the nodes; spikelets subglobose, about 4 mm long; 1st glume broadly ovate, much shorter than the 2nd glume, both 5-nerved; sterile lemma slightly longer than 2nd glume, both 5-nerved; sterile lemma broadly elliptic, strongly convex, smooth, lustrous, about 3 mm long, the inrolled margins enclosing the palea, the latter with shriveled apex at maturity.

Introduced in the United States as a crop plant, native of eastern Asia including Japan.

FIG. 215. **Echinochloa colona,** × 1.

FIG. 216. **Echinochloa utilis,** × 1. (As
E. crus-galli var. **frumentacea** of
Hitchcock & Chase.)

Missouri. Rare and little known, railroad yards, St. Louis County (Muehlenbach 3349 MO), probably not persistent. Flowering in summer.

3. Echinochloa walteri (Pursh) Heller Fig. 217.

Annual; bunch-forming, robust, culms erect, 1–2 m tall; sheath papillose-hairy mostly near summit, sometimes sparsely rough-pubescent, lacking papillae; ligule lacking or obsolete; leaf blades mostly glabrous or scabrous, to 3 cm wide; panicles bushy, the spikelets numerous, on short, ascending branches, becoming purplish; spikelets ovate, hispid, mostly nonpapillose, about 4 mm long; glumes and sterile lemma with prominent veins, the latter usually with awn to 4–5 cm long, or sometimes awnless or nearly so; fertile lemma firm, indurate.

Eastern United States and adjacent parts of Canada to middle Mississippi valley, Mexico, and Central America; wetlands and brackish waters.

Missouri. Marshland, Dresser Island, St. Charles County (Smith 3273 MO); field reconnaissance, especially in eastern counties bordering the Mississippi River, may reveal additional stations for this species, since Iowa and Arkansas are included in its western range. Flowering in summer.

4. Echinochloa crus-galli (L.) P. Beauv. BARNYARD GRASS. Fig. 218.

Annual; culms erect to geniculate-decumbent, branching from lower nodes, to 1.5 m tall; sheaths mostly glabrous, becoming flattened; ligule absent; leaf blades glabrous, 5–10 mm wide, long-tapering; panicles erect to nodding, the thick, spike-like racemes 2–4 cm long; spikelets crowded, bristly-hispid, broadly elliptic, 3–3.5

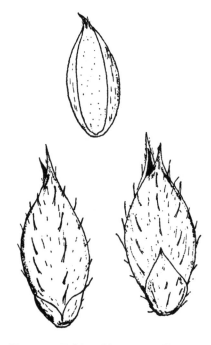

FIG. 217. **Echinochloa walteri,** × 1.

FIG. 218. **Echinochloa crus-galli.** Two views of spikelet, and floret, × 10.

mm long, awned or awnless; 2nd glume and sterile lemma with setae usually lacking papillae at base; fertile lemma smooth, lustrous, encircled below the tip by a ring of minute hairs or bristles, the apex becoming shriveled and dried.

Plants with thick, heavy, nodding panicles and plump, awnless spikelets are separated from typical *crus-galli* as var. *frumentacea* (Link) W. Wight, a cultivar known as billion dollar grass (*E. frumentacea* Link). Vickery (1988) indicated that the description for var. *frumentacea* as employed by Hitchcock (1951) applies to *E. utilis* (no. 2), described by Yabuno (1966). Both taxa are used as small grain and forage crops. Vickery adopted specific status for var. *frumentacea,* since it is thought to be native to India whereas *crus-galli* is traditionally accepted as a European species.

Widespread in the United States; introduced from the Old World.

Missouri. Waste areas, low fields, and alluvial soils, mostly damp ground, generally distributed as typical *crus-galli;* var. *frumentacea* observed as waifs, but not persistent. Flowering in mid- to late summer.

5. Echinochloa muricata (P. Beauv.) Fern. Fig. 219.

Plants resembling *crus-galli* in general habit and panicle development, these not always satisfactorily differentiated; spikelets crowded, ovate, 2.5–4.5 mm long, typically long-awned but some plants awnless or nearly so; 2nd glume and sterile lemma usually with pustular setae or bristles; fertile lemma lacking ring of minute hairs below tip. *E. pungens* (Poir.) Rydb.

Plants with awned spikelets 3.5–4.5 mm long represent typical *muricata;* those with smaller spikelets, 2.5–3.5 mm long and awnless, are separated as var. *microstachya* Wieg. Other plants also awnless with spikelets of similar dimensions, but in which setae lack pustular bases, are separated as var. *wiegandii* Fassett (*E. occiden-*

FIG. 219. **Echinochloa muricata.** Plant, × ½; two views of spikelet, and floret, × 10.

talis (Wieg.) Rydb.); the last variety is distinguishable from species no. 4, both of which lack the pustular condition, by the absence of the ring of minute hairs below the tip of the fertile lemma.

This taxon is considered by most authors to be a native American species, indigenous to the eastern and central United States and adjacent Canada.

Missouri. Lake margins, alluvial flats, and spring branches, on open ground, generally distributed as typical *muricata;* vars. *microstachya* and *wiegandii* scattered and less common. Flowering in mid- to late summer.

67. BRACHIARIA (Trin.) Griseb.

Annuals and perennials; inflorescence consisting of several spreading-ascending, spikelike racemes along the unbranched central axis; spikelets 2-flowered, sessile, solitary, in 2 rows on one side of the rachis, falling entire, only upper floret fertile; 1st glume noticeably shorter than 2nd; 2nd glume and sterile lemma similar, equaling length of spikelet; fertile lemma indurate, awnless, with inrolled margins enclosing palea, the convex side *away* from the rachis. $x = 7, 9$; Kranz.

Key to Missouri Species
a. Spikelets glabrous; racemes few, distant ....1. *B. platyphylla*
a. Spikelets pilose-pubescent; racemes not as above
    b. Spikelets 2–2.5 mm long...2. *B. eruciformis*
    b. Spikelets 5 mm long or more ....3. *B. texana*

1. Brachiaria platyphylla (Munro ex Wright) Nash Fig. 220.

Annual; culms branching, decumbent near base, rooting at the lower nodes, about 50 cm tall; leaf blades coarse-textured, 5–10 mm wide; spikelike racemes few, 3.5–6 cm long, distant along the axis; rachis flat, smooth, about 2 mm wide; spikelets ovate-elliptic, glabrous, 4 mm long; 1st glume thin, broadly ovate about 1.5 mm long, the 2nd glume and sterile lemma three times as long as the first glume, both exceeding the floret; fertile lemma rugose, 3.5 mm long. *B. extensa* Chase; *Urochloa platyphylla* (Monro ex Wright) R. Webster.

Southern United States, from Florida to Texas and Oklahoma, north to southeastern Missouri.

Missouri. On sandy, open ground in the southeast, Scott and Pemiscot Counties. Flowering in late summer and fall.

2. Brachiaria eruciformis (J.E. Smith) Griseb. Fig. 221.

Annual; culms branching, spreading-decumbent, to about 50 cm tall; leaf blades narrow, 3–5 mm wide; spikelike racemes ascending, 1–2 cm long; spikelets oblong-elliptic, hairy, about 2 mm long; 1st glume minute, less than one-fifth the length of the 2nd glume and sterile lemma. *B. erucaeformis; Panicum eruciforme* (J.E. Smith) Griseb.

Sporadic and widely scattered in the United States, an introduction from the Old World.

Missouri. Originally a single station, now the site of Table Rock Dam and Lake, Stone County (Steyermark 80556 MO). Flowering in late summer.

3. Brachiaria texana (Buckley) S.T. Blake Concho Grass. Fig. 222.

Annual; culms coarse, erect to somewhat decumbent, rooting from lower nodes, to 1 m tall or more; sheaths and leaf blades soft-pubescent, the latter cordate at base,

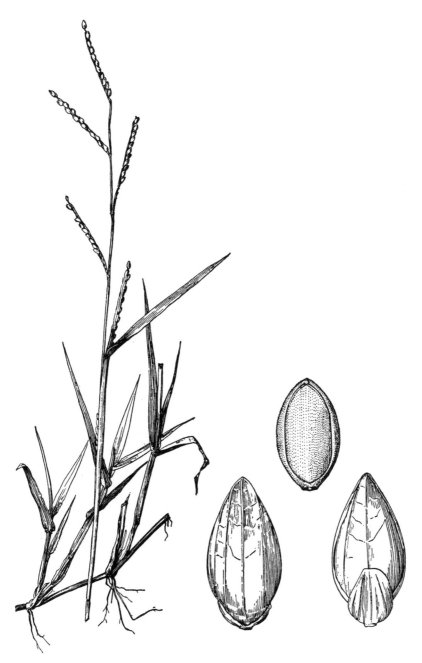

FIG. 220. **Brachiaria platyphylla.** Plant, × ½; two views of spikelet, and floret, × 10.

to 15 mm wide; panicles narrow, 10–20 cm long, with short, appressed-ascending racemes, the central axis and branches pubescent; spikelets fusiform, pilose, about 5 mm long with pointed apex; glumes and sterile lemma conspicuously nerved; 1st glume at least one-half as long as 2nd glume and sterile lemma, or more. *Panicum texanum* Buckley; *Urochloa texana* (Buckley) R. Webster.

Fig. 221. **Brachiaria eruciformis.** Panicle, × 1; two views of spikelet, and floret, × 10.

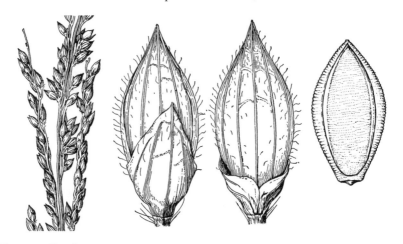

Fig. 222. **Brachiaria texana.** Panicle, × 1; two views of spikelet, and floret, × 10.

Southwestern United States and Mexico, introduced elsewhere.

Missouri. Rare and little known, railroad yards, St. Louis County (Muehlenbach 517 MO), probably not persistent; also roadsides, Dunklin County (Summers 5359 MO). Flowering in summer.

68. ERIOCHLOA Kunth Cupgrass

Annuals and perennials; inflorescence consisting of short, ascending spikelike racemes or contracted panicles; spikelets with 1 perfect floret, sessile or nearly so, solitary or in pairs, forming 2 rows, on one side of the rachis, falling entire; 1st glume *obsolete,* forming with the rachilla joint a thickened ring or minute cuplike structure below the 2nd glume; fertile lemma with convex side *away* from rachis, indurate, with inrolled margins, not flat, awnless or with mucronate tip. *x* = 9; Kranz

Key to Missouri Species

a. Fertile lemma with mucronate tip; inflorescence narrow, contracted ....1. *E. contracta*
a. Fertile lemma lacking prominent tip; inflorescence with spreading branches
    b. Foliage mostly glabrous or with some scattered hairs; internodes glabrous ....
    ....2. *E. acuminata*
    b. Foliage variably hairy; internodes pubescent ....3. *E. villosa*

1. Eriochloa contracta Hitchc. PRAIRIE CUPGRASS. Fig. 223.

Annual, forming small tufts; culms, decumbent at base, 30–80 cm tall; leaf blades soft, lax, short-pubescent, 3–7 mm wide; inflorescence strict with short, appressed, overlapping branches 1–2 cm long; spikelets ovate-oblong, pointed, pubescent, 3–5 mm long; glume tapering to awnlike tip; fertile lemma with abrupt tip, the awnlike projection about 1 mm long.

Southwestern United States, north and east to Colorado and Nebraska; widely scattered elsewhere.

Missouri. Low ground, creek banks, and levees, scattered but not common, Jackson, Ray, Boone, Pike, St. Louis, and Pemiscot Counties. Flowering in July–August.

2. Eriochloa acuminata (C. Presl) Kunth var. **acuminata** Fig. 224.

Annual, mostly coarser than no. 1; culms branching to 1 m tall, decumbent at base; foliage mostly glabrous, the leaf blades to 1 cm wide or more; inflorescence branches spreading, 2–5 cm long, the main axis with short, soft pubescence; spikelets elliptic-pointed, somewhat pubescent, 4–6 mm long; 2nd glume tapering to narrow, sharp-pointed tip; fertile lemma smooth, elliptic, with minute tip. *E. gracilis* (Fourn.) Hitchc.

Southwestern United States and Mexico to Oklahoma, introduced elsewhere.

Missouri. Open ground, Mississippi County (Steyermark 79553), and recently collected along roadside 1 mile north of Rt. Y at I-55, Pemiscot County (McKenzie 1099 MO); probably more common than previously noted.

Specimens with spikelets less than 4 mm long and mostly pubescent foliage are separated from typical *acuminata* as var. *minor* (Vasey) R.B. Shaw, a weedy adventive in the Southwest, not reaching Missouri (Shaw & Webster, 1987).

3. Eriochloa villosa (Thunb.) Kunth Fig. 225.

Annual, culms to 1 m tall, erect, sometimes decumbent near the base, mostly pubescent, rooting at the nodes; sheaths somewhat inflated and partially enveloping inflorescence; leaf blades to 1 cm wide; inflorescence elongate, narrow, the main branches hairy, mostly ascending, 5–7 cm long; spikelets broadly elliptic, 5–6 mm long; cuplike structure noticeably yellow; 2nd glume and sterile lemma about equal,

FIG. 223. **Eriochloa contracta.** Panicle, × 1; floret, × 10.

Fig. 224. **Eriochloa acuminata** var. **acuminata**. Plant, × ½; two views of spikelet, and floret, × 10.

 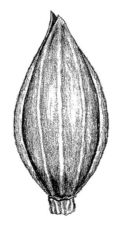 

FIG. 225. **Eriochloa villosa.** Two views of spikelet, and floret, × 10.

sparsely pubescent or puberulent; fertile lemma 3.5–4 mm long, with inrolled margins.

Introduced to United States from eastern Asia.

Missouri. Rare and little-known adventive, fields and open ground, Audrain (Dierker 1802 IPM/UMO) and St. Francois (G. & K. Yatskievych 88-213 MO) Counties. Flowering in late summer.

69. PASPALUM L.

Annuals and perennials; inflorescence consisting of 1 to several spicate racemes or branches along the flower stalk, or sometimes in conjugate pairs at apex; spikelets awnless, with 1 perfect floret, mostly plano-convex, ovate, broad-elliptic to orbicular, solitary or in pairs, subsessile, in 2 or 4 rows on one side of flattened to broadly winged rachis; at maturity, disarticulation below the glumes, the spikelets falling entire; 1st glume usually wanting or minute; 2nd glume and sterile lemma about equal, sometimes with conspicuous nerves; fertile lemma with convex back toward the rachis (adaxial), smooth, indurate, the inrolled margins encircling palea. $x = 10, 12$; Kranz.

Paspalum, with approximately 330 species, is widely distributed in the warm, humid regions of the world, concentrated in the American tropics.

Key to Missouri Species

a. Rachis distinctly winged, as wide or wider than individual spikelets
   b. Racemes numerous, 15–20 or more, the rachis extending beyond the terminal spikelet ..
   ....1. *P. fluitans*
   b. Racemes usually 5 or less on each stalk, the rachis not extended.................2. *P. dissectum*
a. Rachis not winged, narrower than individual spikelets or, if wider, the spikelets in pairs and arranged in 4 rows on the rachis
   c. Spikelets conspicuously villous, with long, soft hairs
     d. Racemes numerous, 10 or more; spikelets about 2.5 mm long............3. *P. urvillei*
     d. Racemes fewer, less than 10; spikelets 3 mm long or more..............4. *P. dilatatum*
   c. Spikelets mostly glabrous or only short-pubescent to puberulent
     e. Spikelets in 4 rows on the rachis...........................5. *P. pubiflorum* var. *glabrum*
     e. Spikelets in 1 or 2 rows

f. Spikelets somewhat biconvex, distant on rachis; 1st glume sometimes present....................
....6. *P. bifidum*
f. Spikelets plano-convex, generally crowded; 1st glume mostly wanting, sometimes present
  g. Spikelets large, broadly ovate, 3.5 mm long or more ....7. *P. floridanum*
  g. Spikelets obtuse or with pointed apex, to 3 mm long
    h. Spikelets solitary, 2.5–3 mm long
      i. Spikelets obtuse..8. *P. laeve*
      i. Spikelets with acute or pointed apex ....9. *P. distichum*
    h. Spikelets mostly in pairs, 1.5–2.5 mm long..10. *P. setaceum*

1. Paspalum fluitans (Elliott) Kunth Water Paspalum. Fig. 226.

Annual, aquatic or terrestrial; culms decumbent, floating or creeping, rooting at the nodes; sheaths inflated, glabrous to papillose-hispid; ligule ciliate, 2–4 mm long; leaf blades thin, soft, 1–2 cm wide; racemes numerous, 2–5 cm long, the rachis winged, tapering to a fine tip *beyond* the terminal spikelet, the whole falling as a unit; spikelets solitary, puberulent, elliptic, about 1.5 mm long. *P. repens* auct. non Bergius.

Virginia to Florida, to Illinois, Kansas, and Texas; also tropical America.

Missouri. Muddy flats, swampy areas, slow-moving water, and wet ground, infrequent and widely scattered, west-central and southern sections, but generally absent from Ozarks region. Flowering in August–September.

2. Paspalum dissectum (L.) L. Fig. 227.

Perennial, decumbent-spreading; culms branching, rooting at the nodes, 20–50 cm long; sheaths somewhat inflated; leaf blades glabrous, narrow-linear, to 5 mm wide; racemes few, 1–5 per floral axis, short, 1–3 cm long, the rachis distinctly foliaceous, leaflike, not extending beyond the terminal spikelet; spikelets solitary, smooth, broad-elliptic, about 2 mm long.

Mid-Mississippi valley to Texas and Gulf region, to Florida and Atlantic Coast.

Missouri. Muddy shores, shallow water, and flats, sporadic and infrequent, Jasper, Howell, and Dunklin Counties. Flowering in late summer.

3. Paspalum urvillei Steud. Vasey Grass. Fig. 228.

Perennial, short-rhizomatous, forming large tufts; culms erect, coarse, 1–2 m tall; sheaths variably glabrous with those near base of culm becoming noticeably

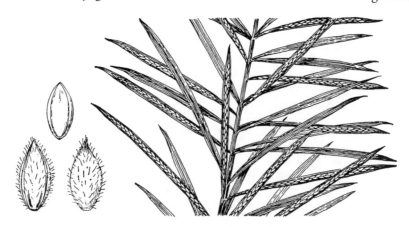

Fig. 226. **Paspalum fluitans.** Panicle, × 1; two views of spikelet, and floret, × 10.

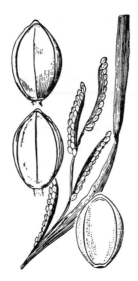

FIG. 227. **Paspalum dissectum.** Panicle, × 1; two views of spikelet, and floret, × 10.

hirsute; ligule conspicuous, to 5 mm long; leaf blades mostly glabrous, elongate, long-tapering, 5–15 mm wide; racemes erect-ascending, overlapping, numerous, to 20 or more on the main flower stalk; spikelets in pairs, ovate-pointed, about 2.5 mm long; 2nd glume and sterile lemma fringed with conspicuous whitish hairs.

Mid-Atlantic and Gulf Coast, from Virginia to Texas, also California; introduced from South America.

Missouri. Rare and little known, railroad freight yards, St. Louis County (Muehlenbach 3070 MO), probably not persistent.

4. Paspalum dilatatum Poir. DALLIS GRASS. Fig. 229.

Perennial, forming tufts or loose sod; culms mostly robust, leafy, erect to somewhat decumbent near base, to 1.5 m tall or more; sheaths glabrous or lower ones variably pubescent; ligule membranous, to 3 mm long; leaf blades mostly glabrous, with tuft of hairs at base; spikelets ovate, acutely pointed, 3–3.5 mm long, arranged closely in 4 rows on the flat rachis; glume and sterile lemma with conspicuous fringe of soft whitish hairs.

Southern United States and Atlantic region, to New York; introduced from South America in last century, becoming an important forage species in warm regions.

Missouri. Rare and little known, railroad freight yards, St. Louis County (Muehlenbach 1355, 1478 MO), probably not persistent, also Newton County (Palmer 66230). Flowering in late summer.

5. Paspalum pubiflorum Rupr. ex Fourn. var. glabrum Vasey ex Scribn. Fig. 230.

Perennial, loosely clumped; culms becoming decumbent at base, rooting at the nodes, to 1 m tall; sheaths mostly glabrous or lower ones somewhat pilose, the hairs with pustular bases; ligule 1–3 mm long; leaf blades mostly glabrous, to 1.5 cm wide; racemes several, generally spreading, about 5–10 cm long; spikelets glabrous, obovate, about 3 mm long, in double pairs, forming 4 rows along the flat rachis, the upper spikelet of each pair sometimes undeveloped.

Southeastern United States and mid-Atlantic region, to Texas.

FIG. 228. **Paspalum urvillei.** Plant, × ½; two views of spikelet, and floret, × 10.

FIG. 229. **Paspalum dilatatum.** Plant, × ½; two views of spikelet, and floret, × 10.

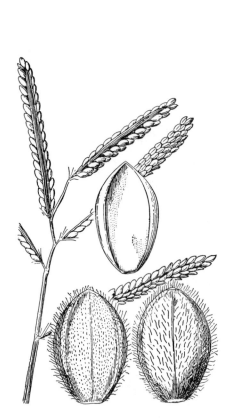

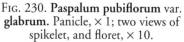

FIG. 230. **Paspalum pubiflorum** var. **glabrum.** Panicle, × 1; two views of spikelet, and floret, × 10.

FIG. 231. **Paspalum bifidum.** Panicle, × 1; two views of spikelet, and floret, × 10.

Missouri. Fields, bottomlands, and damp ground, mainly southern and eastern sections. Flowering in late summer.

The range of typical *pubiflorum* with pubescent spikelets is to the south and east of Missouri.

6. Paspalum bifidum (Bertol.) Nash PITCHFORK PASPALUM. Fig. 231.

Perennial, with short lanate-pubescent rhizomes; culms erect, to 1 m tall or more; sheaths mostly villous; ligule conspicuous, membranous, to 4 mm long; leaf blades variably pubescent, 5–10 mm wide; racemes several, sparsely flowered; spikelets elliptic-obovate, about 3.5 mm long, in pairs, somewhat remote and irregularly spaced on the slender rachis; 1st glume mostly absent or minute, the 2nd glume and sterile lemma with prominent nerves.

Coastal Plain, from mid-Atlantic region to Florida, to Texas, inland to Tennessee, Arkansas, and Oklahoma.

Missouri. Oak-hickory woods on sandy soils of Holly Ridge Conservation Area, Stoddard County (McKenzie & Smith 1520 MO); also sand prairie (Petite Isle), Scott County (McKenzie, Gremaud, & Newman 1480 MO). Flowering in late summer and fall.

7. Paspalum floridanum Michx. Fig. 232.

Perennial, with short rhizomes; culms robust, solitary or forming sparse clumps, to 1.5 m tall or more; sheaths glabrous to variably pubescent; ligule membranous, about 3 mm long; leaf blades mostly glabrous, to somewhat hirsute toward base, 6–10 mm wide, elongate, becoming shorter upward; racemes stiff, coarse, to 10 cm long, 5 or fewer on the central stalk; spikelets large, smooth, suborbicular, about 4 mm long, in pairs or sometimes solitary with the second pedicel present, its spikelet reduced or obsolete.

Plants with increasing pubescence represent typical *floridanum;* those with glabrous foliage, or nearly so, are separated as var. *glabratum* Engelm. ex Vasey.

Southern and eastern United States to Illinois, Kansas, and Texas.

Missouri. Fields and low ground, on moist, sandy soils, widely scattered, south of a line from Vernon to Cape Girardeau Counties, mostly absent from the Ozarks, both varieties equally represented, but not common; var. *floridanum* also reported for Boone, Saline, and Jackson Counties, on I-70 right-of-way. Flowering in August–September.

8. Paspalum laeve Michx. Field Paspalum. Fig. 233a,b.

Perennial, short-rhizomatous, forming tufts; culms erect, to 1 m tall; foliage glabrous to pilose, with keeled or somewhat flattened sheaths, the leaf blades 4–10 mm wide; ligule membranous, 2–3 mm long; racemes several, usually less than 5 to each flower stalk, to 10 cm long; *spikelets mostly solitary,* glabrous, obovate, elliptic-ovate or roundish, 2.5–3 mm long.

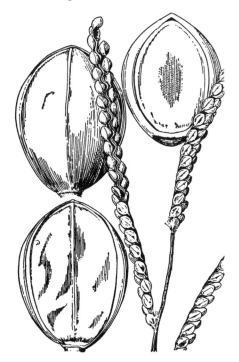

Fig. 232. **Paspalum floridanum.** Panicle, × 1; two views of spikelet, and floret, × 10.

FIG. 233a. **Paspalum laeve** var. **laeve**. Plant, × ½; two views of spikelet, and floret, × 10.

Based on differences in spikelet shape and degree of foliar pubescence, three varieties are recognized for Missouri:

a. Plants identified by generally glabrous sheaths and leaf blades and more or less elliptic-ovate spikelets represent typical *laeve*. (Fig. 233a.)

b. Plants also glabrous, but with more orbicular spikelets are separated as var. *circulare* (Nash) Stone (*P. circulare* Nash). (Fig 233b.)

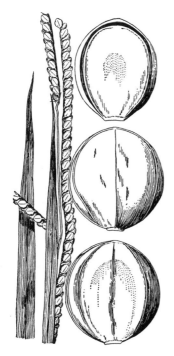

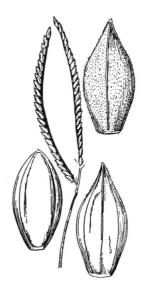

Fig. 233b. **Paspalum laeve** var. **circulare.** Panicle, × 1; two views of spikelet, and floret, × 10.

Fig. 234. **Paspalum distichum.** Panicle, × 1; two views of spikelet, and floret, × 10.

c. Plants with increasing pilosity, with spikelets similar to typical *laeve* are designated as var. *pilosum* Scribn. (*P. longipilum* Nash).

Eastern and southern United States from eastern Texas to southern New England.

Missouri. Upland prairies, woodlands, and spring branches, on moist soils, generally south of a line from Jackson, Shelby, and Lincoln Counties, most common as var. *circulare.* Flowering in mid- to late summer.

9. Paspalum distichum L. KNOTGRASS. Fig. 234.

Perennial, with creeping runners; culms wiry, firm, to 50 cm tall, rooting at the nodes; leaf blades short, 4–8 mm wide, with overlapping sheaths, mostly glabrous or nearly so; inflorescence with 2 conjugate racemes at summit of stalk; spikelets elliptic-pointed, about 3 mm long or more, arranged in a *single* row on a narrow rachis; 1st glume sometimes present, the 2nd with slight pubescence.

Widely distributed from mid-Atlantic and Gulf regions through southern United States to West Coast.

Missouri. Wet banks, ponds, and drainages (Ozark Fisheries, Inc.), Camden County, newly reported for the state (Hudson s.n. MO); well established and probably introduced at a much earlier date. Flowering in summer.

10. Paspalum setaceum Michx. Fig. 235a,b.

Perennial, with short rhizomes, caespitose; culms 40–100 cm tall, foliage glabrous to variably pubescent, from minutely so to densely pilose, or sometimes sparsely long-ciliate; leaf blades 2–15 mm wide or more; racemes slightly curving, 5

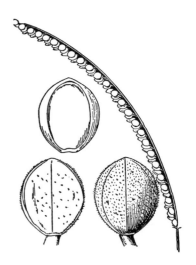

FIG. 235a. **Paspalum setaceum** var. **setaceum.** Raceme, × 1; two views of spikelet, and floret, × 10.

FIG. 235b. **Paspalum setaceum** var. **ciliatifolium.** Raceme, × 1; two views of spikelet, and floret, × 10.

or fewer, sometimes 1, from mostly elongate, slender peduncles, sometimes also axillary; spikelets glabrous to slightly pubescent, ellipsoid to rounded or nearly so, 1.5–2.5 mm broad, mostly in pairs and crowded along the narrow rachis. Incl. *P. ciliatifolium* Michx. (Banks, 1966).

P. setaceum represents a polymorphic complex of intergrading forms with the inclusion of *P. ciliatifolium;* on this basis, four varieties are recognized for Missouri:

a. Plants with varying pilosity of sheaths and leaf blades, combined with mostly single racemes and ellipsoid spikelets, represent typical *setaceum.* (Fig. 235a.)

b. Plants with variably pubescent foliage, 1 to several racemes, and suborbicular spikelets are identified as var. *muhlenbergia* (Nash) D. Banks (*P. ciliatifolium* Michx. var. *muhlenbergia* (Nash) Fern; *P. pubescens* Nash).

c. Specimens with mostly glabrous foliage, sometimes puberulent to sparsely ciliate, with pale yellow-green suborbicular spikelets, 2–2.5 mm wide, are referred to var. *stramineum* (Nash) D. Banks (*P. ciliatifolium* Michx. var. *stramineum* (Nash) Fern; *P. stramineum* Nash).

d. Plants characteristically glabrous or nearly so, having darker, smaller spikelets than *stramineum,* less than 2 mm long, are separated as var. *ciliatifolium* (Michx.) Vasey (*P. ciliatifolium* Michx. var. *ciliatifolium*). (Fig. 235b.)

Atlantic and Gulf regions to Minnesota, Nebraska, and southwestward to Mexico and Central America; also the Caribbean.

Missouri. Dry woods, glades, and prairies; var. *muhlenbergia* widespread throughout the state, var. *stramineum* and var. *ciliatifolium* scattered and infrequent, and var. *setaceum* represented by a single station on Crowley's Ridge, Stoddard County (Steyermark 76726 MO). Flowering in July–August.

70. SETARIA P. Beauv. FOXTAIL

Annuals and perennials; panicles erect to nodding, mostly terminal, spikelike, cylindrical-bristly; spikelets with 1 perfect floret, broadly elliptic, plano-convex, mostly sessile, subtended by hairlike bristles; spikelets separating below the glumes and falling entire, the bristles *remaining* on the rachis; 1st glume to one-half as long as the 2nd glume, the latter and the sterile lemma about equal or sometimes the glume shorter, both awnless; fertile lemma finely to conspicuously rugose, indurate, with inrolled margins; palea equal to lemma. $x = 9, 10$; Kranz.

Key to Missouri Species

a. Perennial, with short, thin, knotty rhizomes; native species............................1. *S. parviflora*

a. Annuals, lacking rhizomes, fibrous-rooted; mostly weedy adventives

    b. Panicles somewhat interrupted, the spikelet clusters, at least on lower axis, in whorls; bristles subtending spikelets retrorsely barbed..2. *S. verticillata*

    b. Panicles more or less continuous, the spikelet clusters not in distinct whorls; bristles smooth or antrorsely barbed

        c. Spikelets subtended by 5 or more bristles; fertile lemma noticeably coarse-rugose ....3. *S. pumila*

        c. Spikelets subtended by fewer bristles, sometimes only 1; fertile lemma mostly smooth or finely rugose

            d. Panicles heavy, to 3 cm thick, with lobulate clusters of spikelets; cultivated species, sometimes an escape ....4. *S. italica*

            d. Panicles narrower, not lobulate; weedy adventives

                e. Panicles about 5 cm long, mostly erect; spikelets about 2 mm long.................. ....5. *S. viridis* var. *viridis*

                e. Panicles much longer, to 10 cm in length, usually nodding; spikelets to 3 mm long ....6. *S. faberi*

1. Setaria parviflora (Poir.) Kerguelen Prairie Foxtail. Fig. 236.

Perennial, with short, knotty rhizomes; culms solitary or few, slender, erect to geniculate, 50–70 cm tall; sheaths keeled, mostly glabrous or with few ciliate hairs on the margins; ligule a short fringe, about 1 mm long; leaf blades mostly glabrous, elongate, 5–7 mm wide; panicles short, 2–5 cm long on long, slender flower stalks with minute pubescence; spikelets 2–3 mm long, exceeded by several tawny bristles with antrorse barbs; fertile lemma with cross wrinkles. *S. geniculata* (Lam.) P. Beauv.

Eastern and southern United States, through lower Midwest to California; also tropical America to Argentina.

Missouri. Moist prairies and low ground, widely scattered, but absent west of a line from Vernon, Johnson, and Putnam Counties, our only native, and perennial, species. Flowering in June–July.

2. Setaria verticillata (L.) P. Beauv. Hooked Bristlegrass. Fig. 237.

Annual, sparsely tufted; culms branching near base, erect to becoming decumbent, to 1 m tall; sheaths mostly glabrous, except lower ones sometimes sparsely pubescent; ligule consisting of cilia about 1 mm long; leaf blades glabrous to ciliate on margins, lax, to 10 mm wide; panicles erect, somewhat interrupted below, the lower clusters of spikelets in distinct whorls; spikelets crowded, about 2 mm long, each subtended by a single bristle to 5 mm long, its barbs retrorse or pointing backward from apex, sometimes antrorse; fertile lemma obscurely rugose or wrinkled.

Plants having bristles with antrorse barbs are separated from typical *verticillata* as var. *ambigua* (Guss.) Parl. (*S. viridis* (L.) P. Beauv. var. *ambigua* (Guss.) Coss. & Durieu).

Widely scattered in the United States, absent northwest, ranging to tropical America; introduced from Europe.

Fig. 236. **Setaria parviflora**, × 1.   Fig. 237. **Setaria verticillata**, × 1.

Missouri. Fields and waste areas, generally distributed, var. *ambigua* known only from St. Louis County (Muehlenbach 1295 MO). Flowering in summer.

3. Setaria pumila (Poir.) Roemer & Schultes Yellow Foxtail. Fig. 238.

Annual, forming loose clumps; culms branching, decumbent near base, to about 1 m tall; sheaths glabrous to sparsely pubescent, the lower ones sharply keeled; ligule a fringe of short hairs; leaf blades glabrous, with few cilia near base, somewhat scabrous on the margins, 5–10 mm wide, tapering to twisted tip; panicles stiff, erect, 5–10 cm long on long peduncles; spikelets about 3 mm long, each exceeded by 5 or more yellowish bristles with antrorse barbs; fertile lemma conspicuously rugose to its apex. *S. glauca* (L.) P. Beauv.

Widely distributed in the United States; adventive from Europe.

Missouri. Cultivated fields, open ground, and waste areas, throughout the state; one of our most common foxtails. Flowering in late June–July.

4. Setaria italica (L.) P. Beauv. Cultivated Foxtail Millet. Fig. 239.

Annual; culms coarse, to 1 m tall or more; sheaths mostly glabrous to slightly pubescent; ligule a fringe of hairs about 1 mm long; leaf blades glabrous to pubescent near base, coarse, 1–2 cm wide; panicles large, lobulate, 3–4 cm thick, to 25–30 cm long, somewhat interrupted near base; spikelets 2–3 mm long, mostly exceeded by a few purplish bristles, separating *above* the glumes and sterile lemma at maturity; fertile lemma mostly smooth or fine-rugose, variously colored, red to yellow or black. Minor variants are recognized, based on color of bristles and fertile lemma, as well as form and relative size of the fruiting panicles.

Widespread in the United States, extensively sown in the Great Plains; introduced in the last century from the Old World as a grain and forage species.

Missouri. Occasionally volunteering in open ground, widely scattered, but gener-

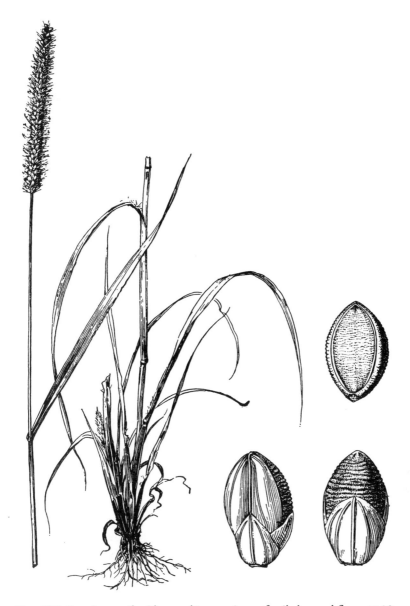

FIG. 238. **Setaria pumila.** Plant, × ½; two views of spikelet, and floret, × 10.

ally not persisting; St. Charles, Cooper, and Miller Counties (McKenzie 1511, 1649, 1672 MO). Flowering in July–August.

5. Setaria viridis (L.) P. Beauv. var. **viridis** GREEN FOXTAIL. Fig. 240.

Annual; culms slender, branching, erect to decumbent-spreading, 20–50 cm tall; sheaths mostly glabrous, sometimes with scattered pubescence; ligule consisting of hairs, 1–1.5 mm long; leaf blades mostly glabrous, about 5–8 mm wide; panicles mostly erect, averaging about 5 cm in length; spikelets about 2 mm long, the 1–3 bristles green, sometimes purplish; fertile lemma obscurely rugose.

Fig. 239. **Setaria italica.** Plant, × ½; floret, × 5.

Fig. 240. **Setaria viridis** var. **viridis,** × 1.

Some plants with thick, lobulate heads, appearing in field situations, but having spikelets disarticulating below the glumes, have been referred to *S. viridis* var. *major* (Gaudin) Pospichal. These are possibly the result of infrequent crosses between nos. 4 and 5 (Pohl, 1966).

Widespread in the United States as a weed species, particularly in the cooler regions; adventive from Europe.

Missouri. Fields, open ground, and waste areas, widely distributed as typical *viridis;* var. *major* reported for St. Louis County (G. & K. Yatskievych 90-272 MO). Flowering in midsummer.

6. Setaria faberi Herrm. Nodding Foxtail. Fig. 241.

Annual; culms tall, coarse, to 1.5 m or more; leaf blades short-pubescent on the upper surface, rarely glabrous, to 1.5 cm wide; ligule consisting of minute hairs; panicles nodding, mostly 10 cm long or more; spikelets 2.5–3 mm long, exceeded by the tawny bristles; fertile lemma rugose, but becoming less so toward the apex.

Widespread in the eastern United States as a weed species; adventive from China and probably introduced as a contaminant of imported millet seed.

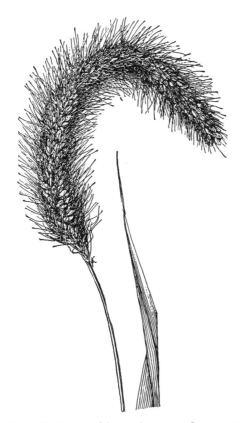

FIG. 241. **Setaria faberi**. Plant, × 1; floret, × 5.

Missouri. Fields, open ground, and waste areas, widely distributed. Flowering in summer.

71. PASPALIDIUM Stapf

Annuals and perennials; inflorescence consisting of short spikelike branches or racemes, appressed-ascending on the central axis, sometimes with distichous secondary branching; spikelet-bearing rachis terminated by a bristlelike tip (in some species, bristles also distributed along the axis); spikelets ovate-elliptic, plano-convex, awnless, with 1 perfect floret, mostly sessile, in a double row on one side of the flattened, sometimes 3-angled rachis, disarticulating below the glumes, falling entire; glumes unequal, the 1st much shorter; 2nd glume and sterile lemma about equal; fertile lemma firm, rugose, with convex side *toward* the rachis; rachilla extending behind the fertile lemma. $x = 9$; Kranz.

1. Paspalidium geminatum (Forssk.) Stapf var. **geminatum** Fig. 242.

Perennial, clump-forming, sometimes with rhizomes; culms erect or decumbent at base, rooting at the nodes, 50–100 cm tall; foliage glabrous, the leaf blades 3–5 mm wide, tapering to involute tip; ligule a short-fringed membrane about 1 mm long; inflorescence narrow, with short, ascending, spikelike racemes 2–3 cm long, somewhat remote on lower axis, the upper becoming shorter and more crowded;

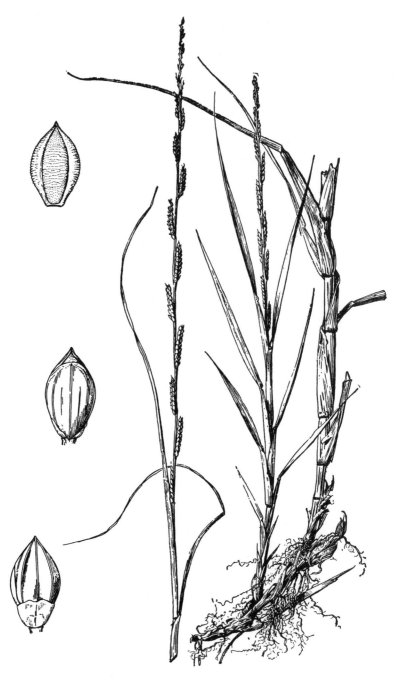

FIG. 242. **Paspalidium geminatum** var. **geminatum**. Plant, × ½; two views of spikelet, and floret, × 10.

spikelets broadly elliptic, 2–2.5 mm long; 1st glume one-fourth the length of 2nd glume, both obtuse, the sterile lemma broadly acute. *Panicum geminatum* Forssk.

The transfer of *Panicum geminatum* to *Paspalidium* is based in part on the 2-seriate arrangement of the sessile spikelets on one side of the rachis terminating in a naked, bristlelike apex (McVaugh, 1983). More recently, Veldcamp (1994), and Webster (1995), joined several species of *Paspalidium* with genus *Setaria* P. Beauv., including *P. geminatum*. In view of no current subgeneric or sectional treatment of *Setaria* to which these species of *Paspalidium* might be transferred, as an alliance distinguishable from previously recognized *Setaria* species, the name *Paspalidium* is provisionally retained.

Introduced in the United States; widely distributed in wet habitats of tropical and subtropical regions of the Old World.

Missouri. Rare and little known, St. Louis County (Muehlenbach 1354 MO).

72. STENOTAPHRUM Trin.

Annuals and perennials; culms decumbent, mat-forming; spreading by stolons or rhizomes, or caespitose; foliage mostly glabrous; inflorescence a short spike, the spikelets partially embedded in a thickened rachis; spikelets awnless, with 1 perfect floret, falling entire with rachis joints; glumes unequal, the 1st much shorter; 2nd glume and sterile lemma about equal. $x = 9$; Kranz.

1. Stenotaphrum secundatum (Walter) Kuntze St. Augustine Grass. Fig. 243.

Perennial, spreading by coarse stolons, forming thick mats; sheaths smooth, folded; ligule short, with fringe of hairs; leaf blades to 1 cm wide, 5–10 cm long, with blunt apex; spikelike racemes with short side branches, terminal or from axils of leaves, mostly less than 10 cm in length; spikelets ovate-oblong, about 5 mm long, on one side of prominent rachis, falling with rachis at maturity; 1st glume about 1 mm long, the 2nd glume and sterile lemma to 5 mm long; fertile lemma shiny, indurate, the margins partially overlapping palea.

Southeastern United States from South Carolina to Texas, Mexico, and tropical America; used as a lawn species in lower South.

Missouri. Rare and little known, a single record, reported as an escape from Stone County (Ellis s.n. MO).

73. DIGITARIA Haller Crabgrass

Annuals and perennials; inflorescence terminal, consisting of several spikelike racemes or branches, digitate to approximate, or an open panicle with diffuse branching; spikelets lanceolate-elliptic, awnless, with 1 perfect floret, short-pedicelled or subsessile, solitary or 2–3 together on one side of rachis, or sometimes single from straight pedicels, falling entire; 1st glume reduced or lacking, the 2nd well developed; sterile lemma conspicuously nerved, equal in length to fertile one, the latter smooth, lacking prominent nerves, with thin, flat margins not inrolled. $x = 9, 15, 17$; Kranz.

Digitaria, numbering approximately 220 species, represents the third largest genus in the tribe Paniceae (after *Panicum* and *Paspalum*). It is widely distributed in the warmer regions of both hemispheres.

FIG. 243. **Stenotaphrum secundatum.** Plant, × ½; two views of spikelet, and fertile floret, × 10.

Key to Missouri Species

a. Inflorescence an open panicle with spreading branches....................................1. *D. cognata*

a. Inflorescence consisting of several digitate or approximate spikelike racemes

    b. Rachis narrow, triangular in cross section ....2. *D. filiformis*

    b. Rachis flat, with winged margins

        c. Foliage mostly glabrous; spikelets about 2 mm long or less ....3. *D. ischaemum*

        c. Foliage variably pilose-pubescent with papillose hairs; spikelets longer than 2 mm

            d. Spikelets to 2.5–3 mm long; foliage conspicuously pilose; common species ....
            ....4. *D. sanguinalis*

            d. Spikelets somewhat larger; foliage sparsely hairy; rare species ....5. *D. ciliaris*

1. Digitaria cognata (J.A. Schultes) Pilger FALL WITCH GRASS. Fig. 244.

Plants tufted; culms with leafy bases, stiffly erect, 30–70 cm tall; lower sheaths mostly pilose; ligule membranous, about 1 mm long; leaf blades pale green, 2–5 mm wide, tapering to fine tip; panicles erect, diffuse, with divergent branching, at maturity separating as a tumbleweed; spikelets elliptic-pointed, purplish, about 3 mm long, on elongate pedicels to 5–7 cm in length; fertile lemma smooth, shiny, about 2 mm long; palea similar to lemma (*Leptoloma cognatum* (J.A. Schultes) Chase) (Webster, 1987).

Eastern and southern United States, west to Minnesota, to Arizona and northern Mexico.

Missouri. Fields, waste ground, and glades, on dry soils, generally distributed. Flowering in June–July.

2. Digitaria filiformis (L.) Koeler Fig. 245.

Annual; culms slender, erect, branching from the base, to about 50 cm or taller; lower sheaths variably pubescent; leaf blades 1–4 mm wide; inflorescence consisting of 1–5 delicate racemes of varying length, subdigitate or remote; rachis triangular, about 0.5 mm wide; spikelets in twos or threes, ovate, 1.5–2.5 mm long; 1st glume absent, the 2nd about three-fourths as long as the sterile lemma; fertile lemma dark.

Coarse plants occasionally exceeding 1 m in height, with densely pilose lower sheaths and spikelets mostly exceeding 2 mm, are separated from typical *filiformis* as var. *villosa* (Walt.) Fern. (*D. villosa* (Walt.) Pers.).

Eastern and central United States, to Kansas, Texas, and Mexico.

Missouri. Open ground, thin woods, and prairies, mainly central and southern counties as typical *filiformis;* var. *villosa* scattered and less common. Flowering in July–August.

3. Digitaria ischaemum (Schreb.) Muhl. SMOOTH CRABGRASS. Fig. 246.

Annual; culms spreading, branching, rooting at the nodes, 20–50 cm (–1 m) tall; foliage glabrous; ligule membranous, about 1.5 mm long; inflorescence consisting of 1 to several racemes, digitate or approximately so; rachis about 1 mm wide, winged; spikelets usually in pairs, ovate, 2 mm long; 1st glume generally absent, the 2nd equal to spikelet length; fertile lemma smooth, dark purplish or blackish.

Robust plants, to 1 m in height, and with numerous racemes are referred to var. *mississippiensis* (Gattinger) Fern., possibly a growth form.

Widespread in the United States, most common in the eastern areas; introduced from Eurasia.

Missouri. Fallow ground, lawns, and gardens, generally distributed. Flowering in midsummer, usually somewhat earlier than the following species.

4. Digitaria sanguinalis (L.) Scop. Fig. 247.

Annual; culms branching, spreading, and rooting at the nodes, to 50 cm or taller; foliage extensively pilose-pubescent, the leaf blades soft, 5–10 mm wide; ligule membranous, about 3 mm long; racemes spikelike, with winged rachis about 1 mm wide; spikelets usually in pairs, elliptic-pointed, averaging 3 mm long; 1st glume minute or obsolete, the 2nd about one-half the spikelet length; sterile lemma strongly nerved, with distinct bristlelike hairs on margin; fertile lemma glabrous, straw-colored.

Widespread in the United States, most common in the east and south; introduced from Europe.

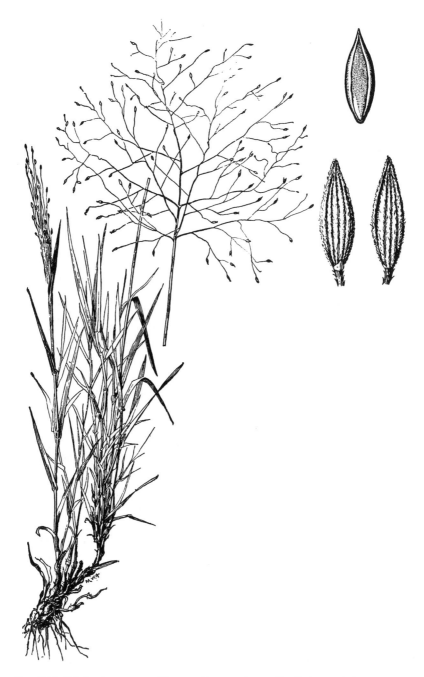

FIG. 244. **Digitaria cognata.** Plant, × ½; two views of spikelet, and floret, × 10.

FIG. 245. **Digitaria filiformis.** Plant, × 1; spikelet and floret, × 10.

FIG. 246. **Digitaria ischaemum.** Plant, × 1; spikelet and floret, × 10.

Missouri. Fields, lawns, and waste ground, generally distributed. Flowering in July–August.

5. **Digitaria ciliaris** (Retz.) Koeler SOUTHERN CRABGRASS.

Annual; similar in general habit to no. 4; foliage sparsely pubescent to becoming glabrous; spikelets to 3.5 mm long; 2nd glume usually more than one-half the spikelet length; sterile lemma not strongly nerved, bristlelike hairs on margin variably present or absent. *Digitaria sanguinalis* (L.) Scop. var. *ciliaris* (Retz.) Parl.

D. sanguinalis, no. 4, is a tetraploid, and *D. ciliaris* is a hexaploid; the latter has a more southerly range (Webster, 1987).

Eastern and southern United States from Virginia to Nebraska and Texas, to Mexico and South America.

Missouri. Fields, lawns, and waste ground, sporadic and widely scattered. Flowering in summer and fall.

74. PENNISETUM L.C. Rich. ex Pers.

Annuals and perennials, the latter forming clumps from hard bases or sometimes spreading by stolons or rhizomes; inflorescence a spicate panicle, cylindrical to short-oblong, mostly terminal, sometimes developing from leafy axillary branches; spikelets with an involucre of simple or plumose bristles fused only at the base, falling entire; 1st glume reduced or wanting, the 2nd glume and sterile lemma about equal or the latter variably longer; fertile lemma shiny, somewhat firm, the thin margins enveloping the palea. $x = 9$; Kranz.

Fig. 247. **Digitaria sanguinalis.** Plant, × ½; two views of spikelet, and floret, × 10.

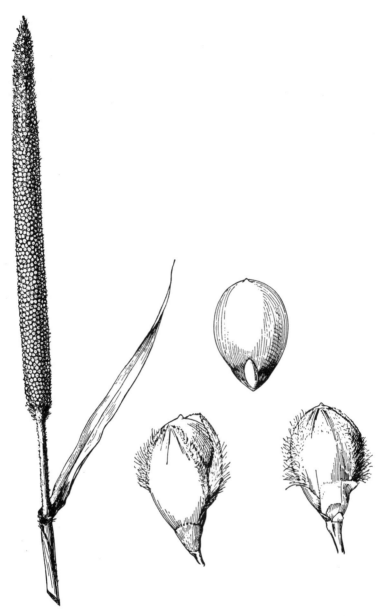

FIG. 248. **Pennisetum glaucum.** Panicle, × ½; two views of spikelet, and grain, × 10.

1. **Pennisetum glaucum** (L.) R. Br. PEARL MILLET. Fig. 248.

Annual; flowering culms robust, leafy, to 2 m tall or more; leaf blades 4–5 cm wide with cordate base; panicle dense, elongate-cylindrical, about 2 cm thick on a heavy, conspicuously villous axis; spikelets plump, obovate, 3–4.5 mm long, in fascicles of 2, not exceeded by the bristles of the involucre; mature grain smooth, emergent from lemma and palea. *P. americanum* (L.) Leeke.

Warm latitudes of Africa and Asia; introduced as a forage and grain species in the southern United States.

Missouri. Roadsides and waste ground as an escape, Howell County (Summers 7280 MO).

75. CENCHRUS L.

Annuals and perennials, erect to weak-stemmed or decumbent; inflorescence consisting of clusters of loose racemes of burlike involucres more or less sessile and falling readily; each bur representing variable connation of bristles or spines derived from much-reduced, sterile branchlets; spikelets awnless, ovate to ovate-acuminate, 1 or more enclosed in each bur, with 1 perfect floret; glumes unequal, the 1st 1-nerved, the 2nd glume and sterile lemma several-nerved; palea of sterile floret usually exceeding its lemma; lemma of fertile floret with inrolled margins about equal to palea. $x = 9, 12$; Kranz. *Pennisetum* L.C. Rich., in part.

1. Cenchrus longispinus (Hackel) Fern. SANDBUR. Fig. 249.

Annual; culms branching, spreading from the base, about 50 cm long; sheaths mostly glabrous, keeled, somewhat inflated; leaf blades smooth to scabrous, 3–6 mm wide; racemes consisting of several burs loosely spaced; burs hard, subglobose, about 5 mm in diameter, with numerous sharp spines; spikelets 1–2 within each bur, ovate-acuminate, the tips protruding. *C. pauciflorus* Benth. of early manuals, misapplied to our taxon.

True *C. pauciflorus,* a later synonym of *C. incertus* M.A. Curtis, is a Coastal Plain species ranging from Virginia to Texas, differing from *C. longispinus* by the relatively few spines of the involucre.

Wide-ranging in the United States and adjacent parts of Canada; also Mexico to South America.

Missouri. Alluvial banks and open ground, on sandy soils, generally distributed. Flowering in midsummer.

2. Cenchrus ciliaris L. BUFFLEGRASS. Fig. 250.

Perennial; culms erect to somewhat reclining, branching at base to 1 m tall; sheaths glabrous to sparsely pubescent, compressed or keeled; blades about 5–10 mm wide; inflorescence spikelike, elongate, 1–2 cm wide; burs purplish, with bristles to 1 cm long, mostly free, fused only at base to form a weak involucre; spikelets ovoid, 2–4 in each bur (fascicle), to 5 mm long. *Pennisetum ciliare* (L.) Link.

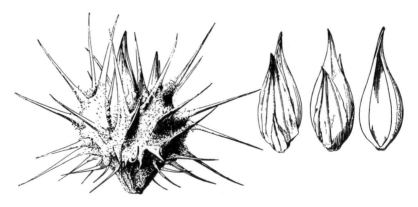

FIG. 249. **Cenchrus longispinus.** Bur, two views of spikelet, and floret, × 5.

Fig. 250. **Cenchrus ciliaris.** Inflorescence, spikelet cluster (bur), and spikelet. (Reprinted from *The Grasses of Texas,* by Frank Gould, by permission of the Texas A&M University Press.)

The transfer of *P. ciliare* to genus *Cenchrus* is based mainly on the slight fusion of the bristles to form an involucre, and their relatively greater width compared to *Pennisetum* (DeLisle, 1963). The bur characteristics of *longispinus* and *ciliare* thus represent a considerable range of variation within the generic limits as currently interpreted.

Introduced in the United States from subcontinental Asia or Australia, possibly in imported wool.

Missouri. Rare and little known, collected from waste ground as *Pennisetum ciliare,* railroad freight yards, St. Louis County (Muehlenbach 1762 MO), probably not persistent.

TRIBE 18. ANDROPOGONEAE

76. SACCHARUM L.

Tall, robust perennials; inflorescence terminal, a conspicuous panicle, broad, soft-woolly, to narrow, more strict, not woolly, the racemelike branches with jointed rachis, fragmenting at maturity; spikelets in pairs, *both* with 1 perfect flower, awned or awnless, the lower one sessile, the upper one pedicellate; spikelets falling entire, the upper one separating from its pedicel, the sessile one falling intact with rachis joint and pedicel. *x* = 5, 10, 12; Kranz. *Erianthus* Michx.

North American authors traditionally recognized *Erianthus* as separate from *Saccharum*. A distinguishing criterion was the awned fertile lemma in the former, particularly for the native species. Presently there is consensus among most taxonomists that separation of these genera on the basis of awned and awnless forms is an artifact of convenience not reflecting a natural dichotomy, and therefore *Erianthus* should be joined with *Saccharum* (Webster & Shaw, 1995).

Key to Missouri Species

a. Awn of fertile lemma about 5 mm long or less; introduced species.................1. *S. ravennae*
a. Awn of fertile lemma 1 cm or more in length; native species
    b. Spikelets with callus hairs few or lacking..2. *S. baldwinii*
    b. Spikelets with copious callus hairs
        c. Awn of fertile lemma flat, becoming twisted, about 1 cm long.....3. *S. alopecuroideum*
        c. Awn of fertile lemma terete, mostly straight, about 2 cm long or more ....
        ....4. *S. giganteum*

1. Saccharum ravennae (L.) L. RAVENNA GRASS.

Plants developing large clumps with elongate, arching leaves; flowering culms hirsute, coarse, 2.5–3 m tall; panicles woolly, silvery, to 50 cm long, 20–30 cm broad. *Erianthus ravennae* (L.) P. Beauv.

Introduced from Mediterranean region as an ornamental, an escape in widely scattered areas.

Missouri. Open ground, on thin soils with dolomite outcrops, highway right-of-way between I-270 and Cragwold Road north of bridge over interstate, St. Louis County (G. & K. Yatskievych 93-323 MO). Flowering in late summer through fall.

2. Saccharum baldwinii Spreng. NARROW PLUMEGRASS. Fig. 251.

Plants forming narrow clumps, from a knotty base; culms slender, 1–2 m tall; nodes with stiff, brownish hairs; sheaths and leaf blades mostly glabrous, the latter about 1 cm wide; panicles brownish, narrow-elongate, with stiffly ascending branches; spikelets somewhat scabrous, 7–10 mm long, with few short hairs at base or none; rachis joint and rachis merely scabrous; lemma with terete, straight awn about 2 cm long. *Erianthus strictus* Baldwin.

A wetland species of the southeastern United States (except sandy coastal plain) north to Tennessee and Missouri.

Missouri. Rare and little known; swampy ground, Dunklin County (Bush 6384 MO). Flowering in late summer.

3. Saccharum alopecuroideum (L.) Nutt. SILVER PLUMEGRASS. Fig. 252.

Plants from thick, heavy rhizomes; culms robust, 1–3 m tall; nodes with villous hairs; leaf blades glabrous or sparsely pilose near base, 1–2 cm wide with conspicuous

FIG. 251. **Saccharum baldwinii**, × ½.

FIG. 252. **Saccharum alopecuroideum**,
× ½.

midrib; panicles dense, woolly, silky-brown, about 25 cm long; upper part of flower stalk appressed-pubescent; spikelets 5 mm long, densely tufted at the base with shiny callus hairs much exceeding the spikelet; rachis joint and pedicel long-villous; awn of fertile lemma flattened, becoming loosely twisted, about 10 mm long or more. *Erianthus alopecuroides* (L.) Elliott.

Southeastern United States and mid-Atlantic region to Oklahoma and Texas.

Missouri. Open woods and sandy prairies, mostly scattered in the southern Ozarks and Bootheel area, south of a line from Barry, Shannon, Reynolds, and Cape Girardeau Counties. Flowering in late summer.

4. **Saccharum giganteum** (Walter) Pers. GIANT PLUMEGRASS. Fig. 253.

Plants robust, rhizomatous, forming colonies, the flowering culms to 3 m tall, with villous nodes; sheaths sparsely pubescent, becoming conspicuously villous at summit and around collar, leaf blades somewhat hispid, 1–2 cm wide, elongate, panicles tawny to purplish, elliptic-oblong, to 50 cm long, the stalk noticeably villous below the inflorescence; spikelets 7–8 mm long with dense, light-brown callous hairs; awn of lemma terete, mostly straight, about 2 cm long. *Erianthus giganteus* (Walter) P. Beauv.

Southern and eastern United States to New York, Kentucky, Arkansas, and Texas.

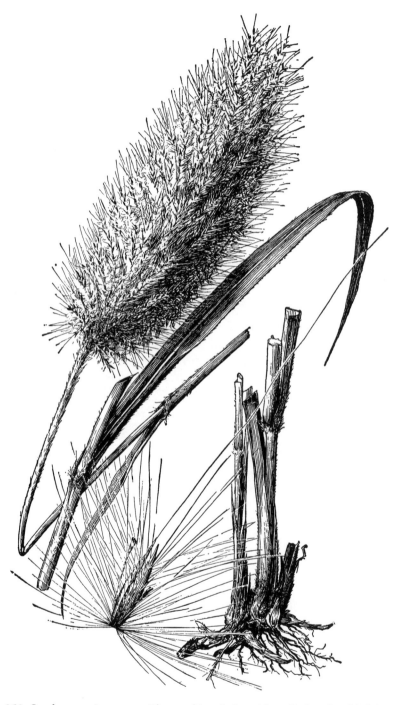

FIG. 253. **Saccharum giganteum.** Plant, × ½; spikelet with pedicel and rachis joint, × 5.

Missouri. Recently collected on low, damp ground, growing in extensive colonies, Butler County (Hudson 331 MO), a new record for the state. Flowering in late summer and fall.

77. MISCANTHUS Anderss.

Perennials; inflorescence a terminal, plumelike panicle of numerous silky racemes on a continuous, *nonfragmenting* rachis, corymbiform (fan-shaped) or subdigitate, to more elongate; spikelets in pairs, similar and pedicellate, *both* with 1 perfect floret, awned or awnless; at maturity the spikelets each falling entire, their pedicels remaining on the rachis. *x* = 19; Kranz.

1. Miscanthus sinensis Anderss. EULALIA. Fig. 254.

Plants developing large clumps, with thick rhizomes; culms leafy, erect, 2–2.5 m tall; leaf blades coarse, elongate to 1 cm wide, variegated to nonvariegated, with scarious margins; panicles corymbose, with leafy axis, whitish brown to purplish brown, the racemes numerous, subdigitate or approximate, 10–20 cm long; spikelets 4.5–5 mm long, with conspicuous tuft of soft hairs at base; lemma with delicate awn.

Plants with grayish brown panicles and variegated leaf blades include var. *zebrinus* (Nikolson) Nakai with white or pale crossbands, commonly called zebra grass, and var. *variegatus* (Beal) Nakai with lengthwise markings; nonvariegated plants with narrow leaf blades and purplish brown panicles include var. *gracillimus* Hitchc. (*Eulalia japonica* Trin. var. *gracillimus* Grier).

M. floridulus (Labill.) Warb. ex K. Schum. & Lauterb. is a robust species to 3–3.5 m tall, with racemiform, more elongate, panicles and somewhat smaller spikelets than *M. sinensis.*

These taxa are from eastern Asia, introduced as ornamentals in landscaping, and are occasionally observed as escapes.

Missouri. M. sinensis, Warren County (Steyermark & Branson 132195 MO); a collection identified as *M. floridulus,* St. Louis County (Muehlenbach 860 MO), is *M. sinensis;* a specimen from Platte County (Pattison 65-10 UMKC) reported as *M. floridulus* is *M. sinensis.*

2. Miscanthus sacchariflorus (Maxim.) Franch.

Perennial, spreading vigorously by creeping rhizomes; culms leafy, 1–5 m tall; leaf blades mostly glabrous, light green, 1–2 cm wide; panicles somewhat loose, feathery, shiny-white; spikelets 4–5 mm long, with unequal pedicels and long silky hairs at base; lemma awnless.

Widely scattered adventive from eastern Asia, forming invasive colonies in some localities as in southeastern Iowa; sometimes cultivated as an ornamental.

Missouri. Sporadic, collected as an escape in Johnson County (Delozier 1315 MO), Callaway County (T48N, R10W, NE ¼, S27), and more recently from a large population on I-70, Wentzville exit, St. Charles County (McKenzie 1490 MO). Flowering in mid- to late summer.

78. MICROSTEGIUM Nees

Annuals; inflorescence consisting of 2 to several subdigitate racemes (occasionally only one); rachis articulate; spikelets in pairs, 1 sessile, the other on short pedicel, *both* perfect with 1 fertile floret; at maturity, spikelets separating below glumes, the

Fig. 254. **Miscanthus sinensis.** Plant, much reduced; raceme, × ½; spikelet, × 5.

pedicel and rachis joint falling with sessile spikelet; fertile lemma awnless. $x = 10$; Kranz. *Eulalia* Kuntze.

1. Microstegium vimineum (Trin.) A. Camus Fig. 255.

Plants with sprawling habit, rooting at the nodes, the culms becoming much branched, 50 cm tall, more or less; sheaths mostly glabrous, sparsely hairy at summit; ligule with few cilia; leaf blades lanceolate-elliptic, 5–10 mm wide, 5–7 cm long; spikelets about 5 mm long; glumes firm, about equal to spikelet length; fertile lemma thin, awnless. *Eulalia viminea* (Trin.) Kuntze.

Southern and east-central United States, widely scattered; adventive from Asia.

Missouri. Low woods and creek banks, infrequent and scattered, Oregon County (Summers & Dodd 3920 MO), also Butler and St. Louis Counties. Flowering in late summer and fall.

79. SORGHUM Moench

Annuals or perennials; inflorescence a terminal panicle with relatively open to compact branching; spikelets in pairs (in threes at the end of each raceme, 2 spikelets of which are pedicellate), the lower spikelet of each pair sessile, perfect, awned, the upper one pedicellate, staminate or sterile, awnless; at maturity spikelet pair falling intact with rachis joint. $x = 5$; Kranz.

The true sorghums are warm-season grasses from the Old World, largely concentrated in eastern Africa and Asia Minor, several of which have been introduced as forage and grain crops in the United States. Under certain weather conditions, such as drought or early frost, that cause a buildup of toxic properties, several sorghums are known to cause prussic acid poisoning in livestock.

1. Sorghum bicolor (L.) Moench GRAIN SORGHUMS, SUDAN GRASS. Fig. 256.

Annuals; culms stout, leafy, 1–3 m tall; sheaths mostly glabrous; ligule 3.5–5 mm long, membranous, with ciliate margin; leaf blades glabrous, to 2–5 cm wide; panicles highly variable, 10–30 cm long, with spreading or drooping branches to dense, compact; sessile spikelets plump, 5–6 mm long, with geniculate awn; pedicellate spikelets similar in size, sometimes narrower than sessile spikelets, mostly awnless. *S. vulgare* Pers.

S. bicolor comprises a complex of subspecies, varieties, and races resulting from cultural selection and spontaneous introgression with wild relatives and "weedy" forms. The well-known grain sorghums such as durra, kafir, and milo, along with broom corn and cane sorghum, are included under ssp. *bicolor;* Sudan grass, widely used as forage, with pyramidal panicles and leaf blades to 1.5 cm wide, is included under ssp. *drummondii* (Steud.) de Wet & Harlan (*S. vulgare* var. *sudanense* Hitch.; *S. sudanense* (Piper) Stapf) (de Wet, 1978).

The sorghums are cultivated over wide areas of the United States.

Missouri. Widely cultivated, sometimes occurring spontaneously in fields and open ground as waifs.

2. Sorghum halepense (L.) Pers. JOHNSON GRASS. Fig. 257.

Perennial, forming extensive stands, spreading aggressively by rhizomes; culms coarse, leafy, 1–2 m tall or more; sheaths mostly glabrous, compressed; ligule conspicuous, ciliate-membranous, about 5 mm long; leaf blades mostly glabrous or becoming pubescent near base, 1–2 cm wide or more; panicles pyramidal, conspicuous;

FIG. 255. **Microstegium vimineum**, × 1.

FIG. 256. **Sorghum bicolor.** Spikelet pair with rachis joint, × 5.

to 30–40 cm long; fertile (sessile) spikelets ovoid, about 5 mm long, with geniculate awn 10–15 mm long, twisted in lower part; pedicellate spikelets lanceolate, usually staminate, not awned.

Widespread throughout the United States; introduced from southern Europe in the early nineteenth century.

Missouri. Open ground, roadsides, and cultivated fields, generally distributed, a noxious weed in some areas. Flowering in summer.

80. SORGHASTRUM Nash

Perennials; inflorescence a terminal panicle, consisting of numerous jointed racemes or branches, fragmenting at maturity; spikelets arranged in pairs, the lower one sessile, with 1 perfect floret, its lemma awned; the upper spikelet reduced to a hairy pedicel; perfect spikelet, pedicel, and rachis joint falling together. $x = 10$; Kranz.

1. Sorghastrum nutans (L.) Nash. INDIAN GRASS. Fig. 258.

Plants forming dense clumps, from short rhizomes; flowering culms erect, to 2.5 m tall; sheaths glabrous to sparsely pilose; ligule conspicuous, rigid, 3–5 mm long; leaf blades mostly glabrous, elongate, 5–10 mm wide, somewhat narrowing toward base; panicles light brownish, shiny, 15–25 cm long, with numerous, delicate branches, each with 1 to several spikelets; sessile spikelets hirsute, 7–8 mm long, with bent, twisted awn to 10 mm in length or more; sterile pedicels and rachis joints with stiff, brownish hairs.

Widespread in the United States, from New England to Florida, to North Dakota and Arizona; also Mexico and adjacent parts of Canada.

Missouri. Upland prairies, glades, open woods, and old fields, generally distributed. Flowering in late summer, the anthers bright yellow, conspicuous.

FIG. 257. **Sorghum halepense.** Plant, × ½; two views of spikelet pair, × 5.

FIG. 258. **Sorghastrum nutans.** Plant, × ½; spikelet with pedicel and rachis joint, × 5.

81. BOTHRIOCHLOA Kuntze

Annuals and perennials; inflorescence a variable panicle consisting of several to many branches, these sometimes with shorter secondary branches, terminal, sometimes also axillary; spikelets in pairs, the lower one sessile with 1 perfect floret, its lemma awned; the pedicellate spikelet of similar size but staminate or neuter, awnless; both spikelets separating below the glumes; 1st glume of sessile spikelet in some forms with 1 to several pits or circular depressions; rachis joint and pedicel with translucent central groove, falling with sessile spikelet. $x = 10$; Kranz. *Andropogon* L., in part.

1. Bothriochloa bladhii (Retz.) S.T. Blake Australian Bluestem. Fig. 259.

Perennial, forming tufts or clumps; culms 50–100 cm tall, with bearded nodes; sheaths mostly glabrous; leaf blades glabrous to sparsely pilose, about 5 mm wide more or less; panicles to 10 cm long with simple branching about 5 cm long; both spikelets of pair 3–4 mm long, similar in shape; lemma of fertile floret (sessile spikelet) with short awn 1–2 mm long. *Bothriochloa intermedia* (R. Br.) A. Camus; *Andropogon intermedius* R.Br.

Introduced forage species in the southern United States; native to subtropical Asia and Australia.

Missouri. Infrequent adventive, waste ground and disturbed areas, Howell County (Bennett 901 UMO), also Warren, Cole, Taney, and Newton Counties. Flowering in summer.

2. Bothriochloa laguroides (DC.) Herter ssp. **torreyana** (Steud.) Allred & Gould Silvery Beardgrass. Fig. 260.

Perennial, forming dense tufts; culms leafy, branching from middle and lower nodes, somewhat decumbent near base, to about 1 m tall; sheaths glabrous to sparsely pilose at summit; ligule conspicuous, about 3 mm long; leaf blades mostly glabrous with glaucous cast, 3–8 mm wide; panicles silvery-pubescent, dense, 5–9 cm long, on extended peduncles, also on shorter stalks from lower nodes; sessile spikelets 4–5 mm long, with bent awn; pedicellate spikelets reduced; pedicel and rachis joint long-villous; awn of fertile lemma 10–15 mm long, twisted below. *Andropogon saccharoides* Sw. var. *torreyanus* (Steud.) Hack.

South-central United States from Alabama to Arizona and Colorado.

Missouri. Upland prairies, limestone bluffs, roadsides, and disturbed areas, on dry soils, scattered throughout the central and southern sections, adventive northward to Boone, Jackson, St. Louis, and St. Charles Counties. Flowering in July–September.

82. ANDROPOGON L.

Perennials; inflorescence consisting of articulate spikelike or feathery racemes, digitate to somewhat paniculate, terminal or axillary, sometimes enclosed in conspicuous spathelike sheaths from middle and upper nodes; spikelets in pairs, the lower one sessile with 1 perfect floret, the upper spikelet pedicellate, and staminate, reduced, or obsolete; at maturity, spikelet pair falling as a unit with attached rachis joint; fertile lemma mostly awned. $x = 5, 10$; Kranz.

Andropogon is a cosmopolitan genus of approximately 100 species distributed in the Americas, Africa, Asia, and Australia, many of which are important forage plants in native grasslands and savannas.

FIG. 259. **Bothriochloa bladhii.** Inflorescence, × ¾. (Reprinted from *The Grasses of Texas,* by Frank Gould, by permission of the Texas A&M University Press.)

FIG. 260. **Bothriochloa laguroides** ssp. **torreyana,** × 1.

Key to Missouri Species

a. Racemes 2 to several, digitate, terminal, on extended peduncles, also from axillary branches

  b. Racemes 2 to several, greenish purple..1. *A. gerardi*

  b. Racemes mostly in V-shaped pairs, silvery-gray, feathery...........................2. *A. ternarius*

a. Racemes several, paniculate, included in bracteate or spathelike sheaths from middle and upper nodes

c. Racemes enveloped in congested, inflated sheaths from upper nodes........3. *A. elliottii*
c. Racemes spaced more uniformly along middle and upper culm and axillary branches.
....4. *A. virginicus*

1. Andropogon gerardi Vitman BIG BLUESTEM. Fig. 261.

Plants forming large, conspicuous clumps, from short rhizomes; flowering culms to 2–2.5 m or more; sheaths glabrous or nearly so, becoming pilose toward base of clump; ligule collar-shaped, 1–2 mm long; leaf blades elongate, spreading, to 1 cm wide, glabrous to sparsely ciliate; spikelike racemes 2–5, digitate, 5–10 cm long, from elongate flower stalks, sometimes on abbreviated peduncles from lower sheaths; sessile spikelet about 8 mm long, with bent awn 10–15 mm long, twisted below, the pedicellate spikelet about the same length, awnless; pedicel and rachis variably hirsute. *A. furcatus* Muhl. ex Willd.

Plants with extensive, creeping rhizomes and the spikelet pair having dense yellow hairs on rachis and pedicel are separated from typical *gerardi* as var. *chrysocomus* (Nash) Fern. (*A. chrysocomus* Nash).

Widespread in the United States and southern Canada, west to Utah, Arizona, and Mexico.

Missouri. Prairies, glades, open woods, and roadsides, generally distributed; var. *chrysocomus* limited mainly to southwestern section including McDonald, Newton, and Barry Counties; also Jackson County. Flowering in late summer and fall.

2. Andropogon ternarius Michx. Fig. 262.

Plants forming tufts; culms leafy, branching from upper culm, to 1 m tall; foliage mostly glabrous to sparsely pilose, the leaf blades narrow, 1–3 mm wide, with inrolled margins; spikelike racemes silvery-white, 3–5 mm long, mostly in V-shaped pairs from exserted peduncles, also from lower nodes; sessile spikelets 5–7 mm long, with delicate awn 10–20 mm long; pedicellate spikelet obsolete; pedicel and rachis joint densely villous, both shorter than sessile spikelet.

Southern United States and mid-Atlantic region, west to southern Kansas and Texas.

Missouri. Glades, thin woods, on dry or sandy soils, scattered and infrequent, south of a line from Barton to St. Genevieve Counties. Flowering in late summer.

3. Andropogon elliottii Chapman Fig. 263.

Plants sparsely tufted, the culms 30–70 cm tall; sheaths inflated, conspicuous, congested in spathelike fascicles from the upper nodes, enveloping the feathery racemes on a slender peduncle; the culm internode subtending the fascicle-aggregates densely villous at its summit; sessile spikelets 4–5 mm long with delicate awn 10–15 mm long; pedicellate spikelets reduced, the pedicel and rachis joint long-villous. *A. gyrans* Ashe var. *gyrans*.

Southeastern United States and mid-Atlantic region from New Jersey to Illinois and Texas, to Central America.

Missouri. Old fields, open woods, and glades, on dry soils; southern and eastern Ozarks, north to Boone County. Flowering in late summer and early fall.

4. Andropogon virginicus L. BROOMSEDGE. Fig. 264.

Plants forming dense tufts or clumps; culms simple, sometimes branching from middle to upper nodes, 0.5–1 m tall, sheaths glabrous to pilose, on lower culm noticeably flattened, sharply keeled; ligule ciliate on the margin, less than 1 mm long;

Fig. 261. **Andropogon gerardi.** Plant, × ½; pair of spikelets, × 5.

FIG. 262. **Andropogon ternarius**, × 1.   FIG. 263. **Andropogon elliottii**, × 1.

leaf blades glabrous to somewhat pilose, 3–5 mm wide; racemes flexuous, feathery, from slender peduncles with narrow spathe; sessile spikelets 3–4 mm long, the awn straight awn delicate, about 10–15 mm long; pedicellate spikelets reduced or absent; pedicel and rachis joint long-villous.

Throughout its range, broomsedge exhibits considerable variation in branching of the flowering culm and crowding of the upper sheaths; generally, Missouri plants have more loosely branched culms, compared to increasing aggregation or congestion of floral branches in specimens from eastern and southern parts of the range.

Eastern United States to Kansas and Texas; also Mexico and West Indies.

Missouri. Old fields, waste ground, and sandbars, common and sometimes locally abundant, scattered northward but generally absent in northern quarter of the state. Flowering in late summer and fall; in winter phase, the foliage is tawny to reddish brown, and a conspicuous feature of the landscape where dense stands occur.

83. SCHIZACHYRIUM Nees

Perennials, forming tufts or clumps, with or without rhizomes; inflorescence a jointed, delicate raceme, 1 to each peduncle, fragmenting at maturity; rachis joint broadened upward, hollow at summit; spikelets in pairs, the lower one sessile with 1 fertile floret, the upper spikelet pedicellate, staminate or reduced; at maturity sessile spikelet falling entire, together with attached rachis joint and pedicel; glumes thick, firm, awnless; fertile lemma thin, with short bent awn. $x = 10$; Kranz. *Andropogon* L., in part.

FIG. 264. **Andropogon virginicus.** Plant, × ½; spikelet with rachis joint and pedicel, × 5.

1. **Schizachyrium scoparium** (Michx.) Nash LITTLE BLUESTEM. Fig. 265.

Plant forming leafy tufts, occasionally with short rhizomes; flowering culms to 1 m tall; foliage glabrous to villous, distinctly bluish green in some forms; sheaths compressed-keeled toward base of clump; ligule firm, 1.5 mm long; leaf blades elongate, about 5 mm wide, curling upon drying; racemes delicate, arching, 3–5 cm long; sessile spikelet 4–8 mm long, with bent awn; pedicellate spikelet and rachis joint pubescent, the latter flattened and expanded upward, truncate, with hollow summit; awn of lemma 8–12 mm long, sometimes twisted in lower part. *Andropogon scoparius* Michx.

Widespread in the United States and adjacent parts of Canada.

Missouri. Upland prairies, glades, thin woods, and open ground, on dry soils, generally distributed; one of our most common prairie grasses. A villous form with bluish green foliage occurs in glades of the White River region. Flowering in late summer.

84. ARTHRAXON P. Beauv.

Annuals and perennials; inflorescence consisting of subdigitate to paniculate spikelike racemes, terminal and axillary; spikelets in pairs, the lower one sessile, with 1 perfect floret, the upper, pedicellate one mostly obsolete, sometimes pedicel wanting; fertile lemma awned dorsally from near base; fresh anthers conspicuously reddish purple. x = 9, 10; Kranz.

1. **Arthraxon hispidus** (Thunb.) Makino var. **hispidus** Fig. 266.

Plants annual, low, spreading, matlike, sometimes rooting at lower nodes; sheaths noticeably hispid; leaf blades ovate-lanceolate with cordate base, about 1 cm wide, 2–5 cm long; racemes several, 3–5 cm long, on extended peduncles; spikelets about 5 mm long; glumes firm; lemma thin with short awn from base.

Mostly southeastern United States to Pennsylvania and Louisiana; weedy adventive from eastern Asia.

Missouri. Rare and little known, reported as a waif from St. Louis County (Steyermark s.n. MO), and more recently on open ground, Cape Girardeau, Crawford, and Lincoln Counties. Flowering in late summer.

85. COELORACHIS Brongn.

Perennials; inflorescence a cylindric or compressed spikelike raceme with hard, thickened rachis joints, fragmenting at maturity; spikelets in pairs, both awnless, the lower one sessile, with 1 perfect floret, appressed to recess in rachis, the upper one much reduced, sterile, on short, thick pedicel; spikelet pair falling with rachis joint; 1st or outer glume thick, hard, the inner glume, thin, recessed; fertile lemma hyaline. x = 9; Kranz. *Manisurus* L.

1. **Coelorachis cylindrica** (Michx.) Nash JOINTGRASS. Fig. 267.

Plants tufted, with short rhizomes; culms erect, to 1 m tall; sheaths smooth, rounded on back; leaf blades elongate, about 3 mm wide; racemes pencil-like, articulate, somewhat arching on long peduncles from the nodes; sessile spikelet about 5 mm long, closely appressed to hollow of rachis joint; 1st glume ovate, conspicuously pitted on back; sterile spikelet reduced to a short tip, the pedicel thick. *Manisurus cylindrica* (Michx.) Kuntze.

FIG. 265. **Schizachyrium scoparium.** Plant, × ½; pair of spikelets, × 5.

FIG. 266. **Arthraxon hispidus** var. **hispidus**, × 1.

Southeastern United States, to Missouri.

Missouri. Infrequent and scattered, open ground, Jackson, Barton, and Mississippi Counties, more recently collected in Paint Brush Prairie, Pettis County (Yatskievych 91-123 MO). Flowering in July–August.

86. TRIPSACUM L. GAMAGRASS

Perennials; plants monoecious; inflorescence terminal, axillary, consisting of 1–3 spikes; upper portion of each spike staminate with continuous rachis, falling entire; lower part of rachis pistillate, fragmenting into rachis joints with the imbedded spikelets; staminate spikelets 2-flowered, in pairs, the lower one sessile, the upper one pedicellate; pistillate spikelets with 1 perfect floret, solitary, appressed in the recess of the thickened rachis joint. $x = 9$; Kranz.

1. **Tripsacum dactyloides** (L.) L. EASTERN GAMAGRASS. Fig. 268.

Plant rhizomatous, forming large clumps with elongate, arching leaves; flowering culms 1–2 m tall or more; ligule a fringe of hairs less than 1 mm long; leaf blades coarse, glabrous, with scabrous margins, 1–2 cm wide; terminal spikes 2–3, digitate, as much as 20–25 cm long, the axillary spikes mostly solitary; staminate spikelets about 10 mm long; pistillate spikelets 8–9 mm long, recessed in the rachis joint.

Eastern United States, west to Nebraska and Texas; also West Indies, Mexico, and South America.

Missouri. Swales, low prairies, and damp waste ground, generally distributed but not common, becoming increasingly important as domestic forage. Flowering in June–July.

87. ZEA L. MAIZE, TEOSINTE

Annuals and perennials; plants monoecious, leafy, variably robust; sheaths overlapping, the leaf blades distichous; staminate inflorescence terminal, consisting of paniculate or subdigitate spicate racemes; pistillate inflorescence axillary, a solid, thickened rachis (cob) supporting multiple rows of paired spikelets, the whole

FIG. 267. **Coelorachis cylindrica.** Plant, × ½; two views of rachis joint with fertile and sterile spikelets attached, × 5.

FIG. 268. **Tripsacum dactyloides.** Plant, × ½; pistillate spikelet with rachis joint, and pair of staminate spikelets with rachis joint, × 5.

assembly enclosed in several husklike spathes, or the rachis thin, fragile, with 2 rows of single spikelets in a simple husk; staminate spikelets in pairs, the lower one sessile, the upper pedicellate, on a continuous rachis; the pistillate spikelets paired (in maize) or single (in teosinte), all sessile, each mostly with 1 perfect floret; glumes of pistillate spikelets, thin, papery, much shorter than the mature grain in maize, or the 1st glume and rachis joint indurate and enclosing grain in teosinte. x = 10; Kranz.

1. Zea mays L. MAIZE, INDIAN CORN. Fig. 269.

Maize has been cultivated as an annual plant in the Americas since prehistoric times and is the only important grain to originate in the Western Hemisphere. It includes numerous races and varieties, all sharing a thickened solid rachis (cob) with several rows of kernels.

Zea mexicana (Schrad.) Kuntze, commonly called teosinte, is a close relative of maize with annual habit, growing wild and untended in mountainous areas of southern Mexico and Guatemala. (*Euchlaena mexicana* Schrad.; *Zea mays* L. ssp. *mexicana* (Schrad.) Iltis.) It bears in varying degree a resemblance to the corn plant, having the staminate spikelets in a terminal tassel-like arrangement and the pistillate spikelets arrayed linearly on a diminutive, axillary spike (rachis), the whole producing a few kernels or grains in two ranks, enclosed in a simple husk. Fertile hybrids have been produced between teosinte and maize, the latter also crossed successfully with *Tripsacum.*

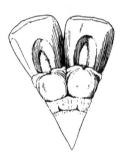

FIG. 269. **Zea mays.** Pair of pistillate spikelets and portion of rachis (cob) with mature grains, and second glumes, × 2.

GLOSSARY

Abaxial. The side away from the central axis.

Acuminate. Pointed, with sides gradually tapering to narrow apex.

Acute. Pointed, short-tapered to apex.

Adaxial. The side near the central axis.

Adnate. Fused or joined, referring to unlike parts, as the seed and ovary wall.

Annual. A plant completing its life cycle in one season. See *winter annual.*

Anther. Pollen-bearing structure of the stamen.

Anthesis. The full opening of the flower.

Antrorse. Pointing upward or forward, as applied to barbs of an awn. See *retrorse.*

Apiculate. With a minute, abruptly pointed apex, not stiff. See *mucronate.*

Appressed. Lying close to axis of surface.

Aristate. Having a minute awn or bristle.

Arm cells. Chlorenchyma cells with projections of inner cell wall extending into the lumina of the cell, characteristic of Bambuseae and related tribes including Oryzeae.

Articulation. Joint of fracture or breaking away, as of a rachis.

Attenuate. Long, narrow-pointed.

Auricle. Ear-shaped appendage, one on each side of sheath summit or base of leaf blade.

Awl-shaped. Narrow, needlelike.

Awn. Slender bristle or hairlike projection from apex or dorsal surface as an extension of the midvein.

Axil. The upper angle formed between a branch or sheath and the main axis.

Axillary. Arising from the axil of a branch, as a lateral or secondary inflorescence.

Axis. The main stem or stalk of the inflorescence or of entire plant.

Bearded. Having a tuft of hairs.

Biennial. A plant with its life cycle completed in two seasons.

Bifid. Two-pointed apex, as in lemmae of *Bromus.*

Bisexual. With both stamens and pistil, referring to perfect flowers.

Blade. In grasses, the part of leaf above its sheath, separated by the collar.

Bract. Generally, a reduced or modified leaf; also refers to the glumes and lemmas of the grass spikelet.

Callus. Pointed, stiff projection at the base of the floret in some grasses including *Stipa* and *Aristida.*

Canescent. With light-colored pubescence.

Capillary. Delicate, hairlike.

Carinate. Forming a keel, flattened laterally, as some grass spikelets.

Caryopsis. The dry, one-seeded fruit of grasses; the mature ovary in which the seed is adnate to the ovary wall. See *grain.*

Cespitose. Growing in tufts or clumps.

Chartaceous. Dry, smooth, thin-textured, or papery.

Chlorenchyma. Thin-walled cells of similar function bearing chlorophyll.

Cilia. Short, usually stiff hairs on the margin.

Ciliate. With fringe of hairs, as on the margins of leaf blades, sheaths, etc.

Cleistogamous. Referring to flowers that remain unopened and are self-fertilized, as in *Danthonia.*

Collar. In grasses, the outside juncture of the leaf blade and its sheath.

Compressed. Flattened, usually forming a keel.

Conduplicate. Folded lengthwise along the midrib, V-shaped, as in the leaf blades of numerous grasses.

Continuous rachis. A rachis that remains intact, not disarticulating.

Contracted inflorescence. An inflorescence that is narrow, with short ascending branches, sometimes dense. See *diffuse inflorescence.*

Culm. The stem of grasses and grasslike plants, characterized by having solid joints or nodes.

Decumbent. Prostrate or touching the ground, as applied mostly to the lower portion of a culm.

Deflexed. Projected downward or backward.

Diffuse inflorescence. An inflorescence that is open, with usually few widespreading branches. See *contracted inflorescence.*

Digitate. Attachment of spikes or racemes from the summit of the main flowering stalk, as in *Digitaria.*

Dioecious. Referring to species in which the staminate and pistillate flowers are borne on separate plants, as in *Buchloe.*

Disarticulating. Separating at a joint when mature, as a rachis, spikelet, or florets on the rachilla. See *continuous rachis.*

Distichous. Two-ranked, referring to leaves in a single plane, alternating on opposite sides of the stalk, as in maize.

Dorsal. Back side, or the side away from the main axis, or abaxial.

Dorsal compression. Referring to spikelets flattened from the dorsal side, not keeled. See *lateral compression.*

Ellipsoid. Elliptic-shaped in 3 dimensions, as a panicle.

Elliptic. Widest in the middle, narrowing to symmetrical ends, referring to a 2-dimensional plane, as a leaf blade.

Erose. Irregular or jagged.

Excurrent. Extending beyond the organ or structure, such as the prolongation of the midvein of the lemma, an awn, or bristle.

Exserted. Extended beyond, as an inflorescence emerging above the summit of its sheath.

Falcate. Tapering as a curving point or apex.

Fasciculate. Closely bunched or in clusters.

Fertile. Producing fruit or grain, referring also to the floret with stamens and pistil. See *perfect.*

Filiform. Threadlike or thin.

Flabellate. Shaped like a fan, as the inflorescence of some *Miscanthus* spp.

Floret. In grasses, the part of the spikelet comprising the lemma, palea, and flower.

Fruit. In grasses, called the *grain* or *caryopsis;* the ripened ovary. See *grain.*

Fusiform. Shaped like a spindle; round in cross-section, tapering toward each end.

Fusoid cells. Large, thin-walled cells of the mesophyll, spindle-shaped in lateral view as observed in transverse section of the leaf blade; characteristic of some bambusoid grasses.

Geniculate. Bent, like a knee, as some awns or lower culms.

Gibbous. Swollen or distended.

Glabrous. Smooth, lacking pubescence of any kind.

Glaucous. With a whitish to bluish green color or coating.

Glomerules. Compact clusters, as an aggregation of spikelets.

Glumes. Lowermost pair of bracts subtending the floret(s).

Grain. The ripened ovary of grasses, sometimes including the lemma and palea that enclose the true fruit or caryopsis.

Habit. Characteristic form of growth; as spreading vs. upright stems, or woody vs. herbaceous.

Habitat. The natural site in which the plant is found.

Hirsute. With mostly slender, somewhat stiff hairs.

Hispid. With rigid, bristly hairs.

Hyaline. Thin or translucent, as some ligules.

Imbricate. Overlapping, as of bracts or sheaths.

Imperfect. Referring to unisexual spikelets with either staminate or pistillate flowers.

Indurate. Hard, firm.

Inflorescence. The flowering part of the plant, as a panicle, raceme, or spike.

Internode. The part of the culm between successive nodes.

Involute. With inrolled margins, as of a leaf blade.

Joint. A section of an articulate rachis; also refers to the swollen node of the culm.

Keel. The ridge or fold formed by the midvein of various structures such as leaf blades, sheaths, glumes, etc.

Kranz syndrome. A set of related anatomical and physiological characters found in C4 plants representing a limited number of plant families including Poaceae; the word *Kranz* refers to the wreathlike or radial arrangement of chlorenchyma cells surrounding the bundle sheath, which is the anatomical basis for partitioning photosynthesis into a two-phase process. See *non-Kranz syndrome.*

Lanate. Woolly-pubescent.

Lanceolate. Narrow-tapering, broadest below the middle.

Lateral compression. Referring to spikelets flattened from the sides, forming the keel at the midvein of the glumes and lemmas as in *Chasmanthium*. See *dorsal compression*.

Lemma. The larger, outer bract of the floret, opposite the palea.

Ligule. In grasses, a membranous or hairy, collarlike appendage at the inside juncture of the leaf blade and sheath.

Lodicules. Minute scales subtending some grass flowers, considered to be vestigial parts of a perianth.

Monoecious. Referring to species with staminate and pistillate flowers on the same plant.

Mucronate. Ending abruptly in a minute, usually stiff tip. See *apiculate*.

Nerve. Vein of a leaf blade or of a bract such as a glume or lemma.

Node. The swollen joint of the culm, where the leaf arises.

Non-Kranz syndrome. The combination of traits in leaf anatomy and physiology characteristic of C3 plants, lacking the radial arrangement of chlorenchyma cells and the division of photosynthesis into two phases typical of C4 plants. See *Kranz syndrome*.

Oblong. Longer than broad, straight-sided, rounded at ends.

Obovate. Broadest above the middle, opposite of *ovate*.

Obsolete. Reduced in size or absent.

Obtuse. Blunt or rounded, as an apex.

Orbicular. Circular in outline.

Ovate. Broadest below the middle, egg-shaped, as a flat surface.

Ovoid. Egg-shaped in 3 dimensions, as an inflorescence.

Ovule. Immature seed, not to be confused with *grain* or *caryopsis*, which is the mature ovary.

Palea. The inner bract of the floret, opposite the lemma, with two lateral veins, lacking a midvein.

Panicle. An inflorescence with compound branching.

Papillose. With minute, pimplelike protuberances at the base of individual hairs, or cilia, as on some leaf blades, sheaths, and spikelets.

Pectinate. The arrangement of spikelets of the rachis similar to teeth of a comb.

Pedicel. In grasses, the stalk of an individual spikelet.

Peduncle. The main stalk of the inflorescence.

Perennial. A plant persisting two or more growing seasons from rootstocks.

Perfect. With both stamens and pistil, referring to bisexual flowers.

Pericarp. The wall of a mature ovary.

Pilose. With soft, straight hairs.

Pistillate. Having a pistil only, lacking stamens.

Plicate. Folded into plaits, usually lengthwise, generally referring to leaf blades.

Plumose. Like the plume of a feather, usually describing awns with delicate side hairs.

Polystichous. Multiple rows, as the grain in maize.

Prophyllum. In grasses, a translucent, sheathlike structure, much reduced, in the axil of the lateral shoot of the axillary branch and main culm, with two lateral veins and lacking a midrib; the first leaf of the axillary branch.

Puberulent. With minute pubescence.

Pubescent. Variable condition of hairiness on different surfaces, as of blades, sheaths, or spikelets.

Pulvinus. In grasses, a glandlike swelling at the base of panicle branches, expanding the inflorescence at maturity.

Pustular. Referring to the minute pimplelike bases of cilia or hairs on foliage and spikelets.

Raceme. In grasses, an inflorescence type consisting of a simple, unbranched axis bearing pedicellate spikelets along its length.

Rachilla. The jointed axis of a grass spikelet on which the florets are borne, sometimes extended as a short stipe beyond uppermost floret.

Rachis. The unbranched axis of a raceme or spike.

Rame. Spikelike branches or racemes bearing spikelets both sessile and with short pedicels.

Retrorse. Pointing backward, as applied to barbs of an awn. See *antrorse.*

Rhizome. A horizontal underground stem that roots at the nodes, producing new plants. See *stolon.*

Rudimentary. Small or imperfectly developed.

Rugose. Wrinkled, as a surface.

Saccate. Baglike, as the second glume of *Sacciolepis.*

Scabrous. Rough to the touch, as the surface of some leaf blades.

Scarious. Thin, membranous, dry, not green.

Secund. Arranged on one side, as spikelets along the rachis.

Serrate. With minute teeth, as the margin of some leaf blades.

Sessile spikelet. A spikelet lacking a pedicel or stalk.

Setaceous. Bristlelike, as an awn.

Sheath. Part of the leaf below the blade that envelops the culm.

Spathelike sheath. Enlarged, somewhat inflated sheath enveloping part of the inflorescence of some grasses.

Spike. In grasses, an inflorescence type consisting of a simple, unbranched axis with sessile spikelets along its length.

Spikelet. In grasses, the basic unit of the inflorescence, consisting of the glumes and one or more florets. See *lemma* and *palea.*

Staminate. Having stamens only, lacking a pistil.

Sterile. Lacking both stamens and pistil.

Stipe. A minute stalk.

Stipitate. With a short stipe.

Stolon. A horizontal stem, usually aboveground, rooting at the nodes and producing new plants. See *rhizome.*

Stramineous. Straw-colored.

Subequal. Somewhat unequal, as the lengths of a glume-pair.

Subsessile. Nearly sessile, as a spikelet with a minute pedicel.

Subulate. Narrow, needlelike, as an apex.

Sulcate. Grooved or furrowed with the long axis of a given structure such as a sheath.

Terete. Round in cross-section, as a grass culm.

Triandrous. With three stamens, the most frequent situation in the grasses.

Trifurcate. With three divisions or branches.

Truncate. Straight across, as if cut off, as of an apex.

Ventral. Inner side, or the side toward the main axis, or adaxial.

Vernation. Disposition of embryonic leaf prior to emergence, appearing in cross-section either rolled or folded (plicate).

Verticillate. Arranged in whorls, as three or more branches of a panicle, on the central axis.

Villous. With long, soft hairs.

Vivipary. When referring to grasses, the development of new plants via bulblet formation from the spikelet, as in some species of *Poa.*

Winter annual. A plant germinating from seed in the fall and overwintering as a seedling, continuing growth and flowering the following season, not persisting afterward.

x. The basic chromosome number of the taxon.

BIBLIOGRAPHY

Aiken, S. G., and L. P. Lefkovitch. 1993. On the separation of two species within *Festuca* subg. Obtusae (Poaceae). Taxon 42: 323–37.

Alexeev, E. B. 1980. *Festuca* L. subgenera et sectiones novae ex America Boreali et Mexica. (In Russian; Latinized title and tables.) Novitates Systematicae Plantarum Vascularum 17: 42–53.

Allen, C. M. 1992. Grasses of Louisiana. 2d ed. Cajun Prairie Habitat Preservation Soc., Eunice, La.

Allred, K. W. 1985. Studies in the *Aristida* (Gramineae) of the southeastern United States, II: Morphometric analysis of *A. intermedia* and *A. longespica*. Rhodora 87: 137–45.

Allred, K. W., and F. W. Gould. 1983. Systematics of the *Bothriochloa saccharoides* complex (Poaceae: Andropogoneae). Syst. Bot. 8: 168–84.

Anderson, D. E. 1961. Taxonomy and distribution of the genus *Phalaris*. Iowa State Coll. J. Sci. 36: 1–96.

Angelo, R. 1991. A new combination in *Panicum* (Poaceae) subgenus Dicanthelium. Phytologia 71: 85–86.

Arnow, L. A. 1987. Gramineae. Pp. 684–788 in S. L. Welsh, N. D. Atwood, S. Goodrich, and L. C. Higgins, eds., A Utah flora, Great Basin Naturalist Mem. 9: 1–894.

Assadi, M., and H. Runemark. 1995. Hybridization, genomic constitution and generic delimitation in *Elymus* s.l. (Poaceae: Triticeae). Pl. Syst. Evol. 194: 189–205.

Avdulov, N. P. 1931. Karyo-systemische untersuchungen der familie Gramineen. (In Russian; German summary.) Supplement 44 to Bull. Appl. Bot., Genet. and Plant Breeding. Smithsonian Institution.

Baldini, R. M. 1995. Revision of the genus *Phalaris* L. (Gramineae). Webbia 49: 265–329.

Banks, D. J. 1966. Taxonomy of *Paspalum setaceum* (Gramineae). Sida 2: 269–84.

Barker, C. M., and C. A. Stace. 1982. Hybridization in the genera *Vulpia* and *Festuca*: The production of artificial F$_1$ plants. Nordic J. Bot. 2: 435–44.

Barkworth, M. E. 1982. Embryological characters and the taxonomy of the Stipeae (Gramineae). Taxon 31: 233–43.

————. 1993. North American Stipeae (Gramineae): Taxonomic changes and other comments. Phytologia 74: 1–25.

Barkworth, M. E., and D. R. Dewey. 1985. Genomically based genera in the perennial Triticeae of North America: Identification and membership. Am. J. Bot. 72: 767–76.

Baum, B. R. 1982. The generic problem in the Triticeae: Numerical taxonomy and related concepts. Pp. 109–43 in J. R. Estes, R. J. Tyrl, and J. N. Brunken, eds., Grasses and grasslands. Univ. of Oklahoma Press, Norman.

Beetle, A. A. 1943. The grass genus *Distichlis*. Revista Argent. Agron. 22: 86–94.

————. 1981. Noteworthy grasses from Mexico VIII. Phytologia 48: 189–93.

Blake, S. T. 1969. Taxonomic and nomenclatural studies in the Gramineae, no. 2. Proc. Roy. Soc. Queensl. 81: 1–26.

Bowden, W. M. 1964. Cytotaxonomy of the species and interspecific hybrids of the genus *Elymus* in Canada and neighboring areas. Can. J. Bot. 42: 547–601.

Brown, W. V. 1958. Leaf anatomy in grass systematics. Bot. Gaz. 119: 170–78.

————. 1961. Grass leaf anatomy: Its use in systematics. Recent Adv. Bot. 9th Int. Bot. Congress (Lectures and Symposia) 1: 105–8.

Brummitt, R. K., and C. E. Powell, eds. 1992. Authors of plant names. Royal Botanic Gardens, Kew.

Brunken, J. N. 1977. A systematic study of *Pennisetum* sect. *Pennisetum* (Gramineae). Am. J. Bot. 64: 161–76.

Campbell, C. S., P. E. Garwood, and L. P. Specht. 1986. Bambusoid affinities of the north temperate genus *Brachyelytrum* (Gramineae). Bull. Torrey Bot. Club 113: 135–41.

Castaner, D. 1983. Additions to the flora of Missouri from Europe. Missouriensis 4: 111–12.

Christ, A. 1988. *Vulpia bromoides* in Missouri. Missouriensis 9: 13–14.

Church, G. L. 1967. Taxonomic and genetic relationships of eastern North American species of *Elymus* with setaceous glumes. Rhodora 69: 121–62.

Clark, L. G. 1990. A new combination in *Chasmanthium* (Poaceae). Ann. Missouri Bot. Gard. 77: 601.

Clausen, R. T. 1952. Suggestion for the assignment of *Torreyochloa* to *Puccinellia.* Rhodora 54: 42–45.

Clayton, W. D. 1965. Studies in the Gramineae, VI. Kew Bull. 19: 287–96.

———. 1968. The correct name of the common reed. Taxon 17: 168–69.

Clayton, W. D., and S. A. Renvoize. 1986. Genera Graminum, grasses of the world. Kew. Bull. Add. Series 13. Royal Botanic Gardens, Kew.

Crooks, P., and C. L. Kucera. 1973. *Tridens* × *oklahomensis* (*T. flavus* × *T. strictus*), an interspecific sterile hybrid in the *Eragrosteae* (Gramineae). Am. J. Bot. 60: 262–67.

Darbyshire, S. J. 1993. Realignment of *Festuca* subgenus *Schedonorus* with genus *Lolium* (Poaceae). Novon 3: 239–43.

Decker, H. F. 1964. An anatomic-systematic study of the classical tribe Festuceae (Gramineae). Am. J. Bot. 51: 453–63.

De Lisle, D. G. 1963. Taxonomy and distribution of the genus *Cenchrus.* Iowa State Coll. J. Sci. 37: 259–351.

De Wet, J. M. J. 1954. The genus *Danthonia* in grass phylogeny. Am. J. Bot. 41: 204–11.

———. 1978. Systematics and evolution of *Sorghum* sect. *Sorghum* (Gramineae). Am. J. Bot. 65: 477–84.

De Wet, J. M. J., and J. R. Harlan. 1966. Morphology of the compilospecies *Bothriochloa intermedia.* Am. J. Bot. 53(1): 94–98.

Dewey, D. R. 1983. Historical and current taxonomic perspectives of *Agropyron, Elymus,* and related genera. Crop Sci. 23: 637–42.

Dierker, W. W. 1989. A new grass for Missouri. Missouriensis 10: 44.

Dunn, D. B. 1982. Problems in "keeping-up" with the flora of Missouri. Trans. Missouri Acad. Sci. 16: 95–98.

Ellis, L. S. 1990. *Stenotaphrum secundatum* (Poaceae) in Stone County, a new grass for Missouri. Missouriensis 11: 7–8.

Erdman, K. S. 1965. Taxonomy of the genus *Sphenopholis* (Gramineae). Iowa State J. Sci. 39: 289–336.

Estes, J. R., and R. J. Tyrl. 1982. The generic concept and generic circumscription in the Triticeae: An end paper. Pp. 145–64 in J. R. Estes, R. J. Tyrl, and J. N. Brunken, eds., Grasses and grasslands. Univ. of Oklahoma Press, Norman.

Freckmann, R. W. 1978. New combinations in *Dichanthelium* (Poaceae). Phytologia 39: 268–72.

Gereau, R. E. 1987. Grasses of Missouri: An annotated checklist. Missouriensis 8: 49–70.

Gould, F. W. 1967. The grass genus *Andropogon* in the United States. Brittonia 19: 70–76.

———. 1974. Nomenclatural changes in the Poaceae. Brittonia 26: 59–60.

———. 1975. The grasses of Texas. Texas A & M Univ. Press, College Station.

Gould, F. W., M. A. Ali, and D. E. Fairbrothers. 1972. A revision of *Echinochloa* in the United States. Am. Midl. Nat. 87: 36–59.

Gould, F. W., and C. A. Clark. 1978. *Dichanthelium* (Poaceae) in the United States and Canada. Ann. Missouri Bot. Gard. 65: 1088–132.

Greuter, W. 1968. Notulae nomenclaturales et bibliographicae 1–4. Candollea 23: 81–108.

Hammel, B. E., and J. R. Reeder. 1979. The genus *Crypsis* (Gramineae) in the United States. Syst. Bot. 4: 267–80.

Heslop-Harrison, J. 1961. The function of the glume pit and the control of cleistogamy in *Bothriochloa decipiens* (Hack.) C.E. Hubbard. Phytomorphology 11: 378–83.

Heumann, B. 1993. *Panicum yadkinense* Ashe (Poaceae) new to Missouri. Missouriensis 14: 23–25.

Hitchcock, A. S. 1951. Manual of the grasses of the United States. 2d ed., revised by A. Chase. USDA Misc. Publ. 200. U.S. Govt. Printing Office, Washington, D.C.

Hudson, S. T. 1994. Three new plants for southeastern Missouri. Missouriensis 15(2): 13–17.

———. 1997. Two introduced species new to Missouri. Missouriensis 17: 10–15.

Iltis, H. H., and J. F. Doebley. 1980. Taxonomy of *Zea* (Gramineae), II: Subspecific categories in the *Zea mays* complex and a generic synopsis. Am. J. Bot. 67: 994–1004.

Kellog, E. A., and C. S. Campbell. 1986. Phylogenetic analysis of the Gramineae. Pp. 310–24 in T. R. Soderstrom, K. W. Hilu, C. S. Campbell, and M. E. Barkworth, eds., Grass systematics and evolution, Int. Symp., Smithsonian Institution, Washington, D.C.

Kiger, R. W. 1971. *Arthraxon hispidus* (Gramineae) in the United States: Taxonomic and floristic status. Rhodora 73: 39–46.

Koch, S. D. 1978. Notes on the genus *Eragrostis* (Gramineae) in the southeastern United States. Rhodora 80: 390–403.

Koyamo, T. 1987. Grasses of Japan and its neighboring regions: An identification manual. Kodansha Ltd., Tokyo.

Kucera, C. L. 1961. The grasses of Missouri. University of Missouri Studies, vol. 34, no. 2. Univ. of Missouri Press, Columbia.

Ladd, D. 1983. *Sclerochloa dura* (L.) Beauv. (Gramineae) in Missouri. Missouriensis 4: 73–75.

Lelong, M. G. 1984. New combinations for *Panicum* and subgenus *Dicanthelium* (Poaceae) of the southeastern United States. Brittonia 36: 262–73.

———. 1986. A taxonomic treatment of the genus *Panicum* (Poaceae) in Mississippi. Phytologia 61: 251–69.

Lonard, R. I., and F. W. Gould. 1974. The North American species of *Vulpia* (Gramineae). Madrono 22: 217–30.

Lorenzoni, G. G. 1966. Revisione del gruppo di *Festuca pratensis* Huds. e *Festuca arundinacea* Schreb. dell' Erbario Veneto dell' Instituto Botanico di Padova. Webbia 21: 601–23.

McClure, F. A. 1973. Genera of bamboos native to the New World (Gramineae: Bambusoideae). Pp. 1–148 in T. R. Soderstrom, ed., Smithsonian Contrib. to Botany, no. 9, Smithsonian Institution, Washington, D.C.

McKenzie, P. M. 1994. *Paspalum bifidum* (Poaceae) new to Missouri, with management recommendations for its recovery in the state. Missouriensis 15(2): 19–27.

———. 1995. *Aristida desmantha* (Poaceae) in Missouri. Sida 16: 589–90.

McKenzie, P. M., and D. Ladd. 1995. Status of *Bromus nottawayanus* (Poaceae) in Missouri. Missouriensis 16: 57–68.

McNeill, J. 1979. *Diplachne* and *Leptochloa* (Poaceae) in North America. Brittonia 31: 399–404.

———. 1981. *Apera,* silky-bent or windgrass, an important weed genus recently discovered in Ontario, Canada. Can. J. Plant Sci. 61: 479–85.

McNeill, J., and W. G. Dore. 1976. Taxonomic and nomenclatural notes on Ontario grasses. Naturaliste Can. 103: 553–67.

McVaugh, R. 1983. Flora Novo-Galiciana. Vol. 14, Gramineae. Univ. of Michigan Press, Ann Arbor, Michigan.

Melleris, A. 1978. Taxonomic notes in the tribe Triticeae (Gramineae) with special reference to the genera *Elymus* L. *sensu lato* and *Agropyron* Gaertner *sensu lato*. Bot. J. Linn. Soc. 76: 369–84.

Mitchell, W. W., and A. C. Wilton. 1964. The *Hordeum jubatum-caespitosum-brachyantherum* complex in Alaska. Madrono 17: 269–80.

Mohlenbrock, R. H. 1986. Guide to the vascular flora of Illinois. Southern Illinois Univ. Press, Carbondale.

Muehlenbach, V. 1969. Adventive plants new to the Missouri flora, III. Ann. Missouri Bot. Gard. 56: 163–71.

———. 1979. Contributions to the synanthropic (adventive) flora of the railroads in St. Louis, Mo. Ann. Missouri Bot. Gard. 66: 1–108.

———. 1983. Supplement to the contributions to the synanthropic (adventive) flora of the railroads in St. Louis, Mo. Ann. Missouri Bot. Gard. 70: 170–78.

Nelson, R. W. 1985. The terrestrial natural communities of Missouri. Missouri Natural Areas Committee (Missouri Department of Natural Resources and the Missouri Department of Conservation) Jefferson City.

Pavlick, L. 1995. *Bromus* L. of North America. Royal British Columbia, Victoria, Canada.

Pilger, R. 1954. Das system der Gramineae. Bot. Jahrb. 76: 281–384.

Pohl, R. W. 1966. The grasses of Iowa. Iowa State J. Sci. 40: 341–566.

———. 1969. *Muhlenbergia,* subgenus *Muhlenbergia* (Gramineae) in North America. Am. Midl. Nat. 82: 512–42.

Prat, H. 1932. L'épiderme des Graminées: Étude anatomique et systématique. Ann. Sci. Nat. Bot. 14: 117–324.

Pyrah, G. L. 1969. Taxonomic and distributional studies in *Leersia* (Gramineae). Iowa State J. Sci. 44: 215–70.

Reed, C. F. 1989. New combinations required for the flora of central eastern United States, III. Phytologia 67: 451–53.

Reeder, C. G. 1975. *Sporobolus* R. Br. Pp. 286–311 in F. W. Gould, The grasses of Texas. Texas A & M Univ. Press, College Station.

Reeder, J. R. 1957. The embryo in grass systematics. Am. J. Bot. 44: 756–68.

———. 1986. Another look at *Eragrostis tephrosanthos* (Gramineae). Phytologia 60: 153–54.

Riggins, R. 1977. A biosystematic study of the *Sporobolus asper* complex (Gramineae). Iowa State J. Res. 51: 287–321.

Runemark, H., and W. K. Heneen. 1968. *Elymus* and *Agropyron,* a problem of generic delimitation. Bot. Notiser. 121: 51–79.

Sauer, J. D. 1972. Revision of *Stenotaphrum* (Gramineae: Paniceae) with attention to its historical geography. Brittonia 24: 202–22.

Schuckman, S. M., and C. L. Kucera. 1984. The hybrid status of *Tridens oklahomensis* (Feath.) Feath. Trans. Missouri Acad. Sci. 18: 11–12.

Seymour, F. C. 1966. *Bromus mollis* and allies in New England. Rhodora 68: 168–74.

Shaw, R. B., and R. D. Webster. 1987. The genus *Eriochloa* (Poaceae: Paniceae) in North and Central America. Sida 12: 165–207.

Shinners, L. H. 1954. Notes on North Texas grasses. Rhodora 56: 25–38.

Smith, B. N., and W. V. Brown. 1973. The Kranz syndrome in the Gramineae as indicated by carbon isotopic ratios. Am. J. Bot. 60: 505–13.

Smith, P. 1968. The *Bromus mollis* aggregate in Britain. Watsonia 6: 327–44.

Smith, T. 1988. *Poa interior* Rydberg (Poaceae), a new record for Missouri. Missouriensis 9: 8–9.

———. 1997. *Echinochloa walteri,* a new grass for Missouri. Missouriensis 17: 32–34.

Snow, N. 1998. Nomenclatural changes in *Leptochloa* P. Beauv. *sensu lato* (Poaceae, Chloridoideae). Novon 8: 7–80.

Stebbins, G. L. 1956. Cytogenetics and the evolution of the grass family. Am. J. Bot. 43: 890–905.

Stebbins, G. L., and B. Crampton. 1961. A suggested revision of the grass genera of temperate North America. Recent Adv. Bot. 9th Int. Bot. Congress (Lectures and Symposia) 1: 133–45.

Stephenson, S. N. 1984. The genus *Dichanthelium* (Poaceae) in Michigan. Mich. Bot. 23: 107–19.

Steyermark, J. A., and C. L. Kucera. 1961. New combinations in grasses. Rhodora 63: 24–26.

Tateoka, T. 1961. A biosystematic study of *Tridens* (Gramineae). Am. J. Bot. 48: 565–73.

Terrell, E. E. 1967. Meadow fescue: *Festuca elatior* L. or *F. pratensis* Hudson? Brittonia 19: 129–32.

———. 1968. A taxonomic revision of the genus *Lolium.* Techn. Bull. U.S.D.A. 1392: 1–65.

Thieret, J. W. 1966. Synopsis of the genus *Calamovilfa* (Gramineae). Castanea 31: 145–52.

Thom, R. H., and J. H. Wilson. 1980. The natural divisions of Missouri. Trans. Missouri Acad. Sci. 14: 9–23.

Tucker, G. C. 1988. The genera of *Bambusoideae* (Gramineae) in the southeastern United States. J. Arnold Arbor. 67: 239–73.

Tzvelev, N. N. 1989. The system of grasses (Poaceae) and their evolution. Bot. Rev. 55(3): 141–204.

Van Welzen, P. C. 1981. A taxonomic revision of the genus *Arthraxon* Beauv.(Gramineae). Blumea 27(1): 255–300.

Veldkamp, J. F. 1973. A revision of *Digitaria* Haller (Gramineae) in Malesia. Blumea 21: 1–80.

———. 1994. Miscellaneous notes on Southeast Asian Gramineae, IX: *Setaria* and *Paspalidium.* Blumea 39: 373–84.

Vickery, J. W. 1975. Flora of New South Wales. No. 19. Gramineae, Part 2. Supplement to Part 1. N.S.W. Dept. of Agric., Sydney, Australia.

Wagnon, H. K. 1952. A revision of the genus *Bromus,* section Bromopsis, of North America. Brittonia 7: 415–80.

Wakeman, A., and P. M. McKenzie. 1997. Rediscovery of *Oryzopsis racemosa* (Poaceae) in Missouri. Missouriensis 17(1,2): 16–23.

Warwick, S. I., and S. G. Aiken. 1986. Electrophoretic evidence for the recognition of two species in annual wild rice (*Zizania,* Poaceae). Syst. Bot. 11: 464–73.

Watson, L., and M. J. Dallwitz. 1992. The grass genera of the world. CAB International, Wallingford, Oxon., U.K.

Weber, W. R., and W. T. Corcoran. 1995. Atlas of Missouri vascular plants. Southwest Missouri State University, Springfield, and the Missouri Plant Society, St. Louis.

Webster, R. D. 1987. Taxonomy of *Digitaria* section *Digitaria* in North America (Poaceae: Paniceae). Sida 12: 209–22.

———. 1988. Genera of the North American Paniceae (Poaceae: Panicoideae). Syst. Bot. 13: 576–609.

———. 1995. Nomenclatural changes in *Setaria* and *Paspalidium* (Poaceae: Paniceae). Sida 16: 439–46.

Webster, R. D., and R. B. Shaw. 1995. Taxonomy of the North American species of *Saccharum* (Poaceae: Andropogoneae). Sida 16: 551–80.

Widén, K. G. 1971. The genus *Agrostis* L. in eastern Fennoscandia: Taxonomy and distribution. Fl. Fenn. 5: 1–209.

Yabuno, T. 1966. Biosystematic study of the genus *Echinochloa.* Jap. Bot. 2: 277–323.

Yates, H. O. 1966. Revision of grasses traditionally referred to *Uniola,* II: *Chasmanthium.* Southwest Nat. 11: 415–55.

Yatskievych, G. 1990. Studies in the flora of Missouri, II. Missouriensis 11: 2–6.

Yatskievych, G., and D. Figg. 1989. Studies in the flora of Missouri, I: New records of introduced taxa. Missouriensis 10: 16–19.

Yatskievych, G., and J. Turner. 1990. Catalogue of the flora of Missouri. Flora of Missouri Project, Monographs in Systematic Botany from the Missouri Botanical Garden, vol. 37.

[The Flora of Missouri Project is a collaborative effort between the Missouri Department of Conservation and the Missouri Botanical Garden.]

Zuloaga, F. O. 1986. Systematics of New World species of *Panicum* (Poaceae: Paniceae). Pp. 287–306 in T. R. Soderstrom, K. W. Hilu, C. S. Campbell, and M. E. Barkworth, eds., Grass systematics and evolution, Int. Symp., Smithsonian Institution, Washington, D.C.

INDEX

Note: Synonyms are in italics. Page numbers for principal descriptions are in boldface.

ABOUT THE AUTHOR

Clair L. Kucera is Professor Emeritus of Biological Sciences at the University of Missouri–Columbia. He is the author of *The Challenge of Ecology* and numerous scientific articles. He has served as the associate editor for the journal *Ecology* and was the editor for *The Proceedings of the Seventh North American Prairie Conference.*

Photo courtesy of University of Missouri Publications and Alumni Communication